REAR ADMIRAL THOMAS H. MORTON, UNITED STATES NAVY, RETIRED

Thomas Howard Morton was born in Annapolis, Maryland, on March 1, 1912, son of Captain James P. Morton, USN and Mrs. (Grace Howard) Morton, both now deceased. He attended Annapolis High School, then was a student at Severn School, Severna Park, Maryland, prior to entering the U. S. Naval Academy, Annapolis, Maryland, on appointment from the State of Missouri in 1929. Graduated with distinction, eighteenth in a class of four hundred and thirty-five members, and commissioned Ensign, June 1, 1933, he subsequently progressed in rank to that of Rear Admiral, to date from July 1, 1961.

Following graduation from the Naval Academy in 1933, his first assignment was in the USS MISSISSIPPI, in which he served as Junior Division Officer, Engineering Division Officer and Gunnery Division Officer until December 1936. He then joined the staff of Commander Battleships, Battle Force, for communication duty, and in January 1938 reported as Chief Engineer on board the USS BORIE. Detached from that destroyer in June 1939, he next had instruction in ordnance engineering at the Postgraduate School, Annapolis, Maryland.

In September 1941 he became a Special Naval Observer in London, England, and continued to serve in that capacity, following the United States entry into World War II, December 8, 1941, until February 1944. In April he reported as Gunnery Officer on board the USS NORTH CAROLINA and while attached to that battleship saw action in the Marianas, Leyte, Luzon, Iwo Jima, Okinawa and Japanese Mainland operations. "For heroic service...(in that battleship) in action against enemy Japanese forces in the Pacific War Area from May 4, 1944 to August 15, 1945..." he was awarded the Bronze Star Medal with Combat "V." The citation further states in part:

"Organizing his men and material into an effective fighting unit, Commander Morton directed his ship's antiaircraft defenses in repulsing heavy enemy air attacks off Saipan and during the Okinawa operation. In addition, he was largely responsible for the NORTH CAROLINA's successful participation in heavy main-battery bombardments of Saipan, Iwo Jima and Okinawa, paving the way for the eventual occupation of each island..."

Detached from the NORTH CAROLINA in December 1945, he served until September 1947 as United States Navy Secretary on the United Nations Staff Committee. In that assignment he attended the initial meetings of the United Nations General Assembly and Security Council in London, England and New York, New York. He assumed command of the USS COMPTON in October 1947 and in November 1949 reported as Assistant to the Director of the Planning Division, Bureau of Ordnance, Navy Department, Washington, D. C. During the period August 1951 to June 1952 he attended the Industrial College of the Armed Forces, Washington, D. C., after which he was Commander Destroyer Division ONE HUNDRED TWENTY-TWO.

DECLARATION OF TRUST

The undersigned does hereby appoint and designate as his (her) Trustee herein, the Secretary-Treasurer and Publisher of the United States Naval Institute to perform and discharge the following duties, powers, and privileges in connection with the possession and use of a certain taped interview between the undersigned and the Oral History Department of the United States Naval Institute.

1. Classification of Transcript.

   ( )a. If classified OPEN, the transcript(s) may be read or the recording(s) audited by the qualified personnel upon presentation of proper credentials, as determined by the Secretary-Treasurer of the U.S. Naval Institute.

   ( )b. If classified PERMISSION REQUIRED TO CITE OR QUOTE, the user will be required to obtain permission in writing from the interviewee prior to quoting or citing from either the transcript(s) or the recording(s).

   ( )c. If classified PERMISSION REQUIRED, permission must be obtained in writing from the interviewee before the transcribed interview(s) can be examined or the tape recording(s) audited.

   ( )d. If classified CLOSED, the transcribed interview(s) and the tape recording(s) will be sealed until a time specified by the interviewee. This may be until the death of the interviewee or for any specified number of years.

2. It is expressly understood that in giving this authorization, I am in no way precluded from placing such restrictions as I may desire upon use of the interview at any time during my lifetime, nor does this authorization in any way affect my rights to the copyright of my literary expressions that may be contained in the interview.

Witness my hand and seal this 11 day of December 1979.

I hereby accept and consent to the foregoing Declaration of Trust and the powers therein conferred upon me as Trustee:

Morton #1 - 1

Interview #1 with Rear Admiral Thomas H. Morton
Place: His residence in Annapolis, Maryland
Date: Tuesday morning, 16 September 1975
Interviewer: John T. Mason, Jr.

Q: Well, Tom, I'm delighted that at last we're going to sit down with a tape recorder and have an account of your most interesting naval career. Would you start an oral biography, which indeed this is, in the proper way by telling me about the date and place of your birth, and then something about your family background, which is exceedingly Navy?

Adm. M.: True. I was born in Annapolis, Maryland in what is known as Murray Hill, March 1, 1912. My father was then Commander James P. Morton and was one of the early heads of the postgraduate school, which was why he was here. My mother was an Annapolis girl, Grace Howard, whose father was Admiral Thomas B. Howard of the Naval Academy Class of 1873. My grandfather - Admiral Howard - in about 1915 was designated as the first four star Commander-in-Chief of the Pacific Fleet. This was largely in connection with the Panama-Pacific Exposition. An interesting sidelight on Admiral Howard: he was retired in about 1916 and then was recalled in World War I as a rear admiral, as the Superintendent of the Naval Observatory in Washington. I spent the war years there, my father being at sea, with my grandfather and my grandmother and my mother, and the thing of interest there is that until about 1930 when it became the CNO's quarters (that house, which I remember well, and the grounds has recently been designated as the Vice President's mansion) and, although I was only five, six, and seven years old I knew the house well and, of course in CNO's receptions in the Sixties I was able to go back and see the house and was amazed to find how small it was!

Q: Do you have any recollections - specific recollections of your years there?

Adm. M.: Well, not particularly, although I remember the technical scientists there were Dr. Hall and Dr. Hill, and we often went over to the big dome and saw the range of Saturn and the mountains on the moon, and so forth. It was a wonderful place to grow up - huge grounds. I used to go shopping with my mother and grandmother, and in those days the Superintendent had a two-horse carriage which we would take all the way downtown, and go to the usual Woodies, Garfinkles, and whatnot. It was quite a thrill. Old William, I think, was the coachman. And, mind you, in those days the Observatory was really out in the country. I mean nothing - nothing but fields at that time all the way down to Upshur and Sheridan Circle on Massachusetts Avenue.

Q: Now, the Cathedral had been begun, had it not?

Adm. M.: I don't remember this really. I can't remember whether they'd started that or not. But, we had a wonderful childhood there.

Q: Was Emily also there?

Adm. M.: Emily was there, but Emily doesn't remember it. She was too young. I was, as I say, five, six, seven. I remember the sirens every day downtown. I think it was noon, or one o'clock. I remember them going off. I remember all the gardens and things there. It was a marvelous place. You had all the acreage - marvelous hill for sleigh riding in the winter - and so on.

Q: Were there lots of parties held in the house?

Adm. M.: Not too many because of course the - well, I mean, we had them. The families had the parties, but the thing is, the Superintendent of the Observatory was not the figure that later the Chief of Operations was when he occupied it; so we didn't have a host of official, big

Morton #1 - 4

parties. My grandfather had known an awful lot of the Members of Congress and they came there quite often with their wives. Congressman Bert Snell of New York; Congressman MacArthur, I think of Oregon, and General and Mrs. Lyman were very good friends (who were the father and mother of Admiral Charlie Lyman, whom I'm sure you'd know.)

Q: Did you, being exposed to the Observatory - did you develop an interest in astronomy as a result of that? Did you want to be an astronomer?

Adm. M.: Well, I never expected to be an astronomer, but I certainly did have a long interest in it during my childhood, in years after that. We had a little telescope right on the veranda at the admirals house which, of course, was peanuts compared to the big dome, but it was there for our own use, and we used to use that a lot. But, the big thrill was going down to the big dome - you really could see it. I've forgotten the magnification of the scope.

Q: And your grandfather had some specific qualifications for that job?

Adm. M.: Not particularly. My grandfather was for a long time just a straight line officer, and I think it was a typical case of needing someone there who was on the retired list, and he happened to be chosen. He had, in addition to this CinC Pacific that I mentioned - he was also one of the captains of the Great White Fleet, and he's in my picture up there taken in Yokohama. He commanded the Tennessee and the Ohio. There was some shift in captains on the way around and he started out, as I remember, with the Tennessee and ended up the cruise with the Ohio. This must have been some sort of promotion - the relative size or prestige of the two ships. That's the old Tennessee, of course.

Q: Yes. Tell me about your own father's naval career.

Adm. M.: Well, my father was, as I say, one of the early people that founded the PG School, and he was first head. That was in 1912-14. Meanwhile, my father got quarters in the Academy after I was born. My sister Emily was born at 7 Porter Road, which then was called Samson Road. And one of my father's distinctions at the Naval Academy - I've been told - was that he was the first Naval Academy officer to have an automobile. The thing of interest about my father was that in 1914 or '15 he was assigned as Naval Attaché to Turkey - and of course we were neutral at that time, and so we had our attaché in Turkey - Istanbul - Constantinople - even though Turkey was fighting

Morton #1 - 6

with the enemy powers. One of the things that really was of interest was, in addition to his duties as Naval Attaché, he was also in command of a station ship - the Scorpion - so when the U.S. got into the war the diplomatic staff (which would have included him as attaché, were released to go home because of their diplomatic status. My father was incarcerated as the skipper of a naval vessel. They took over the Scorpion - that overruled his diplomatic status.

Q: Was he given good treatment?

Adm. M.: Yes, he was given very good treatment because he knew a lot of the senior Turkish people, naval particularly. And, the story of him being spirited out of Turkey to come home through Europe was fascinating. It involved veiled women, and beautiful blondes, and false passports, and everything you can think of. I have a lot of that material.

Q: Cloak and dagger sort of thing.

Adm. M.: It really was that. He wrote his report to the Navy Department when he reached the French Embassy in Paris but he got home alright. He was later in command at sea of the battleships Kentucky and Wisconsin. I'm not sure which order. Then, unfortunately, he died in about '22. No, he retired in about '22, and died in about 1927. So, at that time we had moved here to Annapolis where I really had most of my childhood, although we'd lived in Coronado and Newport, and so forth.

Q: The family didn't think about accompanying him to Turkey in 1914?

Adm. M.: No. I suppose in those days, either they couldn't or with Emily and myself three and one-years-old, it may have been mother's decision. I really can't answer that.

Q: Well, it was a different age and the customs were different from what they are now, certainly.

Adm. M.: I don't know whether the attachés, in those days, had their families with them or not. I can't say. And, it may have also been with Turkey a belligerent, and us neutral, maybe the families were prohibited from going. I don't know this.

Q: How far back do your family roots go in the Navy beyond your grandfather?

Adm. M.: Not beyond my grandfather. If we have time, I can give you an interesting sidelight on that. My grandfather's father was a captain or a major in the Union Army, and he was killed in the Civil War. The Confederates blew up a bridge under the train in which my great-grandfather was riding from one place to another with his troops, and he was killed. Well, his home was Galena, Illinois, where my grandfather and his brothers and sisters were born and raised.

Q: Also the home of Ulysses S. Grant?

Adm. M.: That's part of my story, because when this happened my grandfather had a brother by the name of Douglas Howard, and General Grant when he became President, had known the Howard family so well that when he became President he wrote to the widow Howard and said, "Well, I'm here. What can I do for you and, particularly, your two boys?" And one thing led to another, and so my great Uncle, Douglas Howard, was appointed to West Point by the President, and my grandfather was appointed to Annapolis by the President. Not under the present competitive system, but just as a personal appointment. So, with this long background of Army officers, my grandfather Howard was the first one to defect to the Navy; and that was the reason he went. Grant had two appointments for the Howard

Morton #1 - 9

family - one to West Point and one to Annapolis. So that started my family on this Navy pitch.

Q: Very, very interesting indeed.

Adm. M.: Then, it's been almost primarily Navy, as you realize. I remember, I'd seen a movie when I was a kid here in Annapolis. It was called "West Point", or something to that effect. And, I guess it was in early high school, and I got inspired by whoever was in the cast and came home and announced that I was not going to the Naval Academy, I was going to West Point. I think the family damned near hanged me for being a traitor.

Q: Then it had always been concluded that you would go?

Adm. M.: Yes, it was. Although I was never forced in it. I mean it was just a natural thing to look foward to being a midshipman.

Q: You went to high school here in -

Adm. M.: I went to high school the first two years, and then finished the last two years of the high school equivalent at Severn School at Severna Park.

Q: That was a kind of prep school, was it not?

Adm. M.: That was a prep school in those days predominantly for the Naval Academy. We had three semesters. There were 120 students in those days. I can't remember how many were in the graduating class but - I'd say there were, out of the 120, three or four or five who were prepping for West Point, and the very occasional boy who was not preparing for either service academy. But it was predominantly Naval Academy. In recent years they've very much removed the emphasis on the Academies. And Severn is now very proud that they're sending people to 50 different universities, some of course to West Point and Annapolis, but not many.

Q: They also include girls now?

Adm. S.: Yes. You know Corky Ward, of course. When he was headmaster they were contemplating this coed business. He asked a lot of us individually what we thought of that, and I told Corky, "After all, Princeton and everybody else is doing it, so what's the harm of Severn letting the young ladies in?" I never felt that my school was being ruined by the coed plan.

Q: And, I take it that it was a welcome financial support too?

Adm. M.: I think it was. I think Severn now has about 400 students, as opposed to roughly 120 when I was there. There were a lot of people like me who had gone there for the last year, or last two years of high school. The junior classes - say seventh, eighth, ninth, tenth grade - were very, very small. I think they're bigger now. But, most of the Severn students in those days were in the 11th and 12th grades - going strictly as a prep school.

Q: Focusing on entrance to the Naval Academy; what did you study?

Adm. M.: Well, we got the complete high school education. In other words, my two years got me a high school diploma from Severn, but in addition to that they emphasized the Navy examination subjects, and in fact we studied a lot of old examination papers. In those days the Navy used to print the Naval Academy exams every year in pamphlet form for the use of candidates, prep schools, and so forth. Also, if you'd already had completed one of those courses to the satisfaction of the school - they also were able to give you a course, of say one or two terms of a Naval Academy subject which was useful. For instance, I studied chemistry which I wouldn't have gotten in high school, and that made chemistry down here very easy because I was just repeating what I'd learned at Severn.

Q: Did they help a boy in getting an appointment?

Adm. M.: I don't believe they were able to do that very much because, in those days, the people were from all over the East Coast and some, particularly Navy Juniors, from California and whatnot, and I don't believe the school was able to do that directly. My appointment was an interesting experience, if you want to hear that.

Q: I do, yes.

Adm. M.: The appointments for Maryland were then, very, very hard to get, and not many members of Congress, as they do now, were giving competitive exams. In other words, it was largely appointing someone who was valuable politically, or a personal friend; and so mother practically walked the halls of Congress to try to get me an appointment. Senator Millard Tydings of Maryland had turned her down. He said he didn't have any available, so Mom, somehow ended up with a second alternate from Senator James Read of Missouri - my father having been from Missouri, by the way. One of the reasons Mom had some entree there.

Q: He was quite a power in the Senate.

Adm. M.: He was indeed. I used to exchange Christmas cards with him until he died. But anyway, a second alternate was not very much of a sure thing so I had to study the curriculum for the regular exams. The situation has changed now with the College Board, but the Presidential appointments were based on what they called the regular exams which were six subjects, whereas, if you had an appointment and you had a high school diploma you were able to take one day of exams which was only English and math. So I'd studied the whole year - grinding away at two histories and so on, for the six exams I had to take. Around January, I got a letter from Senator Read saying that the Principal had withdrawn, and so that made me first alternate. So, I sweated through to the six exams for the Presidential appointment and Mom came down. I remember we were playing the Plebes in lacrosse - it must have been around April. And, Mom came down, and between the halves she came over and said that the Principal had withdrawn - my top man on the appointment had dropped out, so I now had the Principal. I could have taken a lot more Naval Academy subjects at Severn if I'd only studied for two exams.

Q: It often happened that way.

Adm. M.: Yes. So I actually went in on a second alternate knowing that I was the principal. I can't think of anything else from the Severn days that would be of any particular interest.

Morton #1 - 14

Q: Well, you came into the Academy without any difficulty?

Adm. M.: Right. As it turned out, yes.

Q: Did many of the lads in your incoming class - Had any of them had college experience?

Adm. M.: Yes, there were a few. I would say not very many, but I can think of three or four right now who had been at least a year at college. Of course, the age limits were different then, and you had to be more than 16, and not more than 20. Now, of course they're taking much older people. I think it's gone to 17 to 22 - 24 if they're veterans. So that the boy that could be young enough to get in under the 20-year-old rule had either gone to college early, or only gone one year or else he would have been too old.

Q: Well, tell me about your Plebe Year.

Adm. M.: Yes, the Navy Junior had a rough time. An Annapolis Navy Junior had an even rougher time.

Q: Now why?

Adm. M.: The First Class, or Upper Class, just had the

tradition then that anybody from Annapolis, particularly a Navy Junior, ought to have more sense than to go into the Naval Academy. It was a sort of a joking thing. It wasn't hazing. They asked us more questions because they figured that a Navy Junior from Annapolis ought to know all the answers, and if I didn't I'd get hell. I was lucky. I think in my class there were probably more Annapolitans than any other class in that day. I think we had about thirty. They were a class of 568. Well, 431 graduated, or something like that. No, I take it back. 568 entered as Plebes, and about 430 graduated. So that 30 was quite a number from one town. Of course, a lot of them, but not necessarily all of them, were Navy Juniors.

Q: And they'd all gone through the same difficult process in getting an appointment I suppose?

Adm. M.: Oh yes, they did. Some of them had come in through the Navy. They used to take about 100, or 120 from the fleet. Well, of course, very few of them were actually from the fleet, but if they had gone to Bainbridge Prep, you know they'd been in the fleet.

Q: They had enlisted as seamen and then had been sent to the prep school?

Adm. M.: And that was a fleet-wide exam, but of course, the boys who had been assigned to Bainbridge from the fleet had a tremendous advantage because they had a full prep year.

Q: Well, even though you had a rough time as a Plebe, tell me about that Plebe year.

Adm. M.: Yes. I'd like to correct that. When I said Bainbridge, I was thinking of the modern-day Bainbridge Prep. I believe the prep school then was Norfolk.

Q: It was Norfolk actually. Yes. Sam Frankel went there.

Adm. M.: Well, Plebe Year I roomed with Ernest Lee Jahncke, Jr., who I'd met at Severn, and Lee Jahncke and I stayed together the whole four years happily.

Q: He was from New Orleans, wasn't he?

Adm. M.: He was from New Orleans, and was from the big Jahncke family down there, and at Severn he almost decided in March '29 that he wouldn't go to the Naval Academy because President Hoover had nominated his father as Assistant Secretary of the Navy just the spring of that year and he always felt that anything he did at the

Academy successfully, they would all say, "Oh well, Secretary Jahncke's son would do this." But he got over that, and so we had a happy four years together, and he's still one of my best friends. Sue and I visited him and his wife not long ago, and we see each other a great deal.

Q: Did he stay in the Navy?

Adm. M.: He stayed in the Navy until 1937 when he had been in cruisers and was sent to destroyers and, he just found out that he couldn't take destroyers. He was prone to seasickness and he had to resign voluntarily. It was strange because Jahncke had been a small boat sailor and yachtsman all of his life. The cruiser was all right, and the small yacht was all right but the destroyer got him.

Q: That isn't too unusual is it?

Adm. M.: Well, no. I think the destroyer of course is one of the worst riding, if he was prone that way but, on the other hand, you'd think someone who'd been around the water like he had, and had really been an excellent young sailor - you wouldn't think about him being affected by seasickness. He came back during the war as a reserve officer and served the whole war successfully.

Q: As a Plebe, you had no difficulty submitting to the discipline?

Adm. M.: None at all. You heard, in those days, about ruthless hazing and so forth. I never really witnessed any of that. I mean, of course we were given questions to look up the answers to and we occasionally washed upper classmen's clothes and shined their shoes, and that sort of thing, but as far as the brutal beating - there was very little of it.

Q: That was behind you wasn't it? That was in an earlier day?

Adm. M.: The very bad hazing and beating was earlier. I'd say about the mid-Twenties, or early-Twenties. But there was some. I mean, you'd have bad apples in every crowd, and there were some Third Classmen who were just plain sundowners, and took it out on you - any Plebe that they thought deserved it.

Q: Inasmuch as you lived in Annapolis, I suppose your home was a sort of mecca for midshipmen when you had time off.

Adm. M.: It really was, yes. Of course, through the four years you got more and more time off. Plebe Year, I think

think you could only go to Sunday dinner as I remember, with a special dining-out slip, as we called it and then the next year, maybe Saturday night came in, and so on – up to First Class Year when we had liberty every afternoon. But, my roommate and I and three or four classmates would invariably come out. Mom would have these figures that we've eaten X number of potatoes and a dozen ears of corn, and all that – and we actually did – particularly Plebe Year.

Q: Well, Plebe Year you were limited in vacation time too, were you not?

Adm. M.: We got none. The first leave we got in those days was Christmas week. In other words, Plebe Summer went through – right up to academic year, and they didn't have the September weekends. We didn't have the Parent's Forum, and all that that they have now for the Plebes. So we were in the Academy – except for these Sunday dining-out privileges – right up to Christmas week without any real extended break.

Q: Did that prove difficult for some of the boys from other parts of the country – that long isolation from their family?

Adm. M.: I don't think it did particularly because, as a Plebe, this Sunday dining out had to be on a special permit. In other words, you had to know someone in town who'd invited you to dinner, or someone at the Naval Academy. And the boys from distant places - they didn't miss anything because they didn't have anywhere to go really. Probably the biggest hardship was that Christmas leave is relatively short and some of them just didn't have enough Christmas leave to get home. It was kind of rough on them.

Q: Yes, it was traveling by train in those days?

Adm. M.: Yes, right. I think we had about - maybe ten days, something like that you know. A couple of days before Christmas and a couple of days after New Year's and that's all. One of the things that the Plebes had - (in fact any other midshipmen during Christmas leave) - they were permitted to have full 24-hour leave - I mean around-the-clock leave - and were permitted to stay in Bancroft Hall, and one of the highlights of the Christmas scene was a big midshipman dance at -

Q: Carvel Hall?

Adm. M.: Well, actually we had it at the Hamilton Hotel in Washington. It happened to be sort of a tradition.

Of course, Carvel Hall had the tea dances and that sort of thing - but this Hotel Hamilton thing had been organized by the middies for - oh, five or ten years before that, and continued some time after. And that was a big event, particularly for the ones who were not home on leave; but of course, all of us went anyway as a real gala occasion. It was just one of those traditions. It was around - I'd say 27th or 28th December or something like that.

Q: How did you fit into the course of study in the Plebe Year. Some of it was repetition was it not?

Adm. M.: Yes, it was. As I mentioned, Chemistry 1, and I think I was probably a little ahead in Algebra, or whatever the math would of been at that time - Algebra. I really - not blowing my own horn. I had no trouble academically at the Naval Academy, at all. I stood three Plebe Year, largely because it was repetition, and then I stood, over all for the four years, eighteenth. I'm not saying that immodestly but I never had any trouble. In my Lucky Bag, my roommate, Jahncke, says that "While 2200 brains were buzzing during study hour every evening, Tom was casually sitting at his desk reading the New Yorker magazine," which, to some extent might have been true.

Q: You're addicted to the New Yorker?

Adm. M.: Yes. A great aunt gave me a New Yorker. She brought me my first one down Plebe Summer - 1929. Never heard of the New Yorker. It had only been running about four years; and I liked it so much I subscribed right there and I'm still getting it 46 years later - we've always had the New Yorker. That's how it started, and that's mentioned in the Lucky Bag.

Q: Yes, I know. Well, tell me about the course of study in your time at the Academy. In retrospect, was it an adequate course of study for the kind of career you were developing?

Adm. M.: I think it was really. We got, certainly I think, an adequate liberal arts course. We had, of course - English, and History all through most of the four years. You have to remember then, that every one of those - well, practically every one of those 600-odd that entered the Naval Academy, were signing up for a full Navy career. There was none of this avoiding the draft or a free college education. Now that doesn't mean that some didn't resign on graduation, but on the other hand, every one of those Plebe classmates of mine was bound and determined, and believed that he'd stay in the Navy say, 30 years after the Naval Academy. There were very few who went there for the so-called free education.

Q: That's an interesting point to make. Of course, you were there. You went in - what? The year of the market crash did you not?

Adm. M.: That was our Plebe October. We'd only been in the Academy a few months. And that's why it today makes me a little annoyed to see things in the paper about how many graduates have resigned, because in those days they didn't.

Q: The attrition was largely due to scholastic failure?

Adm. M.: Scholastic failure or illness, physical disability - not many at that age of course, but some, and a minimum number of deaths, but largely academic failure - mostly in the first two years. We had semi-annual exams then, in February and May, and Plebe Year in February and the end of the Plebe Year in June, the attrition on exams was pretty high. A few were turned back to start again the next year in the Class of '34. A few got re-exams which might have passed. Some did, some didn't. But, after Youngster Year - the third class year, sophomore - there was practically no loss at all, except in the first class year, and anybody that did sort of stumble on some particular subject, if he didn't pass the re-exam he was

Morton #1 - 24

almost invariably turned back. We had several of those from the Class of '32 in our class, '33. But the last two years attrition was almost nil.

Q: That's in contrast to now, isn't it?

Adm. M.: I don't think it's very different now. In fact I don't know. I think the person who scholastically is able or is unable to get through, is found out by his marks the first year. In other words, it's sort of a weeding-out process. I can't quote today's figures but I don't think they're very different.

Q: Say something about the faculty in that time. What was the proportion of civilians to officers?

Adm. M.: There were very few civilians in the strictly Naval tech courses. In other words, the Ordnance Department, the Engineering Department, the Navigation, Seamanship were almost 100 percent naval officers faculty. There might of been one or two people. On the other hand, physics for instance, chemistry, electrical engineering. They were, I'd say, about half and half, and English, history were almost 100 percent civilian. There were one or two officers, particularly well qualified, but basically the liberal arts were almost entirely civilian; the strictly naval subjects were almost entirely navy.

Q: Did that make any difference in the status of the various departments? I mean, now in an almost entirely civilian faculty, did that department enjoy a similar status to a professional faculty?

Adm. M.: I'm sure it did. I mean, I know some of my professors who are still living around here, and I don't know of any that felt any friction between them. As a matter of fact, the head of English and history was a civilian and lived on Porter Road. I mean the head of department. I think he was probably the only one. But then when you got back to the ones I mentioned - strictly Navy, including leadership programs and that sort of thing. They were nearly always naval officers.

Q: Who were the Superintendents when you were there?

Adm. M.: I had two. The first two years, Admiral S. S. Robison. And the second two years was Admiral Tommy Hart who came down with his Hoover type collar and really put the screws on the Naval Academy. Although we liked him he was totally different from the old German who preceded him.

Q: He was not an easygoing man?

Adm. M.: He was not, that's true.

Q: He was in fact a sundowner, was he not?

Adm. M.: And he brought some sundowners with him.

Q: Did he?

Adm. M.: Whether it was coincidence or not, we don't know.

Q: You mean staff people?

Adm. M.: Well, an occasional new lieutenant in this department brought up by Tommy Hart. Whether they were or not I don't know (laughter). But it did become stricter the last two years. Of course it was a little easier on us because we'd gotten some seniority in junior and senior years, but Admiral Hart was a disciplinarian, there's no question about it.

Q: And yet you had very little personal contact?

Adm. M.: No, practically none at all; reviewing parades and occasionally meeting him walking around the Naval Academy, and even the commandant was the type that you'd see only if you were in trouble, usually like any other situation, and, I suppose our senior contact was one called the Executive Officer of Bancroft Hall who was number two in the executive department under the commandant. No, you just felt the changes in regulations and changes in emphasis on shoe-shines and that sort of thing. Not that it hadn't been before, but to a much greater degree.

Q: In that day you went in formation to class?

Adm. M.: That's right. We'd march to class - march to and from every class, and of course, as now, the meal formations were the same. We marched to chapel. Didn't march back from chapel. This was long before the recent putting chapel on a voluntary basis. But, I don't know when they abolished that marching to class - that was about ten years ago, maybe?

Q: Tell me about your first cruise.

Adm. M.: The first cruise was 1930. We had three battleships - the Arkansas, Florida, and Utah - and we had a good cruise. It was the full three months, June, July, and August. We went to France, Norway, Germany, and Scotland; that is Kiel, Germany, and Edinburgh, Scotland; and Cherbourg, France, and Oslo in Norway. It was a fine cruise and we were also delighted to find that all of those ships were oil burners, so we were one of the first classes, if not the first, that had no coaling ship.

Morton #1 - 28

Q: You were well aware of that coaling tradition though?

Adm. M.: Oh, we'd seen them in the papers and the <u>Lucky Bags</u> and all that. The last coaling ship class, I guess, was about, maybe two years ahead of us. Some of the ship's were oil and some were not. And, one of the highlights of that cruise was the fact that one of my classmates - John Danenhower - whose father was a retired naval officer had attempted to lead a submarine expedition to the North Pole - a privately financed thing. I can't remember who the senior scientist was. It sort of makes me think it was Wilkins.

Q: Sir Hubert Wilkins.

Adm. M.: That was it. Well, Danenhower's father was working with Wilkins on it and one of our ships, somewhere in the North Sea or near the English Channel, had to break off and tow the <u>Nautilus</u> into port because she was having some trouble. I don't think that expedition really got off to any serious success. It was one of those things you remember.

Q: It was highly publicized.

Adm. M.: Yes. Then of course, from Cherbourgh a lot of us voluntarily went to Paris. In Kiel, you had a choice between Hamburg and Berlin, and of course, Oslo, itself was a good liberty town; and in Edinburgh, the Firth of Forth. You were allowed to go to London if you wanted to take in the town. It was a great experience. It was a very fine cruise. The First Class cruise, two years later, was slightly different. Do you want me to tell you that now, or wait?

Q: Yes. But tell me first about the first cruise you went on. What kind of duties did you have as midshipmen?

Adm. M.: They divided us into divisions which rotated. In other words, you had a certain number of weeks in an Engineering Division, and a certain number of weeks in a Deck Division, and Gunnery.

Q: Were you the equivalent of enlisted men?

Adm. M.: Yes, exactly. The enlisted petty officers; they had taken some of the younger seamen off these ships to make room for us, but in addition to the regular standard Division Officer, the division petty officer's and the first class actually administered the Plebes, and the First Classman was, more-or-less sort of part junior officer, part petty officer. He did mostly officer's duties but he was training for it.

Q: In retrospect, was there great value in having the whole class involved in a similar Summer operation, in contrast to now?

Adm. M.: Well, we like it, and we liked it much better than our next cruise which - the First Class cruise, between Second and First Class Year, and I won't go into that in detail yet if you don't want me to. The scarcity of ships made it so that in 1932 only the Wyoming was available for the midshipmen cruise and, this was long before they included destroyers, and so forth. So that was a split cruise with half the First and Third Classes getting two months leave and then a two months cruise and vice versa, so that the old September leave disappeared that particular year because you not only got one month but you got two months leave and two months cruise and they went to different ports, and so forth - and I think, for knowing your classmates and knowing the people in the Class of '35 - two years behind us - we didn't see as many as we would have seen in one single cruise. So I can't speak of the wide variety types of cruises they get now. I don't know how they feel.

Q: What kind of instruction did you get on this earlier cruise? Were there instructors, professors from the Academy?

Adm. M.: Yes, there were some there but they were really more-or-less on for the experience and the pleasure, or a sort of short sabbatical. The civilian professors went in some numbers on the cruise, but we didn't actually have any exams - I mean classroom instruction. We had to keep Engineering notebooks and we had to keep Navigation notebooks, but that was sort of picking up the practical sense. In other words, diagramming a fuel system or fresh water system, or something like that.

Q: In a way, it was beginning to be an application of what you were learning during the school year?

Adm. M.: This is true. But you were taught it as you would be if you were just a new enlisted fireman or an enlisted seaman. In other words, you learned by doing under supervision. Of course, First Class year was entirely different because then you'd become supervisors.

Q: You spoke earlier about the first two years in the Academy as being kind of a culling out time for those who were weaker scholastically. Did these early cruises also work in that way? Was there a culling out of boys who decided then that they didn't want a naval career?

Adm. M.: None that I remember. Not to any number at least. In other words, after Youngster cruise, as I say, there were a few more that were lost Youngster year, but only in the academic year. I don't recall any that actually resigned at the end of the cruise, and neither do I recall any system of weeding them out scholastically because it wasn't a scholastic period really.

Q: No. What was your own personal reaction to this cruise in battleships? I mean, was it a confirmation of the rightness of your choice?

Adm. M.: Oh yes, I think so. I thoroughly enjoyed the cruises - both of them - and it, as you say, it probably confirmed, this is what I came here for. Of course we had experience being messengers on the bridge, and that sort of thing. The Youngster, the former Plebe, was given all these seaman/fireman duties and, I never thought that I wouldn't like it because the combination of being at sea that way, and also excellent liberty ports, which is one of the main attractions of course. We thought we couldn't have done better in those forms.

Q: Did you have much pocket money to spend on these -

Adm. M.: You're familiar with the graduation allowance for uniforms and all that. Well now, of that amount that had built up Plebe Year, there was a small amount given us, in increments on the cruise. In other words, in addition to our $4 a month, there was provision for a certain amount for each Plebe, and a little more for each First classman, in each port, from his reserve. But, in fact, nearly all the families just gave their sons something - what's the use of sending a boy to Europe if he's going to only have $10 or $15 to spend in each port - and there for four, or five, or six days? So, practically every family did, at least every family that could just sent their sons some cash to use on the cruise. Although it wasn't supposed to be done, it was done universally.

Q: Well, you came back and entered your Youngster Year.

Adm. M.: Youngster Year - sophomore year if you want to call it; third class; and that went along pretty much - except for the fact that you were carrying on as an upper classman instead of bracing up as a Plebe, it wasn't a great deal different. Meanwhile, having played lacrosse at Severn for two years, I was on the Plebe lacrosse team and continued that career for all three years.

Q: That was the principal sport for you?

Adm. M.: That was the principal one. I didn't go out for the swimming team Plebe Year but, Youngster Year I got inspired to go out for swimming and made the team, but the pool was too cold so I decided my last two years I'd quit swimming.

Q: It wasn't heated in any sense?

Adm. Morton: Not enough - and again, in The Lucky Bag, my roommate's writeup on me says that, "Youngster Year Tom went out for swimming, made a success of it, but quit because the pool was too cold. Tom likes his comfort." Which was all too true. But, scholastically it wasn't a great deal different.

Q: But, you had one elective in terms of language, didn't you? What had you selected?

Adm. M.: I took French. When I went in the only choice was French or Spanish - somewhere along in the four years - they added two more, which I think were German and Italian, so that the subsequent classes in those days came in with a choice of four languages. Some of my class shifted to German and Italian - some because they'd had the language in high school, some because they might have been of German or Italian extraction - I mean ancestry. But, because it hit us in the middle of the course there were very few that gave up their French and Spanish to take the others, but some did. And, I think two were German and Italian. I'm not sure. There were then four battalions, and the First and Third Battalions were the Spanish students and the Second and Fourth Battalions were the French.

Q: That was just a convenient way of doing it?

Adm. M.: Really, yes.

Q: Because there was no special affinity was there?

Adm. M.: No, none at all except, of course when one class in one battalion went to a language course, they all went to the usual classrooms, say Spanish or French. You didn't march in formation and then split up some to take one language, or something. It was convenience more than anything else; and it was surprisingly equally divided too, by the way. I don't think there was any significant difference in size.

Q: You spoke about taking up lacrosse. Tell me about that career at the Academy. It's a very fast game isn't it?

Adm. M.: Yes, it was a very fast game and we had a rather successful team. I played all four years, as I've said, and it was not only a great game, and that sort of thing, but you've got a lot of friendship with your team mates which you may not have known too well, from another battalion, or something like that - of all classes. And, then the trips were fascinating. We went to Kent State, Harvard, the University of Pennsylvania, and so on.

Q: But, lacrosse was played largely on the Eastern Seaboard?

Adm. M.: Pretty much so, and pretty much concentrated right here in Maryland. Maryland, the Navy, and Hopkins, and then St. John's here were the leading teams for years - the main ones. A few of the others did play, not as widespread as it is now. Kent State was one; Harvard, Yale, Princeton. I don't think it had gotten down to Duke in North Carolina at that time - and, of course, Army. The Army situation was unfortunate when I was a midshipman. In 1928, I believe it was, Army did not have the eligibility rules that Navy did and they were playing - either playing their freshmen, or they were playing people who had already had one or two years experience in college, and so they broke off all sports for the Army.

Q: The Navy?

Adm. M.: The same thing was true of Johns Hopkins. I never played Johns Hopkins in lacrosse because we didn't play them any of those years. We did play Army the last - my First Class year because Army had come around to the same eligibility laws.

Q: Did this mean there was a hiatus in the Army-Navy game?

Adm. M.: Completely, yes sir. We played Dartmouth in 19 - my Plebe Year as the final game. I'm talking football now. I don't remember - Youngster Year - who we played then. Then, we played a charity game in Yankee Stadium. But, in any case, that was the first Army-Navy game and it was done on a basis of - the excuse was that it was a charity game so that we could waive the rule. Then, my First Class Year the whole situation was renewed. It was, from roughly, '28 to '32. It was a complete blank in all sports; and the same way with Johns Hopkins.

Q: What would you say about the value of the sports program at the Naval Academy to the mishipmen, themselves?

Morton #1 - 38

Adm. M.: I still felt that whether my class or not, that my lacrosse team mates are still good friends - I look on them as old team mates.

Q: They're the closest ones?

Adm. M.: Among the closest, particularly a few of them are still my closest friends. The same way with the swimming team - and that had the advantage of not only was your class but it was the classes above and behind you, and it goes along for a long time. I mean, I don't like to sound like a Jock particularly. But it meant a lot to us through the years, plus what I mentioned of seeing other colleges, even for just an afternoon on a weekend was an experience. I mean, I would never have been to any of those otherwise. On the swimming team we went to Syracuse and we went to Princeton and, it's just another place you've seen, another group of opponents that you've met, gotten to know.

Q: Well, various people have emphasized the team spirit, the cooperation that is necessary, as it is on a ship.

Adm. M.: Yes. I think this is true, and I think that it's a lasting thing, as I mentioned too. We had the big advantage of conditioning, because we were automatically conditioned down there. No booze, and quitting cigarettes, if you smoked, during the season. But, I think the physical training, and so forth, at the Naval Academy - and I think this is still true - gives the service academies a big advantage. I may be wrong, but I'm sure it was true when I was there. You just expected to, you might say, you hoped to wear them down by the, say, third quarter, fourth quarter. Now it didn't always happen.

Q: Because you had more stamina?

Adm. M.: Yes, really, yes, and also, when you think that the Academy was only 2200 then, and is, what is it, 4200 now, that's a lot more than the college equivalent because you've got coeds, and you've got people who have no physical requirements to pass, and so you might say that 2200 midshipmen was worth four or 5,000 in an ordinary university.

Q: Men in the prime they were.

Adm. M.: Yes, right. They had to be physically fit to a large extent, and then they were all men - no coeds (laughter) so this was some equalizer that allowed us to play in different sports with a university of ten or 15,000.

Q: In your time there, was there any attempt on the part of the Academy at recruitment of men with athletic abilities?

Adm. M.: I think there was. Yes, especially in football. I think there was some football effort to encourage them to go to the Naval Academy. I don't think there was any other sport that was really subject to recruiting. The guy who played lacrosse didn't, the guy who played baseball didn't.

Q: Football was the first sport wasn't it?

Adm. M.: Well, it was as it is now. It was the one that carried the cost of all the other programs, as it does today.

Q: Is that a wise arrangement, do you think?

Adm. M.: Well, I think it's the only way. As you know, the government contributes nothing to athletics down here, and where is the money coming from, as the saying goes? I think it almost has to be, and yet, with the possible exception of some basketball games nowadays, football is the only one that can ask you for $6 or $8 a ticket, and get it. Now, there are a few wrestling meets, and a few basketball games, if not all of them, and even a few lacrosse games where you pay for a ticket, but what's 50 cents or $1 compared to the football, getting $4, $5, $6, $8 per ticket - and to much larger crowds. So, I don't know of any way that - at least the Naval Academy, could support an athletic program, including the intra-mural - the class teams and battalion teams. It's the only way to do it. You might say, "I know it's wrong, but it's still our policy."

Q: Would it be to the advantage of the Academy and the whole program if the Federal government would subsidize the Athletic program?

Adm. M.: I think it's better the way it is. It's always been this way, to my knowledge, and I wouldn't like to see it change. I don't think it's a great deal different from a college or university where, my understanding is, very little of that money comes out of the university budget. It's done by the alumni and the athletic association, as near as I can make out, just like it is down here. And, I think also, it's freer of pressures - I'd say, congressional interference -

government interference and control - the way it is now. I think that the Congress feel that the athletic program has a value, but wouldn't want to pay for it.

Q: I remember, in talking with Admiral Harry Hill, who was superintendent some time later, he put tremendous stress on the athletic program.

Adm. M.: I know. He was very enthusiastic.

Q: As a morale builder and everything else, in terms of training midshipmen. Tell me about the value of the Chapel program? What value did it have to you and your classmates?

Adm. M.: It's hard to say, because we - I hate to use the term we - we had to go to Chapel; we had no choice. Either that, or to join a group going to say, the Catholic Church or, even St. Anne's Episcopal. The Chapel itself was inspiring. We had excellent chaplains when I was there and I think we got a lot out of it spiritually, I really do - in spite of the fact that we marched there, and were mustered and all that. I don't know how it's working on a volunteer basis now. I can't speak to that. Well, I feel that the sermons we got were excellent. They had, usually a visiting minister, not always. I

Morton #1 - 43

think the Navy Hymn was always a sort of high water thing at the end. I think it was a very fine program.

Q: So the Chapel that was just bulging - filled with people - was an exciting thing?

Adm. M.: It was, yes. And then all the various windows - the memorial windows. Of course, we didn't have a little Chapel in those days, as you know - St. Andrew.

Q: The argument was used, by Admiral Moorer and others, when they were testifying in Court that the Chapel experience for midshipmen was of importance and was essential in that these midshipmen were going out to command men.

Adm. M.: Yes, I remember that.

Q: Was that a valid argument?

Adm. M.: I never felt that strongly about it. And, I know that Tom Moorer, and others, used the same thing, but - I also remember he was critical - and criticized by some who figured that possibly an atheist could be a good leader too. I don't know whether this is true or not. I think Tom Moorer overemphasized it in that case, really. I think it definitely improved the midshipman in his four years, helped him, inspired him, and so forth, but to say that compulsory Chapel is necessary because you're going to lead in the fleet - I don't think this is true. I think it's much better really probably if the man goes to Chapel voluntarily, as they're doing now. It's a controversial thing and I don't know the answer. I didn't entirely agree with Tom Moorer and the others.

Q: Well, tell me about the rest of your scholastic career then. Were there any highlights to it?

Adm. M.: Well, of course, we were the first class that had what they call Second Class Summer - Aviation Summer - so we didn't have our second cruise. In other words, we made the First and Third Class Cruises, but we had no Second. It was what they called Aviation Summer, and we stayed here, with the other two classes on a cruise; so we had that experience.

Q: It was less expensive for you.

Adm. M.: Yes, it was, but of course you felt you'd missed another trip to Europe, for instance.

Q: What did you do with Aviation Summer?

Adm. M.: As a class we had drills and rifle range, some classroom work, but not much - mostly practical; and we'd go up in these old type seaplanes - and they really were seaplanes; boat hull and all that, and have a sort of exposure to aerial navigation as it was in those days, and camera gun firing at targets - camera gun, with sites showing on the film to show you how you did; and a whole lot on, aircraft engines, aircraft structures and that sort of thing from a frightful laboratory. Not to make us experts but just one way of teaching us.

Q: You didn't go down to Norfolk?

Adm. M.: No, they didn't have the Little Creek program in those days. When they first started the variation on Second Class Summer, I think they'd actually go to Pensacola and Little Creek. This was the first year they did this so we were right here at the Naval Academy.

Q: Did it strike a spark in you? Were you interested, at all, in aviation?

Adm. M.: I never was. I don't know why; I like to fly; don't mind it a bit, but, I never was interested in being a naval aviator - never thought about it. I just figured, the Navy line, seagoing fit best for me. The other thing I might mention: prior to this, and still, nowadays, a few graduating ensigns - graduating midshipmen - helped to administer the Plebes. Of course, that was a big part of our Second Class Summer. We had many, many more people to administer the Plebes in infantry drill and administration, and all that; and so that was good experience. In other words, as Second Classmen, having just been Youngsters, at the end of two years at the Academy we found ourselves officer of the watch in Bancroft Hall, and that sort of thing, which was an experience we wouldn't have gotten that early. And, we had our own organization - regimental, battalion commander, right on down for the summer. So it had it's advantages there - probably more than the Third Cruise would have had; I'm not sure of this.

Q: All of those were factors, I suppose, they took into consideration when -

Adm. M.: I think so, yes. I think part of it was this shortage of ships which was all in this one battleship split cruise - my last cruise. That, plus the fact that aviation was coming along.

Q: It was a respectable endeavor now, wasn't it, in the Navy?

Adm. M.: Oh yes. Oh yes.

Q: A few years before it was a dead end.

Adm. M.: That's true. That's right. We had those big carrier conversions - the old Saratoga and the old Lexington. As a matter of fact, our class is the first one that put an aircraft symbol as part of the engraving on a ring. There's a propeller and a radio engine there, and we proclaimed that we were the first to recognize aviation. I think we were too.

Q: Were there a lot of the boys who joined aviation as a result of Aviation Summer?

Adm. M.: I can't really say, Jack. Whether any of them were converted then or not, I don't really know, but the idea was not so much to, as I remember it, to proselyte for aviation candidates as it was to have the general line of the Navy know something about aviation. I think it was more that than encouraging them to, for instance, apply to Pensacola.

Q: It was a new horizon, and men in training should know about this.

Adm. M.: That's right, and of course, contrary to the way they do it now, where some go right to Pensacola for instance, in those days you did a year or two in the fleet before you even got to Pensacola. One of the strange things there was - if I can skip to graduation. I mentioned that 434 had graduated. Because of the economy, and cutting of the Navy, and so forth, they divided our class scholastically - exactly 217. The top 217 went into the Navy. The others "a thank you very much," - and they were discharged.

Q: They were given reserve commissions weren't they?

Adm. M.: Well no, they were given a year or two's pay, I think - something like that. Now this doesn't mean that the 217th man was the last one. Coming down the line, they took out the people who'd applied for Supply Corps or Marine Corps and that sort of thing. So that the actual last man was the 217th in the Navy line so, I would say that maybe 100 got their "Thank you very much." They did all sorts of things. They went in the merchant marine; they went as trainees in business companies, and, it's all in that 20-year book, as to what they did in that year, but then the building program came along and they called them back - gave them the option of coming back. And, I'm guessing when I say maybe 100 did.

Morton #1 - 49

Q: Came back into the Navy?

Adm. M.: Came back into the Navy, to rank with the next class, which is where they would rank anyway because they ranked above the next class you see. The reason I mention this - we were talking about the year or two in the fleet before you went to flight training. About ten or 12 of my class who were not high enough to make a commission - to get a commission - they went to Kelly Field and Randolph Field as Army aviation cadets, and when they were called back in - or given the option of returning to the Navy - they returned to the Navy with their wings from the Army - then Army Air Force, and they were given a month or two at Pensacola just for the Navy side of aviation.

Q: Navy orientation?

Adm. M.: Yes, right. Orientation is exactly it, including seaplanes, and that sort of thing. So those boys got their wings, including the wings in the Navy, long before our classmates even got to Pensacola.

Q: So that route was a faster one really for the aviators? Very interesting. Of course, when the class was divided and they got thank you letters - those who were in the

Morton #1 - 50

lower half - it was an awfully tough time to be let out.

Adm. M.: I know it was.

Q: It was the height of the Depression.

Adm. M.: It certainly was, but they did all sorts of interesting things. Merchant marine was, naturally, one attraction. Draper Kauffman did that, for instance. He was one of them.

Q: Now, he went into the French Foreign Legion didn't he?

Adm. M.: Well, later on. He went to England and then he got in the Royal Navy as a bomb expert, and so forth. But, there were a lot of them: Jim Reedy, if you know Jim. He had the Antarctic expedition about ten years ago. He was the admiral down there. And he was our football captain. He was one of the ones that went to Kelly Field and got his wings down there. And there were others. But, they always laughed at that, that the ones not savvy enough to get a commission got their wings way ahead of the bright boys - relatively bright.

Q: Tell me about your last cruise - your First Class cruise.

Adm. M.: Our First Class cruise was, as I said, one ship - the Wyoming, and I happened to make the second cruise, as I remember - our battalion did.

Q: This was limited I suppose because of Depression too, wasn't it?

Adm. M.: Yes, it was and in the meanwhile we'd had this pay freeze too. The Wyoming had gone - we went to the Azores and Halifax in the two months cruise. That's all we had time for, we couldn't even include Europe. The other group, the second cruise, went to - I beg your pardon, that was the second cruise. The first cruise had gone in June and July - went to San Juan and somewhere else down that area. One of the highlights of that cruise was the fact that the Wyoming skipper was the father of one of my near classmates - Ben Dutton - Benjamin Dutton, who was a real navigator, or one of them. We went through a terrific gale - I can't remember whether it was actually a hurricane or not, but they told us that we had rolled 34 degrees which, for one of those old battleships, was a hell of a lot, and this was official - 34 degrees in the storm.

Q: This was en route to the Azores?

Adm. M.: It was between the Azores and Halifax as I remember it; and Captain Dutton, who we all highly respected because we'd studied his tome - he sent by a notice in the plan of the day that we could tell our friends and family that we'd really been through one of the worst storms he had seen, and so on, and if we don't believe it, 'refer em to me.' That sort of thing. It really was an experience, but no damage just uncomfortable, but still an experience. 34 degrees is not much for a destroyer occasionally but for something like the old Wyoming it was a lot.

Q: Did you anchor at Ponta Delgada, and did you go in?

Adm. M.: I'm sure we anchored there. Ponta Delgada was a port, yes, if that's what you think, yes, and Halifax was the other one - the other port. And then we came home from that cruise - ours being the second - and went right into the academic year because we'd already had two months leave.

Q: What did you do with your leave?

Adm. M.: I don't remember now what I did - Washington and Baltimore a lot. One of the September leaves I went to Texas where an uncle and aunt lived but, we just thoroughly enjoyed that extra month.

Q: Is there anything you recall from your classrooms first year, First Class Year?

Adm. M.: No, I can't think of anything. Of course, going back to the cruise though, by then you became more-or-less junior officers, instead of assisting therein, you actually were the midshipman officer of the deck and sometimes they let you do the conning and that sort of thing, but we had no ship with us to maneuver in formation, so that detracted some of it.

I'll never forget. One of my memories - As much as I'd personally known Captain Dutton, through the family and through his son being a year behind me at the Naval Academy - when I was midshipman officer of the deck they told me to make the 8 o'clock reports to the captain - I think the OD told me to do that, so I got this little seaman who I thought was one of these real experienced seaman, that had been around, and I told this boy, "Go down to Captain Dutton and make the usual 8 o'clock reports." Well, the phone began to ring and the messages - orderlies came screaming up to know who the midshipman was 'cos that's exactly what this boy had told the skipper. He said, "The officer of the deck makes the usual 8 o'clock reports", and that was it. Dutton didn't like that.

Q: So you got called on the carpet?

Adm. M.: Yes, I sure did, and after that I had the thing down, "8 o'clock, galley fires out", and that sort of thing. Of course, I knew it then but I just assumed this seaman was an expert, which he was not, or else he was good enough to say exactly what I told him to say.

Q: He turned out to be a parrot. Did you get involved in any disciplinary problems while you were at the Academy?

Adm. M.: No. I guess you might say I was one of the sensible ones or one of the sissies, one or the other because I never attempted to go over the wall and I never had to do time on the ship - the Reina.

Q: The Reina was there?

Adm. M.: The Reina was there, sure. In other words, I had no serious disciplinary problem because it never occurred to me to take French leave and that sort of thing. I don't know how much those boys really enjoyed it - most of them got caught anyway, so what was the use of putting on a sweater and hoping to have some gal take you to Washington, and that sort of thing. It just wasn't worth it.

Q: We're approaching time for graduation. Did you have

Morton #1 - 55

any selection as to the first duty, that first assignment. Did you have any choice?

Adm. M.: Yes, we were given a sort of breakdown on type of ship, which fleet - Atlantic or Pacific and then individual choices, categories, and then individual ships in each category.

Q: Then this depended upon your scholastic standing?

Adm. M.: No, as I remember, it was drawn by lot; I don't think it was scholastic. In any case, I asked for battleships and I got one. I got my first choice which was the Mississippi, then overhauling - or modernizing, I should say, in Norfolk with her sister, New Mexico, going through the same process in Philadelphia.

Q: Why did you select the Mississippi?

Adm. M.: Because due to the modernization, that class was the Navy's latest. In other words, it wasn't the newest class - the Big Five, so called, came after that - California, Tennessee, West Virginia, Colorado, Maryland. But, the Mississippi and her sisters, because of this three-year modernization - three years - was coming out with the latest equipment, ordnance and everything else -

and the profile of her, you see was the - the West Virginia, which was my second ship, as you can see, still had the cage masts, whereas the Mississippi had this pagoda-like super structure which was the new Navy. But there were enough people who preferred going to the Pacific Fleet, and that sort of thing, so that I somehow got the Mississippi.

Q: She was Atlantic?

Adm. M.: Well, she was Atlantic at times. Of course, when they finished this job in Norfolk, about a year later, we went around to the Pacific Fleet.

Q: Did you know anything about the officer complement on board?

Adm. M.: Did I, at the time? No.

Q: Yes, before you made your selection. This, I would think would be a factor wouldn't it?

Adm. M.: Yes. Well, I had an uncle who'd retired along about that time as a captain in the Navy and bringing up personalities - I needn't name them but -

Q: His name was Morton, too?

Adm. M.: Howard. One of my mother's brothers. He very much liked the skipper of the New Mexico in Philadelphia and didn't think too much of the skipper of the Mississippi.

Q: Who was the skipper of the Mississippi?

Adm. M.: Well, he won't know I said it will he? Bill Puleston, and Weaver was exec and Uncle Doug said, "You mark my words, if you don't change that to New Mexico you're going to regret it." Well, I didn't really regret it but old Pulee was a little rough but that was my own fault. I think it was a case of preferring to go to Norfolk rather than Philadelphia for the several months that was left of it.

Q: Were you swayed perhaps by the fact that some of your own classmates were going there too?

Adm. M.: Well, there might have been, yes. Some of my closest friends did end up in Mississippi, but also in New Mexico. I mention those two because they were the only ones. The Idaho was the other member of that class, but she was a year or two behind and we were not sent to the Idaho. She was not one of the ones we could have picked, but the Mississippi is another chapter; it was a good ship and great experience, and we somehow got along with Pulee.

Interview #2 with Rear Admiral Thomas H. Morton
Place: His residence in Annapolis, Maryland
Date: Friday, 26 September 1975
Interviewer: John T. Mason, Jr.

Q: Well Tom, it's nice to see you this morning, even though it's a wet, wet day.

Adm. M.: I'm glad you got here safely.

Q: And, we'll begin Chapter Two by lapping back for just a second to have you talk about the graduation exercises in the year 1933 at the Naval Academy.

Adm. M.: Well, in those days Inauguration, as you remember, was March 4, and FDR came in as President on 4 March '33, and one of the first actions he took, as far as the Naval Academy was concerned - he let it be known that he would like to be the guest speaker at our graduation and present the diplomas, which was arranged. The remarkable thing about the President at that occasion, which was the first time most of us had seen him, was the complete ignorance of us and the general public as to his infirmities. We knew there were ramps and rails, and so forth, but no one was really conscious of the fact it must have been a physical struggle for Roosevelt to make it to the platform and to the speakers rostrum. He must have faced the same difficulty on every occasion but, the thing was not a highlight. You were not really conscious of the fact that the man was so physically handicapped. He gave us a marvelous graduation address, and in those days the classes were smaller. Instead of presenting the Company Commanders with the diplomas each one of us filed past the President to receive his individual diploma. One of the inspiring things which I think is of interest is that when we all gathered out in Lover's Lane, in that area after graduation it was natural for us to compare notes on what the President had said to us as each got his diploma. To show his outgoing personality, and you might call it public relations, it seems that he must have had about four or five stock phrases that he alternated. For instance, I've forgotten exactly what he told me, but I remember mine and the others. He told one - he said, "As you know, I'm a Navy man and I hope we'll be shipmates some day," as he shook your hand. And he said, "I hope your career in the Fleet will be as successful as your four years here have been," and that sort of thing. I don't remember, specifically, any of the others, but it was remarkable that he had that sort of set of little phrases so that he made you feel that you're the one he came down to see, and it was quite remarkable, and I think typical of FDR, whether you like him or not.

Q: He related to the individual?

Adm. M.: He did indeed, and it was quite, quite impressive.

Q: Well, I'm glad you included that bit, Tom. And now, would you go on to the Mississippi. Your first tour of duty was on the battleship Mississippi?

Adm. M.: Right, and as I told you, we reported ten-strong to the Mississippi in the Norfolk Navy Yard where she was approaching the end of her three-year modernization. The crew had been almost stripped down to nothing during these three years and was just building up, and in order to build up the Junior Officer's Mess to Approximately 30 ensigns - there were ten of us, and then they took one or two from each of the battleships then in commission and assigned them to the Mississippi, so that we had a full JO mess of the Classes of '31, 1, 2, and 3. One of the interesting things that happened - one of the first, well the first operation - was, in about

September, '33, the New Mexico was pulled out of
Philadelphia - our sister ship - going through the
same modernization and the same schedule, and we left
Norfolk to go down and patrol off Havana. This was in
the time, as you remember, when there were three or
four Presidential regimes in Cuba, and I believe Sumner
Welles was working on the situation, so the New Mexico
and Mississippi went to Dry Tortugas, off the tip of
Florida, and anchored there and then took turns in patrolling off Havana. The Navy Department, or State Department had told the ship patrolling to make every effort
to give the feeling that the American presence was
there. We had the biggest ensign - the biggest national
colors flying at the gaff. We had our turret guns
elevated to maximum elevation, and we steamed up and
down a five or ten mile line, reversing course, and
continued that, I would say, for maybe six or eight
miles off shore. We also had - made preparations for
a landing force. How effective this would have been,
nobody knows, but we had the standard landing force
organization. We took the officers' and mens' whites
and dyed them in coffee to give them a khaki appearance,
and we had continual drills. We had briefing on the
terrain in Havana - where certain landmarks were and had
maps and charts, and so forth, showing the - the National
Hotel I remember was one, and two or three country clubs
was another, school, and so forth. Of course the landing

never came off. Meanwhile, I think we continued that for, say five, six days and then would change places with the New Mexico and go back at night.

Q: Now the supposition was that you were there in order to protect American citizens?

Adm. M.: Right. That was it, and to go in by force if necessary. Whether we would ever of really done that nobody knows.

Q: It really had a larger purpose than just that however, didn't it?

Adm. M.: It was just to make the maximum effort to show the flag there. Now the thing that nobody knew in those days - the public didn't know it - was that in the hurry to get out of the yard, we didn't have one piece of ammunition aboard, of any kind - except the landing force guns and our own rifle range. These greatly elevated turrets didn't have one shell to put in them, and neither did our 5-inch. But, it was still a public display of the American presence.

Q: Well, it was a facade.

Adm. M.: Yes, it was. And of course, that was kept

highly secret but, the reason for it was they wanted us there in a hurry and they didn't want to wait for a day or twos loading of ammunition, which would have been at least two days. We were down there, I would say about four to six weeks is my recollection. That was our first operation. Then we went back to actually finish the overhaul and complete our loading, and the next thing of any moment, I think was we joined the Atlantic Fleet with the idea that we would go west to the Pacific later on, and the schedule was such that the President, Roosevelt, again was going to touch base with the Navy and have a huge review off the port of New York City. So we waited for a lot of the Pacific Fleet to come around. Meanwhile, we were operating out of Norfolk and Newport, and then, at the Presidential Review, we joined them and then we were on the way to the West Coast - later on.

Q: Now the Presidential Review took place in the year 1935?

Adm. M.: May '34. It was very close to Memorial Day. I'd say it was the 25th or the First of June of '34. Then the Fleets - such units of the Fleet that had come around from the Pacific, stayed in the Atlantic until they all went back together.

Q: I understand that was a very impressive array of naval power?

Adm. M.: It was. It was typically Roosevelt showing his interest in the Navy, and keeping close to it.

Q: What are your recollections of the Review itself?

Adm. M.: The President - he was in the cruiser Indianapolis, as I remember. Of course, we were all in our full dress with the fore and aft tack sword, and so forth, for the whole area. The only thing that lessened the impressiveness of it was the fact that it was a rather misty, foggy day. I don't mean dense fog but, it was an ugly day and visibility was not more than three or four miles so that the large expanse of the whole Fleet, there for him to see, he couldn't get the whole picture of it. In other words, it was confined by the visibility. But, it was a great thrill.

Q: There must have been a lot of foreign visitors reviewing the Fleet?

Adm. M.: I don't know what party he had aboard. I remember pictures of him later in the papers and also, I think, circulated to the ship showing Roosevelt up on the bridge, or quarterdeck - whatever it was, of the

<u>Indianapolis</u>, his flagship, at the time.

Q: Now, did this have any noticeable effect on the morale in the Fleet? This was a low period in the history of our Navy with the depression, and salaries cut back, and all that sort of thing, and ships decommissioned.

Adm. M.: Well, I would say it did. Of course, about the same time - and we all credited Roosevelt with this, too - they were recalling the people that had been mustered out the year before, that is my classmates were being recalled and, I think at that time, were reporting, and maybe reported right in New York City. Then, the cruiser building program was well underway, and we knew that the Navy strength was going up. I think in the case of enlisted men - at that time the enlisted men were very stable. They were in it for a career. Partly because they'd come into the Navy for that purpose and also, because of conditions on the outside, and it was worthwhile staying in the Navy.

Q: And, you had a fairly high caliber of man coming in?

Adm. M.: We did, yes we did. Not as intelligent and savvy as the average man today is but, at the same time, they were real seamen. I mean, they'd come into the Navy because that's what they wanted to do - no draft or anything like that, of course.

Q: Do you recall the reactions in the ward room to this participation in the great Review of the Fleet?

Adm. M.: Well, not particularly, except we all looked forward to it. We felt that we were in something rather important at that time, involved with the President of the United States, and with an enormous concentration of naval power there for him to see, and I don't recall any particular reaction except for a sort of excitement of the whole thing. Lot's of joshing about, "why put on a sword and a fore and aft hat when the President probably wouldn't notice what you had on, he's looking at the ships and not the people," but whether this was right or not, I don't know. I can't remember the distance we passed from the flagship, but it was quite an experience; one of those things that is still a highlight for all of us, I think.

Q: Well, you said after that gathering of the Atlantic and Pacific Fleets, then you went down to the Panama Canal, did you not?

Adm. M.: Not until October or November. Most of that

between Review and that, we were at Newport or Norfolk.

Q: And how did they busy the crew?

Adm. M.: Well, of course, after three years of cruelest inactivity, our ship and the New Mexico had to go through intensive training, and of course that included the period at Guantanamo which is, as you know, an excellent place to build up a ship's efficiency, and excellent services, good will, and that sort of thing.

Q: Were there any new and significant pieces of ordnance being added to the battleships?

Adm. M.: Yes, in this modernization we got the latest in antiaircraft directors and computers - they didn't call them computers then. Then I think they called them range keepers. In any case, we had, I believe those two ships and the Idaho, a year later - our other sister. They had the - I believe among the earliest stereo rangefinders for antiaircraft work which, combined with the range keepers, gave them a much improved antiaircraft pattern. This was before the days of VT fuses, of course. We still had to depend on the time fuses, but the stereo range finder improved the accuracy tremendously, as opposed to so-called coincent range finder. We still had the coincent range finders in the main battery but not in antiaircraft.

Q: What was the speed of the Mississippi? What was she capable of?

Adm. M.: Well, all the battleships were pretty much restricted to maximum speed of 22 knots, 21, 22.

Q: Had they not been slowed a bit because of the - Didn't they add the, what do you call them, bulges, or something?

Adm. M.: Yes, the blisters. They didn't affect us too much. See, the engineering plant was pretty much the original one - steam turbine. We didn't look on that class as being smaller than the others. In other words, if Fleet maximum speed was 21, 22, and we usually looked upon 18 knots as normal high speed, and cruising was 12, 15. It wasn't until the later, so-called, fast battleships came along early in the war, when they came in, they got a 27, and then, even a later class up to 31.

Q: You said earlier that you stopped by Dry Tortugas. Of what use was that particular island?

Adm. M.: It was of no use at all, except it was a place out of the Cuban area where the alternate ship could anchor rather than just steam around. In other words, it was a rest period for the crew and for the ship.

It's famous, you know, as the place where Dr. Mudd was incarcerated and, of course, we were tremendously interested in that.

Q: What facilities were available at Guantanamo in that time?

Adm. M.: Well, Guantanamo had pretty much what she has now, except of course, it was the year 1933. They had target tow, tug and target tow, and they had aircraft towing facilities for antiaircraft fire. They had the usual shipboard observers - ship riders as they called them, that not only took care of gunnery but gave advice and observed exercises in engineering damage control, navigation, seamanship. Incidentally, when those ships were commissioned - I wouldn't say commissioned. When they had completed this modernization they were the first ones - or at that time the fleet had gone to have the first lieutenant the head of department, and also designated by name as damage control officer because damage control was just coming in, and a lot of our drills were on that subject - closing of doors and marking of fittings, X, Y, Z, and so on. Our damage control officer was next senior to the exec. In other words, he was number three on the ship, which was another indication on the emphasis we put on this activity.

Q: New technique? What inspired the development of damage control on those ships?

Adm. M.: Well, I'm really not sure of that. I think it was a gradual fleet thing. I think it was just one of the things that, probably in the Bureau of Ships and CNO's people had worked out these techniques and decided to put them in, and to make sure that they were properly used and highlighted when they put in this very senior head of department. I don't think any one instance had ever influenced this.

Q: Did we, at that time, use any other facilities in the Caribbean area? Did you put in anywhere else? Roosevelt Roads or -

Adm. M.: No, not Roosevelt Roads. I was there much later, several times, but with the <u>Mississippi</u> - we did visit Ponce, Puerto Rico. Now, whether we did that from Guantanamo, or whether we did that en route to the canal, I'm not sure, but we did go into Ponce - not San Juan, Ponce being on the south coast. We also went to St. Thomas somewhere along the line; Charlotte Amalie. Again, I'm not sure whether this was during the Guantanamo phase or on the way to the canal.

Q: Did you pretend to visit that famous town across the

bay from Guantanamo?

Adm. M.: Oh, yes. We went up to Caimanera. Caimanera was a famous town, as you say, and the Red Barn at Boqueron was another one although we -

Q: At where?

Adm. M.: A town called Boqueron on the opposite side of the bay from Caimanera. The regular boat trips made town every evening - and every afternoon. And then there was an old, very lanky, lean colored woman - I've forgotten her name - who was always on the pier at Caimanera and she had one of these beautiful British West Indies accents. And she would greet us with a slogan: "Officer's peanuts". I have to point out that enlisted men could not go to town. But, she did a roaring trade there with her "Officers peanuts". But, the fine watering place there was called Pepes. There were others of lesser glamor and lesser - you might say morality - but Pepes was the place to go, and it was right at the dock. For the crew, in addition to the usual softball, baseball, and tennis, and that sort of recreation, they could take a motor launch, with two or three officers with them, and go up a little estuary called Fresh Water River and the ship's were allowed to load them with gear and take them up and anchor. There wasn't much to do except go ashore up there and enjoy their beer. Of course, the men also had their own NCO Club, and that sort of thing, just as the petty officer's had.

Q: Did the native Cubans have a ready access to the Guantanamo Bay facilities?

Adm. M.: You'd see the occasional, I suppose fisherman, and that sort of thing. A great number of the civilian labor force, clerical force, was Cuban, and you'd see them come in every day and go home. There was also a place for recreation called Guantanamo City which was some 12 or 15 miles inland from the base itself, and they had a regular train schedule, and you were authorized to go there. It was a reasonably sizeable town where enlisted men could go and have a real liberty rather than just on the base. As usual, we sent our own shore patrol on the train - but I never saw that. Speaking of beer, I can't remember when prohibition was repealed, which was another thing we thanked Roosevelt for. Whether we were in Newport, or later on in California - the joy of going ashore and enjoying a Scotch and soda or a martini, or whatever you had, legally. That was quite an event too.

Q: That was a morale builder?

Adm. M.: Yes, indeed it was.

Q: You mentioned sports, and the crew playing baseball and what have you. Were you, as a young officer, involved in sports? Did you have any obligations in this area?

Adm. M.: Well, they always planned on some of us to be things like referee or umpire, and we all had a turn at that. We also had an officers team which played in softball, as I remember, and I don't remember if we had a formal league in the Mississippi, or not, but divisions and departments had teams and, as I recall, we also had an officer's team. All the officers played with their divisions.

Q: What was your complement at that time?

Adm. M.: I'm guessing when I say 1,400. That could be way off but it's in that ballpark. I was going to say 100 officers - I don't think it was quite that many - 85 perhaps. But, my memory is a little hazy on the exact figures there.

Q: Well, eventually you transited the canal?

Adm. M.: Yes, we did, and that was pretty much in the news at that time because we took the whole fleet, as it was, through the canal in record time for the number of ships. I don't remember whether it was 48 hours or 72 hours, but whatever the number of ships were, it was a record in transit time per ship at least for the Navy, and that was one of those things that we were rather proud of. We went through to the West Coast - I think it was late in November or early December of '34.

Any other highlights of East Coast experience, I can't remember offhand. One of the things we mentioned the other day - we mentioned Captain Puleston. One of the amusing incidents there - A class mate of mine, and also a roommate of mine in the ship, named Charlie Moore, now unfortuantely deceased, was a junior officer of the watch, teamed with a wonderful lieutenant named Zoluka - Benny Zoluka - and Zoluka/Moore was 18 on the deck watch list. Captain Puleston had a habit of coming out to the bridge and leaning on the bridge windows and whistling through his teeth, it was just one of the things that everyone expected him to do. He'd just come out and whistle to himself - but through his teeth. So Zoluka and Moore got the habit, when the captain wasn't around, that they'd do it too - usually getting quiet laughter out of the messengers, and bosuns mates, and quartermaster. One night, one of them came up to the other and started whistling through his teeth as a signal to whistle back, and the whistle came back but it wasn't the other watch officer, he was the captain. We never knew whether he was aware of what was happening, but when he left the bridge the bridge watch just had a tremendous guffaw over what had happened. That's one of those silly things you remember.

Then, our Pacific Coast time, besides the usual gunnery practices and drills, and so forth, was taken up with what they then called fleet problems. They were numbered and say fleet problem 13 went to the Panama area as a destination, and they were putting in battle problems, and that sort of thing, going down and coming back. Another one went to the Hawaiian Islands, as a place to go for recreation in the midst of this two or three month problem.

Q: Was Admiral Reeves still in command?

Adm. M.: I've forgotten my sequence but, I believe Yarnell had the Asiatic Fleet. Admiral Sellers had left to go to the Naval Academy. I think Reeves was then called CinCUS - C-in-C US. And his flag was normally the Pennsylvania which, I think, still was in Pearl Harbor. Of course, the aircraft carriers were few and far between there. We had the Saratoga and Lexington.

Q: But, they were coming on in importance, were they not?

Adm. M.: Oh, yes, very much so, very much so, and Admiral King, later had the Lexington.

Q: <u>Lexington</u>?

Adm. M.: Yes, and then he went to the Patrol Planes Pacific Fleet, still as a captain. And they were very much in the show in the fleet problem, as well as the fighters and bombers.

Q: Patrol planes were flying boats, were they?

Adm. M.: Yes, they were flying boats. I don't remember the designation of them.

Q: What kind of planes did you have on the <u>Mississippi</u>?

Adm. M.: We had two OST-U, I believe they were called, but they were strictly for gunnery spotting and that's all. Very low armament and, in fact, I don't think they had any. And we had the catapult. I can't remember if we had one or two catapults. In any case, we carried the two planes and had a complement of two or three aviators - three, I think - in the flight crew, and enlisted men.

Q: Did the aviators stand watch for the other officers?

Adm. M.: Yes, they did. At that time, they were developing, or had developed, the Baker Cast method we called them. We had these aviation cranes with the sleds on them to retrieve the thing, and the Baker method the ship would make a turn so that they passed through the wind and had a slip there which the plane could land on and taxi up to the slip. Then they developed the Charlie method - Cast method, then it was called, in which the ship headed into the wind and made no turns - just let the planes taxi up on each side. And, they had hooks in them to hook on a carrier plane.

Q: Grappling hook?

Adm. M.: Well, an automatic hook and the sled was so fixed - hanging in the water - fixed so it had a manilla netting, the plane's hook catching foward there while the observer fastened the plane to the crane's hook.

Q: It must have been very good coordination between the spotters and the gunnery crews, because your turret got an E didn't it?

Adm. M.: Yes, yes. I was lucky on that. But, of course, the E's were then given to the main batteries for short-range practice and the turret that I had, number 1, the second year I was out in the Pacific Fleet, we got highest 14-inch score. In fact, we got what would amount to a perfect score. We got all hits and in less than the required time.

Q: That got some notice from SecNav?

Adm. M.: Yes, I got a letter of commendation from SecNav, who was then Claude Swanson, and that E went on the turret and on the uniform of all the crew.

Q: Was Puleston still captain?

Adm. M.: No, I was trying to think who the others we had...I can't remember when Captain Puleston was relieved. He must have taken us to the West Coast. Then, the order I'm not sure of, but the other skippers that were there when I was were - as I say, I don't know the order. Captain Loomis and Captain Gaddis.

Q: Tell me about some of the fleet exercises - the one that took you to Hawaii.

Adm. M.: Well, they were all based on a series - they were called fleet problems and they were based on a series of exercises. We had all sorts of maneuvers. We had flipped them off into two fleets and had the standard battle line approach and marked gunnery, and so forth. There were a lot of night exercises in darkened ship, and night maneuvers - search lights, starshells, that sort of thing. They were actual make-believe battles. They had torpedo attacks, they had bombing attacks, and so forth.

Q: And, at that point, the battleship was still considered supreme?

Adm. M.: Yes, it was. Largely because there just weren't that many carriers to bring aviation up to supremacy. The battleship was the queen of the sea, and battleship admirals were top dogs.

Q: What was the status of things in Pearl Harbor in that time?

Adm. M.: Well, they could do standard repairs, such as tenders could do. They also had several large dry docks. One of the famous ones was called Ten-Ten, I don't know why that number, but Ten-Ten was a famous dry dock. They had the big ship mooring along the east side of Ford Island - there were gigantic concrete mooring piers which, of course, the fleet was using when they were hit by the Japanese later, if you remember pictures of Ford Island. Most of the moorings there were battleships, and I think the cruisers were either moored at piers elsewhere, or anchored. And, of course, the destroyers were nested at buoys, which was standard practice. There were no major overhauls scheduled, but the facilities were there to use. Ford Island, of course, was a naval air station. You've often heard it discussed, I'm sure, that if the Japs had put more of an effort on the yard rather than the fleet, that things might have been different, because the way the yard, with all the outside help they got in the way of salvage crews, were able to put most of them back in in 1942, if you remember; and the yard was relatively lightly damaged. I often wonder what would have happened if they'd sunk fewer of the ships, but completely blasted the yard that recovery might not have been as fast. That's one theory. Then, of course, going back to that stay there in Pearl Harbor: it was a marvelous liberty port for all hands - at Honolulu, and the rest of the island, because Waikiki had not been built up and the town was not crowded. None of the high-rises were there. The two big hotels, or the two main hotels were the Royal Hawaiian, and then the Muona, which were right next door to each other, and then the one downtown which was called Alexander King. That may not be quite right, but they were the three big hotels, and then, of course, there were lots of shops and restaurants - Chinese restaurants. There was one called Larrie Chi which was very famous, and very pretty and excellent food. The Larrie Chi was actually the best, but it always had the name of Lousy Chow because it sounded that way. The chow was by no means lousy, and the old proprietor which we all got to know - seems to me he was named Pe Y Chong, but I'm not sure of this. But, his was a great hangout, and you just didn't have all these Miami Beach-type high rises along that Waikiki Beach. Actually, for swimming and body surfing, and that sort of thing, the north shore was even better than Waikiki. Waikiki, you needed a board, and you had to be good at it to enjoy it, and we were just never there long enough to really practice but, the northern beaches - Kayloa and Kaneohe - were really the best swimming. Then, we saw a lot of the Army there. There was no Air Force as such. They were called the Army Air Forces then. We'd be invited up to parties at Scofield Barracks and Fort de Russey and Fort Shafter - all of those Army posts were very hospitable.

Q: Did you get out as far as Midway?

Adm. M.: Yes, we did. We didn't stay there, but we did go out - past French Frigate Shoal and Midway. We were way offshore. Some of the fleet maneuvers were out that far, as I recall. These fleet problems were a rather busy time. The excellent liberty in Panama and Hawaii was welcome but it was well-deserved, I think.

Q: How many ships would participate in a maneuver?

Adm. M.: Well, everything that wasn't under overhaul or in some special assignment. Let's see, that's ten battleships, and by that time the new cruisers were coming out. I couldn't give you a guess on that but, it was, in effect, the whole Pacific Fleet.

Q: Tell me about the operation off Panama. I mean, this was the defense of the canal, was it?

Adm. M.: That was part of it, yes.

Q: Now, planes played a part - a big part - in it?

Adm. M.: Yes, yes they did, as I remember it. They did indeed. Then, of course, planes and submarines and Coco Solo played a part, too. But in general, the fleet problem although it was based on one thing, like the defense of the canal or the defense of Hawaii, it was a period where they could almost schedule anything they wanted. Of course, an operational of this thing came out months in advance, so that the destination, such as the canal or the Hawaiian Islands, was really known. You might say it was partly operational but mainly to have a place that we were heading to - a different port for the men to get ashore in rather than the California ports.

Q: Was there much problem with men when they did have leave ashore?

Adm. M.: Not much. Then, of course, we had our own assigned shore patrol, as a fleet unit, and they could take care of things and there was very little serious trouble, as I recall; almost none.

Q: Were there any particular steps taken; especially when you were along the West Coast, to prevent espionage?

Adm. M.: I can't answer your question specifically but, along that line, we used to sort of snicker at the number of Japanese tankers that came into Long Beach and San Pedro. I don't think that many people foresaw what was coming, but it was obvious that we were giving the Japs all the oil that they required, and these huge ships would come in and load steel, and flying the Japanese flag. But, I don't think there was any animosity. We'd get to wondering among ourselves, why are we giving them all this oil, and all this steel, and so forth. Of course, no one foresaw that it would be coming back at us.

Q: There was also a great deal of traffic in scrap iron, wasn't there?

Adm. M.: Yes, but when I said steel, I mean that. But, I don't recall any particular fleet directions at least none that would get down to my level, as an ensign and a jg - none that I remember passing on to me, or to the enlisted men. Of course, everybody was quite accustomed to the fact that Honolulu population is something like five percent Hawaiian, and the rest of it was Chinese-

Hawaiian, Japanese, Japanese-Hawaiian, some Portuguese who had been out there working in the cane fields, pineapple plantations. I don't remember any real fear of being accosted by a spy, for instance.

Q: Were there any organized athletic events in that period?

Adm. M.: Yes, there definitely were. I'm guessing when I say that the Twenties and Thirties were probably the peak time for fleet sports. The famous old Ironman trophy was still being given to the lead ship. They had whale boat races, on a really organized basis. They had football, baseball. Those were the main sports.

Q: There was wrestling too, wasn't there?

Adm. M.: Yes, and boxing, by all means - boxing and wrestling. And in those days, with the fleet at a slower tempo than it has been since the war, they were real events. I mean, if the Arizona boxing team came over to the Mississippi, they'd bring as many people as they could to cheer them on, and the whole crew turned out to cheer the Mississippi. They were big events. And, whaleboat racing to football, wrestling and boxing. They never regained in the fleet since World War II began, the same prestigious basis they had then.

Q: Do you think this is a loss?

Adm. M.: Well, I think it's a loss as far as what we were talking about, as far as the Academy sports, a team spirit was very much there. If a man was not on one of the teams, he was still an ardent spectator. They had done away with the service teams - they were at the peak in the Twenties, and had brought it back to an individual ship team basis. Of course, in the Twenties the Army-Navy - when I say that, I mean the fleet - teams against the Armys' team - not West Point and Annapolis - they were a big game and the Navy-Marine game was a big thing. But, they were chosen from all over the service, and in the Thirties, they got more back to, as I say, ship teams. But, they were big events, and the competition for the trophy was quite keen - especially in the bigger ships.

Q: Did they have a golf team?

Adm. M.: I don't remember that being too prominent. Of course, the Leech Cup tennis matches were an annual thing in those days - Army-Navy matches. Again, these were drawn from all over the fleet and from all over the Army posts, and to make the Leech Cup tennis team was quite an honor; you had to be pretty good. I mean, on the Navy team we often had former captains of the tennis team down here, for instance. But, golf? I don't remember there

Morton #2 - 86

being a golf team. There might have been.

Q: That came later, I guess. Did the Mississippi get involved in the flower circuit or visitations, that sort of thing?

Adm. M.: You mean in the way of celebrations and ceremonies?

Q: Tournament of the Roses -

Adm. M.: Oh, yes. We didn't have to go to Portland for that. One of the highlights of that Mississippi cruise was that we were fortunate enough to go up to San Francisco to the opening of the two bridges - separately; it was separate years. And, of course, that was a real event - the opening of the Golden Gate Bridge and Oakland Bay Bridge. It was also interesting that we had been up there enough times for just standard fleet visits - that we actually saw these two bridges coming along; the piers being put in and the towers being built, and the first cable being chimed. It was rather interesting, I often thought that if someone had taken a picture of each of those bridges each time we'd been in there it would have been a nice progress report. They were big events in that town which, incidentally, is one of my favorites, as it is for a lot of people. Then, of course, we had the visit to Seattle and Tacoma, which was just a periodic refuel of ships, as I remember. A lot of the ships went to the Rose Festival in Portland, Oregon. We never happened to make that. The Rose Bowl, speaking of roses. The Rose Bowl parade and football game were highlights of that stay. We got there in about November, '34, as I told you, and some of us simply rode in and asked for tickets and got them - got our tickets and went up and enjoyed the game and then, once you got on the mailing list you got an application every year. Now, you couldn't get one for $1,000, I'm sure, and as an ensign or a jg, we did. Let's see, two of those: New Year's Day '35 and '36. More monumental was Alabama's victory over Stanford. The famous combination of Hal Hutson took charge. That was fantastic - something like 28 to 13, Stanford having been the favorite. But, that passing combination was marvelous. Of course, Hutson went on to play in those for ten, fifteen, twenty years as a very famous receiver. In the next year after that we rooted for Alabama, complete with pennants and things - we went up to try to see SMU beat Stanford, but Stanford put it on. We were still all ardent Easterners as far as sports went.

Q: Toward the end of '36, you left the Mississippi and joined the West Virginia -

Adm. M.: Well, the West Virginia was the flagship of,

then called Commander Battleships - ComBatShips. He was Admiral Kalbfus, and I was assigned to be the senior CWO. They had four communication watch officers, three of them usually being ensigns or junior jgs. Well, they were ensigns, and they had one jg in charge to coordinate the four, including himself, under the staff communication officer, and I relieved Ralph Johnston, who now lives here, as a senior jg. That was a tremendously interesting job because, going from the Mississippi, where I'd had gunnery, communication, and engineering - the usual rotation - the volume of communication traffic coming into a major flagship like that made it tremendously interesting.

Q: And demanding, too?

Adm. M.: Right. The senior CWO, which I became, was also in charge of the staff communication officer, in charge of the communication competition in the battleship group, and we had top-ranking radiomen - chiefs and first class - who were monitoring each circuit, and we were very meticulous to point out errors in procedure or sloppy procedure, and all of this went into a formula to pick out the battleship with the best communication overall, which included flag hoists, semifore, blinker, and of course radio. In that connection, when I got there I found out that the bull chief signalman, who

I'd been with in the Mississippi, lived up in the heights of San Diego, and he would come down and give the signal gang hell the next day, because he'd sit on his lawn or porch at night and watch the Mississippi up to the wee hours and catch the guy who was making mistakes, or when some other ship was calling the Mississippi he'd come back the next day at 8 o'clock and give the signal gang hell. "The Arizona called you for 12 minutes last night at 1:15. Why didn't you answer faster than that?"

Q: This was the blinker system then?

Adm. M.: Yes, the yardarm blinkers or searchlight, whichever the case.

Q: So you were really being spied upon by an old timer?

Adm. M.: He was an old timer.

Q: What was Admiral Kalbfus like?

Adm. M.: Well, as jg's - I'm sure, as most people - we loved the old gent. He was very good to all of his staff and he had a very convenient way of handling us; sense of humor, and so forth. He was very well liked; so were his two Chiefs of Staff who rated - They were captains then but - Captain Richmuth, who was the first Chief of

Staff when I was there, and he was relieved by Captain Roland Brainard, who later set up the amphibious forces - vice admiral, early in World War II. Captain Brainard, I had known for a long, long time, through the family. He was one of the Navy's best.

Q: What role did the amphibious forces play in the fleet?

Adm. M.: There were none.

Q: There were none?

Adm. M.: There were none. We had fitted up motor launches and such, to carry the landing force guns and, of course, troops, but, amphibious force as such, with all of the things that World War II led to, such as LSTs, LSDs, LCIs - they were non-existent. I think Admiral Brainard commissioned them in March '42, as I recall. I remember that from my days later in the amphibious force as an anniversary date.

Q: But, even at this early date in the mid-30s, the Marines, at least, were working in this area and beginning to develop techniques.

Adm. M.: True, but nothing like later came along. I mean, all we had were motor launches to carry the troops to the deck divisions assigned to the landing force and the guns but, as far as any real, deep thinking, or major problems on amphibious warfare, as such; it was very, very low priority.

Q: In addition to the use of motor launches, was there any attempt at shore bombardment in preparation?

Adm. M.: Yes, we had that. We had land firing going back to the Guantanamo days with the Mississippi. We had land firing exercises at Culbra which, by the way, has just been withdrawn as a target island - within the last few months, as I remember. And, we did have bombardment down there with air and shore spotters. The shore spotters were in pillboxes, platforms, wherever - in a safe area. So, we had done that. I'd forgotten that. That included star shell, and both 5-inch and 14 inch; but, there was no coordination of gunfire and landing craft.

Q: What kind of codes did you use for your communications when you used radio?

Adm. M.: Well, they had three variations then, called restricted, confidential, and secret. The restricted was a sort of administrative message that they just didn't want to be putting out on the broadcast circuits and

various other circuits. It was a simple substitution
cipher: Amen; J and B meant something, which any cryptog-
rapher could decipher - any good person, with cryptology
as a hobby, could easily break; but they were not used
for real important messages. They were used for something, as I say, that they just didn't want to put in
plain on the air. And the confidential and secrets were
the large variety. The one I remember the best, and
which probably is most used, is called strip cypher,
which I'm sure you're familiar with. And, then there
was a very voluminous code book - codebook, vocabulary
or glossary - which, in general was a consonant, vowel,
consonant, vowel, consonant, for accuracy in transmitting
and receiving. T-O-L-U-M was a typical one, for instance.
That vocabulary was large enough so that you could almost
put any naval message into this code. It was a lot more
tedious using that than using the strip cypher. The
strip cypher was fastest but the effectiveness, compara-
tive effectiveness, I'm not sure of. Then there was
another one that we did use for landing force exercises,
which was a cylindrical cypher similar to the strip cypher
in that the 26 wheels were put in order, as from the code
book, for that day or that month, and you were simply
using them - same techniques as the strip cypher; you
would spell out your English and then put a certain
letter or line on the machine. There was also the -
I've forgotten the name of it but it was the first really

crypto machine. It worked on a principal of every letter that went in shifted the setup. You may remember these.

Q: That made it more difficult to break a code, didn't -

Adm. M.: Right. Each one was a successive step but, that had the advantage of being really faster because you simply typed the English to this and came out with a tape which you transmitted. The others were fairly tedious because you either had every letter or every word to decipher as you went along. We used all of those particularly in fleet exercises as a part of the battle training; the modifications operations orders, for instance.

Q: Did you have to have any special training for this particular job?

Adm. M.: No, but you see, as a junior officer in the Mississippi, as I've said before, we were all rotated through, at least, six months in each department. Most of mine was deck and gunnery but, I had my usual six months as a boiler division officer, after being on deck, then I had the communication watch officer's job in the Mississippi, which, as I said, was the same sort of thing but, the traffic was much lighter. We were all encouraged, on our watches, at quiet times, to take up the fox broadcast —

as it was called in those days - the cape broadcast - which was transmitted at about 18 words per minute, so that in the Mississippi I had the standard training that all of us had, which made me qualified to take over the West Virginia job.

Q: And this, in your watch periods, this was to acquire a greater facility in speed? In the area of courses, did you have any correspondence courses with the Naval War College?

Adm. M.: Yes, we did. I think they had started in; I'm sure they had. I took a couple of them, and I can't even tell you now what they were; but, one of the things we had in the Mississippi, just as I mentioned on the Midshipman Cruise, is that we all had to keep these notebooks on engineering and, another thing that we had to study considerably for was the department then had a system of giving examinations to ensigns after two years, fleet, work Navy-wide, and that combined with the Naval Academy standing, combined with your fitness reports to date, resulted in a re-shuffling of the seniority of each class member so that with attrition, and with transfers from the Marine Corps, and that sort of thing, I think I moved up from 18 on the list at graduation to about 10.

Q: But, there was that feed-in. I mean the practical development of the man.

Adm. M.: That's right. Contrasted to the nominal examination, the exams - six or eight of them, as I remember - were all promulgated by the Bureau of Personnel and then the Bureau of Navigation, and marked, and they covered exactly what you were supposed to be doing.

Q: Sounds like -

Adm. M.: Navigation, gunnery, ordnance, engineering, plus the things that you'd learned a little bit at the Naval Academy but get more by practicing with the fleet - such things as Courts and Boards, military law.

Q: It sounds like an awfully good system.

Adm. M.: I don't know when that went out. I suppose that was one of the many things that went out with World War II; and, I don't remember when it started. I hesitate to say, really, the first class that had that two year exam but we might have been - It wasn't a very old system. Normally, you just kept the same number on the seniority list that you came to the Academy with.

Q: But, it kept you -

Adm. M.: Oh yes, we knew it was coming. We studied when we could for two years, particularly in the last few weeks.

Q: Yes, naturally.

Adm. M.: If you were in; for instance, in a deck division, gunnery division you had to brush up on your engineering a little bit because you may have been out of engineering for a year. But, of course, you could do that with your colleagues who were in the other departments - discuss these things, and we had reference books.

Q: I would think it would be a good way of keeping your hand in, with text books, and with study, in preparation for postgraduate school. I mean, it was just a lead-in?

Adm. M.: They were all good - just practical examinations. I mean there was no more math, as such. It was totally shipboard experience. Speaking of that, we also had organized admission procedures - Navywide entry of enlisted men into the Academy Prep School, or directly to the Academy. Six of us ensigns set up classes for a handful of enlisted men, and this again, is in the Mississippi, and taught them the six subjects which they were going to face. Some of them had history. I can't remember who had that - I had physics, I remember that.

Q: Well, this was a volunteer thing on your part?

Adm. M.: Yes, it was. It was encouraged by the skipper, but we were all volunteers - picked our own subjects. We sent two men in from the Mississippi direct - not through Norfolk Prep but right into the Academy.

Q: That was a rewarding kind of service.

Adm. M.: Yes, it was, and it was very interesting. It was one of the things I overlooked when we were talking about the Mississippi. We sent an engineer, Fears, and a deckman named Reisenberg, I think his name was. His father was quite a maritime expert in naval architecture - Felix Reisenberg. These boys both got in and Chuck Fears became one of my best friends in the Navy in the later years, and just retired in the last couple of years as an engineer officer - EDO. He married one of Captain Jim Compton's daughters. I don't know whether you know Captain Compton; he lives down on Ferry Point Road here. Chuck Fears married one of the Compton daughters and became very, very good friends of ours.

Q: You mentioned Courts and Boards, and that draws forth a question from me as to any particular experience you may have had in that area - with representing somebody who was -

Adm. M.: No, I was never a counsellor, or that I recall. My actual court experience came along later in higher rank - in one or two investigations - several court marshalls, and stuff like that. But, I had no real experience, except just talking to the people who were serving the court, as far as proceedings went. Of course, at the Naval Academy you had a pretty good short course in naval justice.

Q: Were you required, or were you permitted to attend a Captain's Mast?

Adm. M.: Yes, we often attended there as a division officer. In other words, a division officer, or one of his assistants always had to go with a man in his division, to Captain's Mast. So, that's where you got most of the experience. You were there really to listen in and help the guy - fleet proficiency, whatever you might be able to do. In nearly all ships, there is the executive officer at the first screening, then the more serious ones, he'd take them up to the captain.

Q: Well, all of this was tremendous and valuable experience in the development of a young naval officer?

Adm. M.: Yes, I can't speak for a JO these days, but, this concentration on a training of the ensigns was really very well done, I think.

Q: Many sided, many faceted, wasn't it?

Adm. M.: Yes. But, again, it was probably due to the slower tempo, is the only reason I can think of. A lot of the things we were required to do, or were able to do, it just seems that there's no time for this any more. Now maybe, maybe this is a good thing. The old, Long Beach Navy was too slow, in operational time.

Q: If you pass judgment on it, I think you have to pass judgment also on our civilization as a whole, because the Navy was keeping pace with what went on ashore. The tempo was the same on shore.

Adm. M.: Oh, yes, that's right. I wasn't criticizing the Navy, but you often hear about the Battleship Admiral's and the Long Beach Navy, and that sort of thing, and, as you say, it was just part of the times.

Q: Well, now you went on, in 1938, I guess it was, to the next step in your training in development. You went to destroyers?

Adm. M.: I went to the USS Borie, who was DD-215, and I first went to her for two months as first lieutenant,

Morton #2 - 100

but in training to relieve the engineer officer, which I did, and served as engineer officer for, I think, about a year.

Q: What was the Borie, now?

Adm. M.: The Borie was a so-called four-stacker.

Q: Oh, she was a four-stacker?

Adm. M.: She was a four-stacker, and up through the Twenties I think, she had a long service in China Station - Asiatic Fleet.

Q: Had she been decommissioned and recommissioned?

Adm. M.: No, she was still active. See, those days, the squadron flagships - she was a squadron flagship, then as the so-called gold platers came along - the 1650s, 1800s - they became the squadron flagship so that really, at that time, the four stacker destroyers were our destroyers - right up to about '37 or '38. Well, we did the routine things is all I can say, except it was from a destroyer angle instead of a big ship, anyway. The home port was San Diego, rather than Long Beach. In fact, I think, no destroyers were based at Long Beach in those days. There was a policy then to build up the facilities and expertise, I guess you'd call it, at Pearl Harbor, and we happened to get to Pearl Harbor, as a division, which, again, I don't want to say we were the first, but we were one of the early ones because of this policy in '38.

Q: This was a part of the development of Pearl Harbor as a base?

Adm. M.: Right. Well, of course, the base had been there, and so had the yard, but, they'd gotten very little work. People had been going to Mare Island and Bremerton, and so on, and they made it an honest effort to give Pearl Harbor more business you might say - and they did a good job.

Q: That was pleasing to the crew?

Adm. M.: Yes. Plus being in a wonderful spot. Then, from Pearl Harbor we were assigned to the Atlantic Fleet, and so we came around, again through the canal, and went up to Boston as a home port, at that time.

Q: Did you take to the new life on destroyers?

Adm. M.: Oh, yes. Very much so.

Q: You preferred that to the battleship?

Adm. M.: No, I wouldn't say I preferred it. I think that there were a few people around the Class of '31 and '32 who went right from the Academy to destroyers. I don't think there were any in my class. And, of course, there's a never-ending argument about whether a destroyers gives you more responsibility and requires more knowledge quicker - maybe too soon - than a big ship, as a first ship. I personally think that I liked the order that I happened to get. I liked the training in the big ships - not only training, but real experience - qualifying with Officer of the Deck, and that sort of thing.

Q: Sort of, ease-into responsibility?

Adm. M.: Right. Exactly. And so, when I got to a destroyer the watch-standing and the administration, and all that was that much easier, plus the fact that it was a tie-in entity, relatively speaking. During the time down there in San Diego, before we came around to the East Coast, I had gotten various notices for postgraduate school; and I had put in for postgraduate study in ordnance engineering. And so, in Boston in June, I was detached to port to PG School which, in those days, as you know, was here rather than Monterey.

Q: So, your experience on board the Borie was a very brief one?

Adm. M.: A year and a half approximately, I think. And, so my request went in and I was accepted for this two-year postgraduate training.

Q: This was in ordnance?

Adm. M.: Ordnance engineering was the exact title.

Q: You were one of the elitists?

Adm. M.: Well, we liked to think so. Some people proudly called it the Gun Club and others contemptuously call it the Gun Club, so you sort of, take your choice but, you had to have a high standing down here, and you had to have considerable experience in gunnery or, they wouldn't look at you. There were only ten or twelve of us in that year. And, they had a system then of overlapping the Naval Academy classes. For instance, some went at the end of six years, and some went at the end of seven; so the group that I came here with was half 1932 and half 1933. That was so that, if they sort-of missed a guy they thought they could use - whether it was meteorology or ordnance engineering, or metallurgy, or whatever - he had a second chance. And it worked out that they were about a half and half every year. I can tell you a little bit about PG School, unless you've got something else.

Q: I do. Yes, I want to hear about it.

Adm. M.: Well, of course, this was 1939 and the events of Europe were happening, as you know, and did happen in August and, for a while there, the postgraduate possibilities were rather tenuous. When the 50 destroyers were turned over to Britain, they took all the so-called one-year postgraduates, and just closed those courses, to man these ships.

Q: These were the non-ordnance men?

Adm. M.: Yes. Well, what they had. These one-year courses were far less technical and, really more operational. They had what they called applied communications and applied engineering, applied - some others. And, that group was completely dissolved, to man, mostly these four-stackers who were coming out of reserve. Some to go to Britain, and some to stay in the U.S. Navy. And so, the so-called technical courses, at which we were probably 50-strong, never knew when they would go. But, fortunately, for our education, and our future, the decision was to continue these courses; and to continue entry the next year, but only in the highly technical courses. So that, somehow, we got through the two years.

Q: Without being called?

Adm. M.: Right, and were given the full course, as such. Now, the third year, a few were sent to such universities as MIT for fire control, which was largely electrical engineering; Michigan for metallurgy, Carnegie Tech, at that time. I think it's called Mellon now, isn't it? Carnegie-Mellon - in Pittsburgh for - that was metallurgy, and the Michigan was for explosives - power and explosion. The others would normally have spent the third year in what we called the Cook's tour. It was a sort-of joke - visits to such places as ammunition depots, ordnance plants, proving grounds, and so forth.

Q: But, you were denied that?

Adm. M.: Yes. Well, I was rather fortunate, I think. They picked two of us to do the third year in England. We were working with the Royal Navy. The reason they sent two of us was that the Royal Navy set-up was such that they had a Director of Naval Ordnance and a Director of Torpedoes and Mines, instead of having the one Bureau of Ordnance, like we had. So that, you might say that the surface of the water was a division line. I was sent for the naval ordnance part which was gunnery attack and that sort of thing, and my colleague who went with me was mines and torpedoes, nets. In other words, underwater.

Q: Who was that - Muddy Waters?

Adm. M.: Len Frazer. Muddy Waters and Mo Archer were our two predecessors.

Q: Well, first tell me about the two years here in Annapolis. Something about the course.

Adm. M.: Well, the course was heavily mathematics. We had one of the famous postgraduate professors, who's still living. Lefty Bramble - C.C. Bramble. Called Lefty for obvious reasons, at the blackboard. And, that was the full two years of math - real advanced math - into differentials, and on up. Much more than we'd gotten at the Academy. We had a heavy dose of electrical engineering because of the automatic control devices which were on the turrets gun mounts - Selsens, they were called in those days. We still had some, what you might call - I guess you'd call them liberal arts. We had to make a study of - each one of us had to make - regardless of what course we were in - a study of some world figure, at any particular time, and then write a thesis on him and give an oral presentation.

Q: Whom did you select?

Adm. M.: I selected Mussolini.

Q: Was he a hero?

Adm. M.: No, he didn't have to be a hero. Someone else - my driving partner - picked Stalin. Then, we had leadership. We had a man who you may know. His first name escapes me - from Columbia - down about once a week on history. Hunter? Is that the name? Mean anything to you? I can't remember his first name. He was excellent. We had metallurgy; we had mechanics, torsion, sheer, stress, and so forth. They even gave refreshers on such things as navigation and mooring board and maneuvering board, just to keep us in touch.

Q: Was there any noticeable feed-in because of new developments in the Navy? You were on the threshold of -

Adm. M.: Yes, we were. Again, not talking about the world leaders, such as Mussolini, we also had a thesis we had to present, very near the end of the course, on some new development - exactly what you were talking about - and, so each of us selected something that was either just getting into the fleet or just about to get in.

Morton #2 - 108

Q: What was your selection?

Adm. M.: I remember, mine was called "The Star Shell Computer". Mark something. All of those were very much pointed towards the new developments that you've mentioned. That came in the last semester.

Q: I don't suppose radar was introduced?

Adm. M.: No, as I said - you noticed my own write-up in that book - radar was too secret for a graduate of PG, to even know about. And, I'll touch on that a little later. Lloyd Mustin, Ed Hooper, etc.

Q: They were at the PG School when you were here?

Adm. M.: Well, their second year was when I -

Q: The Four Horsemen?

Adm. M.: Right, only they went to MIT. I can't remember who our MIT people were at that time. I don't know. Victor Smith was one, but I think Victor was in the next year. I think he was a year behind me. In fact, I know he was because we didn't have any in '34. But, he was an MIT-er. I think Hal Bowen was one. Do you know Hal?

Morton #2 - 109

Q: No. Well, I suppose you had to apply yourself even more rigorously because of the impending struggle?

Adm. M.: Yes. The homework was considerable, there's no question about it, at the postgraduate school, and the workload was fairly heavy. They did give us the usual, occasional, study periods, though. But, the only real break you got was the school course - first year course closed, and we'll say that was end of May perhaps, and the school didn't open until September, and you were still attached to the PG school, but you had absolutely no duties. You didn't check in anywhere. In other words, you had three months leave at home, is what it amounted to. The Naval Academy people encouraged us to volunteer as assistant coaches and I -

Q: You mean in the Summertime?

Adm. M.: Yes. Well, no, actually not. I was able to be the assistant coach of the Plebe lacrosse game my first year, from, say March to June and July, but, of course, the Midshipmen's formation was 6.30 or so, so we just had that afternoon, and you got home as early as anyone else would.

Q: I would think it would be perfectly good for you, too, to take you away from the books.

Adm. M.: It was a lot of fun. I found out the second year that I really didn't have the time, so I only coached that one year. There were rewards too. You had complimentary tickets to such things as the Hubbard Hall luncheons, or in the case of a crew race on the Severn.

Q: But, there was no compensation - monetary compensation?

Adm. M.: No. You got an automatic invitation every time there was a Navy crew race, that you came to this big function for the visiting officials and coaches and athletic directors. And, that was regardless of what sport you coached; baseball, football - but, you got that much reward for your time; and it was fun, too.

Q: With all the stress on - all the requirements, during this intensive course, were there any of the members who just didn't make it?

Adm. M.: Well, I only remember one. He was not in ordnance; at least, I don't think he was - but, there were practically no dropouts at that point.

Q: You'd been so culled through before you came.

Adm. M.: Probably that was it; yes. That would be my guess. I don't remember anyone withdrawing. And both of

Morton #2 - 111

these years, as you know, was at Halligan Hall then by Gate 8. The school didn't move to Monterey until about 1950.

Q: Your third year was to be in London, and you were stationed where?

Adm. M.: First of all, Frazer and I were sent to the Yorktown Mine Depot to attend the Naval Mine School there, because that was one of the things that neither of us had had any fleet experience in, and it was not emphasized too much at postgraduate school. So, in preparation for this London assignment we were down there for, I'd say, two months, three months, maybe.

Q: Incidentally, it was quite an honor for the two of you to be selected from the group, was it not?

Adm. M.: We were both very pleased about it, yes, we were.

Q: How was the selection made?

Adm. M.: I have no idea of this. Now, the ones that went on to the universities I mentioned - they had been selected for that before they came to Annapolis. In other words, they were scheduled to go to MIT, Michigan.

Q: Before they ever began their course?

Adm. M.: Right. So, how we were singled out, we - I don't know.

So, you might consider that the Yorktown course was a part of the Cooks tour, although the people who would have normally visited Yorktown would not have taken a course. They would simply have been there a week or two absorbing what the station did.

Q: It was merely to fill you two in on what you were going to be learning in -

Adm. M.: Well, it was the one gap - with the exception of radar - that we didn't get down here, and hadn't had any experience in mine craft in the fleet. It was really just to fill in a vacancy in our experience.

Q: Here, you might pause for a moment and tell me about the status of mine warfare in the fleet prior to our entry into World War II.

Adm. M.: Yes, well, the new devices were just coming on, and in addition to the course at Yorktown, I overlooked the fact we were also assigned, about a month, in the Naval

Mine Laboratory which was then in the Washington Navy Yard, in the Gun Factory. And, there we were taught all the things that were just coming into development - not production but development. There was a lot of experience given us on magnetometers in connection with degaussing. We also were told about the magnetic mine firing devices. There were several different types of them depending on whether they worked with a needle or a magnetic detection device. There were also dreams of a pressure mine, but that hadn't come along at that time. They were working on mines for submarine launching. They were working on mines for aircraft launching. And, all of these had been more-or-less neglected, I would say. The scientists that they had at the mine lab in Washington, which is now - White Oak grew out from this. They had scientists from a lot of our top universities working on these projects - each one as a project officer, whatever his specialty was. At Yorktown, we then got the practical application of the things that were already in existence.

Q: Would you say -

Adm. M.: Degaussing was a great emphasis too.

Q: Would you say that this whole area received a great incentive from what was happening in the Royal Navy?

Adm. M.: Oh, very much so, very much so.

Q: This was the inspiration for our resurgence?

Adm. M.: Right. The degaussing had become a must - not only the British, but the German mine techniques. We just suddenly woke up and said, "Woops, we've got to do something in mining," which hadn't been very much emphasized before.

Q: Now, why was that? I am rather curious as to why this aspect was overlooked by the fleet.

Adm. M.: This I don't know. It was also - I'm not casting any aspersions. It was also overlooked by our design and development people too, because the standard mine that was available in numbers was the one developed in World War I. I would guess it was about Mach 6; I could be wrong, but whatever it was, it was well known as, "That's it, that's all we got."

Q: It was just an area where R&D was not particularly alert?

Adm. M.: Not particularly active. It was a sort of - with all due respect to the people who served in the mine craft - it was very low key in the fleet. They were small commands and the emphasis, such as on engineering, gunnery, and all that, was just not there in that particular field.

Q: There was a certain amount, was there not, emanating out of Pearl Harbor? Were there not minesweepers there and —

Adm. M.: Yes, they had minesweepers, but they had one mine layer which was called the Oglala, and she must have been about, oh, 40-years-old, converted from something or other, and it was just that. As I say, we were being taught that because no one else had taught it to us, or had we seen it in the fleet.

Q: So, after this course of sprouts, you were then ready to go.

Adm. M.: Since Len Frazer was assigned to the underwater part of it, he stayed in Yorktown.

Q: Was this a tossup between the two of you or —

Adm. M.: No, this was the way we were assigned, and he got even more time at Yorktown and at the Naval Gun Factory so he joined me a few months later.

Q: Did you have any specific preparation for your

assignment in Britain, other than -

Adm. M.: Other than knowing where it was going to be. Because, after all, we'd just finished the first graduate course, and we'd both had considerable experience in ordnance.

Q: You said a little while back that it was mine-laying and mines, and radar which had not been given you. Was there any intimation that radar existed and was coming on stream?

Adm. M.: Yes, but we had no idea what it really was. In other words, an occasional government officer who had been exposed to it somewhere would tell us this thing was happening, but no details, and usually they didn't know how it worked. We had no idea. I had visualized it when I first heard about it as sort of like a modern television screen. Perhaps in an airplane which, of course, is not the principal or the presentation at all, but this is how little we knew about it. It was never mentioned down here.

Q: Was that, in retrospect was it really a wise policy? To be so secretive about it?

Adm. M.: Well, no, it wasn't a wise policy, but the fact was that we were so far behind in it that it probably was not only very hush and secret, but it was also something that, possibly, we thought we didn't need then; and that's why, as you mentioned, and, I'm not going ahead of my story but, the first thing my boss told me in London; he said, "What do you know about radar?" And, I said, "Nothing." The British called it RDF for disguise purposes. So, that's how he happened to send me down to this four-months course, I think it was, in Portsmouth, England. There was another thing in line with what I said about radar - what we have said. I remember when, after Pearl Harbor, and after the battle in the Java Sea, and so forth, after that one of the things I had to do in working with the admiral was find out what ships were in this action and which ones had radar. And, the answer came back from the Navy Department, "None," whereas they had air defense radars in the ships, and on shore for, I don't know how long. I mean, they'd played a part in the Battle of Britain.

Q: Why, they played a crucial part in the Battle of Britain.

Adm. M.: Yes. What I mean is, you see, they had to have it, and somehow they did. Now, I don't think the Navy but everything, all the services had just lagged behind. We were way behind - way behind. So, to deal with this, I just had to have this course, which was right from the basics on up to their equipment.

Q: Well, tell me about your trip over to Britain.

Adm. M.: Yes, I went over in a convoy leaving New York in the fall. It happened to be the Dutch passenger ship, I guess you'd call it, Maasdam. Now there were two sisters. Whether mine was the Maasdam or the Werdam, I can't tell you now. I've just forgotten which one of the two - but, it was in a multi-ship convoy -

Q: What was this? An 8-knot convoy?

Adm. M.: Probably, couldn't have been much more. The particular ship that I was in had left New York and went to Halifax to join up. The convoy was formed there.

Q: Was your buddy with you?

Adm. M.: No, he came a little later because of the extra time on this mine work. And, of course, we had practically no escorts, as I remember, going to Halifax. You see, this was before Pearl Harbor. This was September.

Q: This was neutrality patrol?

Adm. M.: It was a neutrality patrol and the Greer had been

fired at, and the Reuben James had been sunk, I think, by this time. I think the attack on the Greer was during passage with the convoy. It was, I'd say 70 ships, perhaps; and we had British escorts.

Q: And Canadian corvettes.

Adm. M.: British and Canadian corvettes. And, there were no incidents at all, fortunately.

Q: Did you have any of the old four-stackers? Were they under British flag?

Adm. M.: I'm sure we did. The Maasdam could carry about 15 or 20 passengers.

Q: Thousand?

Adm. M.: Passengers.

Q: Just 15 or 20?

Adm. M.: Yes, it was a cargo ship with the usual quarters and mess for the officers and passengers combined. I had one officer and about eight or ten enlisted men of all ranks - all petty officers. They were going over to continue the work with the British that Muddy Waters and

Archer had done on bomb and mine disposal, and I happened to just be the senior one going along with them. One of the interesting things that happened on there is that the skipper asked me if we could assist in manning the anti-aircraft guns, which were nothing more than 20-mm., if that - probably caliber 50. But, in any case, I did some soul-searching on what would happen to American sailor boys defending a ship when we were not at war. But, I got them all together and one or two officers and all the men all volunteered enthusiastically. And, so they set up their watch list. I think she had two machine guns rigged - and we had a night and day watch manned by the American petty officers, all the way over.

Q: Well, German submarine activity was intense at that period?

Adm. M.: It was. We were just skillfully routed, or lucky, or something. There was not even a scare the whole way.

Q: Was there any zig-zagging?

Adm. M.: Oh, yes; there was that; and complete darkened ship and all that.

Q: Did you have any air protection when you neared the UK?

Adm. M.: Yes. When we got into the UK - near the UK. I remember seeing the first Sunderland, I think she was, patrol.

Q: That was the most dangerous part of the voyage?

Adm. M.: That's right, yes. We were very glad to see them, I remember when the first one came over - and they stuck with us all the way. We went up into Belfast and the convoy ended there, and then the U.S. naval contingent, including myself, crossed the Irish Sea to somewhere near Liverpool to catch the train down. But, having heard about the Reuben James and the Greer, we always had it in mind as to what would happen if we got a Nazi air attack, or if we got a sudden explosion at night, but the convoy was fortunate. Well, that was my trip. And then I saw a lot of those men. They worked in and out of the embassy's technical section, as it was called.

Q: Then, what was your status? I mean, were you an assistant naval attaché, a SPENAVO type?

Adm. M.: No. We were on what they called a special passport. The assistant attachés, as such, had the usual peacetime diplomatic status. I mean, they were assistants to the naval attaché. We were in what they call the, as

I say, special passport rather than a diplomatic, and we were special naval observers, was our actual job title. We had a commander who later made captain who was the head of the technical section, and he had Frazer and myself for two ordnance assistants. We had one radar officer. We had one naval constructor, and we had one naval engineer, plus an additional civilian scientist.

Q: Then, you were all SPENAVOs?

Adm. M.: We were all SNOs - senior naval observers, a special naval officer.

Q: We used to call them SPENAVOs.

Adm. M.: Well, maybe that's it then. And, then later on we were working in the embassy staff, but really under the admiral - what do you call it? ComNavU - AlUSNA.

Q: AlUSNA was Lockwood, wasn't it?

Adm. M.: Lockwood was that when I first reported and, of course, when Admiral English was killed in a plane crash Lockwood was designated Commander Submarines.

Q: And then Kirk came in?

Adm. M.: And Alan Kirk came. And, the admiral was Ghormley when I arrived and, of course, after Pearl Harbor, in the Admiral King shake-up, Admiral Stark, former CNO, came over as ComNavU. My bosses were Captain Lee, who I was with only a few months.

Q: Which Lee was this?

Adm. M.: He was called General Lee, and I'd have to look him up and see. He was with the Class of 1915. (General Raymond E. Lee). And, then he was relieved by Captain Solberg. And, Captain T. A. Solberg took over the section and he and I left together.

Q: Tell me about your first duties when you arrived there.

Adm. M.: Well, there was liaison both ways really. In other words, we would catch ideas, devices, plans, all this for technical equipment from the British, and then occasionally, they would ask us for some information on what we were doing.

Q: Now, when you caught information from them; this was prepared for ONI, or what?

Adm. M.: It was prepared as an intelligence report to ONI;

right. Done on a regular form, regardless of number of pages and number of enclosures and that sort of thing, it went to ONI.

Q: We were inundated by them.

Adm. M.: Were you there then? I'll be darned. Now, as I say, I'll leave out the torpedo and mining part because that was mainly my good flat-mate, as we called it in London, as they phrase it. My dealings were with the Gunnery Division, Admiralty, which was, you might say, a sort of gunnery - staff gunnery outfit as we might have in CNO, although there was no real counterpart. And, with the Director of Naval Ordnance, who was a century out, Chief of BuOrd, minus the underwater. And he had been relocated to Bath. The gunnery division had to stay right in their division. There were other people that I had liaison with, fairly continually. One was called the Ordnance Board, which was located down in Kent. One was with the Chief Superintendent of Research and Development, who was in Shropshire, in Shrewsbury, I believe. And, then the chief engineer on the design, plus a lot more liaison with my friends and faculty at Portsmouth - the radar school, which I often went back to. They worked very closely with HMS Excellent, which was the Royal Navy's gunnery school down in Portsmouth, and that's where they took their (it's sort of like our PG School but more operational - more practical), where they took the young officer who had been designated to go into gunnery. They were line officers, but had become gunnery specialists; and that was at Whale Island, Portsmouth. Now, other than the Navy places that I mentioned, one of the interesting things I found over there was the Ministry of Supply - a big tri-service research and development outfit and it really was. The name is a little misleading. There was a Ministry of Defense, who I think was Churchill himself, but the Minister of Supply, as far as the phase of the work that I was involved in, was a tri-service thing. The Ordnance Board was tri-service, the Chief Engineer of Armoured Design was tri-service, and the Chief Suerintendent of Research and Development. But, now these - An interesting thing struck me over there. They lived in this tri-service setup, and I don't know how old it was. They had all three services involved, officers of all ranks, with the normal -

Q: This was a unified command.

Adm. M.: Unified command for whatever it was - research or development or ordnance background. And they would use, for instance, a naval officer who might be an expert on fuses, so that was his job. He was the fuse man. An RAF officer might have been the best qualified on explosives, so that was his job. So, you had people in all of these various units where, regardless of service, he worked on his particular specialty for all three services. Now, we were talking about the U.S. being behind them in radar and in mining and mine warfare. One of the interesting things about them in my time there was the fact that we were ahead of them in some things too. They had gone way ahead of us in SONOR, which they called ASDIC. They had gone way ahead of us, maybe not in research, but in operational equipment in radar. But, some of the things that we had developed they were very interested in. One of them was our new 5-inch antiaircraft system, and they took a ship called Delhi, a small cruiser - a light cruiser - and completely fitted her with the 5-inch anti-aircraft batteries, including the director and range keeper and so forth. So, it was a case of, we weren't behind in everything. We weren't ahead in everything. It was a nice - as it turned out - a nice blend. Now, the antisubmarine stuff was way ahead of ours.

Q: Because of need, I suppose?

Adm. M.: That's right. The same way with radar.

Q: Perhaps at this point it would be well for you to make a statement on the exchange procedure. Was it completely free on both sides?

Adm. M.: I'm sure it was. I'm certain it was. When you got into our top secret, or theirs, we had to have special authority to discuss it with them. Not many weapon systems were top secret.

Q: That was not so much in ordnance. Most of the ordnance was —

Adm. M.: Was less than top secret.

Q: Yes, yes; was secret.

Adm. M.: From my point of view, the exchange was right. It was perfectly open and subject to your own classification, and so forth. And a lot of those people I have seen in later years, who were stationed in Washington.

Q: Purchasing Commission?

Adm. M.: No, BJSM, after the war. A lot of my colleagues came over and we continued to be fast friends. But, being exposed mostly to the Navy working over there but, to some extent the Air Force and Army developments. There were a lot of things that came to mind in this exchange, and also in the emphasis that we put on certain things there. For instance, in the saturation raids that came at Cologne (I think was the first one) and then Hamburg —

the way that the two air forces had developed their equipment in different ways for different uses really enabled this 24-hour bombing of certain cities - whether it did the job is something else. I mean, that can be argued but - It was possible because they had built these large capacity planes carrying five and ten tons of explosives, with the most simple bomb sight, and they were able to use them for night work. But, when our B-17s came along, equipped with an excellent bomb sight but very light loaded as far as explosive work was concerned, but with their defensive armament - 8 to 10 guns, as I remember - and with the - originally called Norden - bomb sight, which we had studied when we were at the postgraduate school, we could do the pinpoint, relatively light, daytime bombing, whereas they could do the heavy, far less accurate jobs at night; but, each had its uses, and I've often mentioned that when I've given things at research seminars. It was a striking thing. You could say it was lucky we didn't both emphasize the same thing.

Q: To use Churchill's word, it melded.

Adm. M.: Right, exactly.

Q: It melded, one into the other. Well now you said back a little while ago that one of the first things you did when you went there was to learn something about radar. Tell me about that.

Adm. M.: Well, the school at Portsmouth was for - I was a lieutenant then, that was for fleet officers of the school who would be exposed to - search radars, fire control radars. And, they started right from the push-pull vacuum tubes there, as they called it, right on up through the circuit. You weren't supposed to become an expert repairman or technician, at all, but it was just enough background so that you not only later learned what radar could do - it's limitations, capacities, but you also had some idea of how and why it did it.

Q: The capabilities?

Adm. M.: Yes, that was the main thing. They had all sorts of courses running down there at that radar school, and then they had a radar technician course. But, the officers course was strictly a familiarization, as you say, limitations.

Q: Did you move out from there? Did you go to Bowdsey Manor?

Adm. M.: No. One of our officers in that section was a radar electronic man so he may have gone. My interest was only in connection with gunnery. Now, the other thing

Morton #2 - 130

that came up while I was there - talking about things that we got ahead of them - they were tremendously interested in and used, to a great extent the so-called VT fuse.

Q: When that came along.

Adm. M.: When that came along. VT fuse - variable time fuse, Mach-32, whatever you want to call it. And, that was something that they hadn't - either hadn't worked on or hadn't developed - so it was a two-way street really. We had quite a bit of experience with their fleet units, not in action but in shakedown cruises and that sort of thing.

Q: You went to Scapa?

Adm. M.: I went up to Scapa to go out on the - either Anson or Howe. It was one of the two sisters - who were sisters of the King George V, who had, of course, been out operating -

Q: They were later sisters.

Adm. M.: Yes, they were the last two I believe, and my friend Frazer went out with one of their mine layers on an actual mine laying operation.

Q: Where? In the Med or?

Adm. M.: No, off the French coast, as far as I know, or North Sea, or somewhere, and, speaking of the King George V-class, do you remember the Repulse and the Prince of Wales? They were heavily shattered, battered the 10th or 12th of December, I guess it was. Well, that was a striking thing with the Gunnery Division Admiral. I had been sort of lightly and jokingly joshed about Pearl Harbor, and once this happened to them, much smaller outfit, they didn't joke about it as much as they had before.

Q: That was a tremendous psychological blow to them, wasn't it?

Adm. M.: It was, it was, and it took the edge off their - I don't want to use the word kiddingness about Pearl Harbor, but that's what they were. How could such a thing happen? They suddenly realized it could happen to them, for a different reason.

Q: Now, had they realized that the Japanese were using aerial torpedoes?

Adm. M.: Oh, yes, I think so. But they had completely - either didn't have it or completely overlooked air cover. You know more about that than I do, I think.

Q: You mentioned Pearl Harbor and the reaction of some of the British naval people. What was your reaction to Pearl Harbor?

Adm. M.: Well, the first reaction - you just didn't believe it, I'll put it that way. Some of us were at dinner late in one of the London restaurants, and a fellow named Foster, I had gotten to know socially, who is the British or European head of Colgate-Palmolive Peet, a very nice fellow whose first name I can't remember; but, anyway, he spotted us and came over and said, "Did you know that the Japs have bombed Honolulu?" Of course, no one called it Pearl Harbor then because outside of our Navy, it was Honolulu as far as the British were concerned. And, I said something like - you are kidding - and that sort of thing, and he said "No, it was on the 9 o'clock BBC news." By the way, we were in civilian clothes, except for making these visits to their services there.

Q: Why was that?

Adm. M.: To decrease the American presence in London, I suppose. We were all in civilian clothes - at the office.

Q: You mean Ghormley's staff was too?

Adm. M.: Well, no. We were - just that technical staff. Of course, we wore a uniform for the trip to any establishment - Navy, Army, RAF.

We just decided well, maybe the best thing to do is go back to the embassy; so we went back to the embassy and everyone else, apparently, had had the same reaction: The best thing to do is go down to see what's happening. What are we going to do? What's happened out there? So that was the last time we were in civilian clothes. We stayed there 'til late in the evening trying to pick up what the press had on it, and the next morning we reported in uniform. Incidentally, that night - I don't know this first hand, but it's common knowledge in that group - the Japanese had an office somewhere on Grosvenor Square where we were and, whether they had anything to do with it or not we never knew, but our phone systems went completely out that night in that whole American complex in Grosvenor Square. You see, we had the embassy number one, where we were, and then we had the admiral and his various staffs in 18 and 20 Grosvenor Square. The present embassy is exactly opposite there - number one. But, we found out that it sure was true. The BBC News had it straight.

Q: Well, you all knew that you were going to get into conflict one way or another?

Adm. M.: Oh, yes, right, yes, and we suddenly became combatants and put on our uniforms.

Q: Tell me about London and the raids, and their effect on your operations.

Adm. M.: Well, they had, as you know, the various phases there. They had the Battle of Britain phase, and then the heavy night bombing. By Pearl Harbor time - 1941-42 - the heavy scale bombing of London was finished long ago, you know.

Q: Yes, the Battle of Britain had taken place and that was before you arrived.

Adm. M.: Yes, right. That was long before, and of course, what we had mainly was the occasional night intruder or small formation would come over and they - by that time had loaded their parks with these rockets, and so forth - antiaircraft rockets, you would get the very definite alarm - sirens, and so forth, and you would very definitely get the gunfire and rocket fire - enormous quantities of noise, and you'd get the occasional bomb. But, the whole time I was there it was relatively light in the city and also throughout the country. The major damage had already been done; and they had also developed the balloon barrage and that sort of thing. Very rarely did they come over during the daytime, very rarely.

Q: Except to the coastal towns?

Adm. M.: Yes, I'm talking now of London. So, as far as that disrupting whatever we were doing, it didn't -

Q: After a time, I suppose, it didn't even disrupt your sleep, did it?

Adm. M.: Well, you would always get up and see what was happening. We were always taught never to look through a glass window but to leave it open. Of course, the town, the working classes were using the subways to a great extent for shelter.

Q: You, too, were assigned to one, I suppose?

Adm. M.: No, we really weren't. The dangerous place was underneath these rockets, and you would go somewhere else if you were in the open street - go into a doorway, or something, because the debris from these things could do as much damage as the bomb as far as hitting an individual person. Now, Portsmouth had - in an occasional time when I went down there to Portsmouth, including school and after that - they were still getting it fairly badly, but not to the extent of mass raids. All the outlying areas were getting an occasional one, including daytime. But, they were nothing compared to the bombing of London.

Q: Where did you live in London, Tom?

Adm. M.: I lived in three places. I lived at Cumberland Hotel, Marble Arch, which was a sort of standard place for the Americans to live, and then about the Summer of '42, Len Frazer and I decided that we'd had enough of the hotel and so we got ourselves an apartment, and we lived in three different apartments.

Q: Wasn't that, didn't that complicate your lives in terms of food, or did you eat in restaurants?

Adm. M.: No, no. We had our favorite little restaurants around the embassy and, of course, the food was rationed; it wasn't very fancy, but, somewhere along the line there the American services took over a big restaurant near Grosvenor House which let us avoid the British rationed food. In addition, we had commissary, a limited capability commissary and post exchange. We had things like canned Argentine beef and that sort of thing that was sent over and available to us. Fortunately, Len was a good cook so we had our evening meal at home and, then they served - off Park Lane and below the Grosvenor House, they set up a regular officer's luncheon club, which we invariably went to for lunch, on a working day - and working days, of course, were very day but Sunday, and sometimes Sunday. Saturday was a full day, after Pearl Harbor specially. You see, we had to conform to Admiralty hours, and we did it, in my opinion, the wrong way. We still went to work at 8:15 like Uncle Sam's Navy always has done ashore.

Q: 8 o'clock, isn't it?

Adm. M.: Or 8 or 8:15, yes. You couldn't get any contact with the Admiralty 'til 9:30 or 10 o'clock because that was just their routine. It's just like 8 o'clock was ours - but, then they'd work on 'til 6, 7 and 8, and, of course, we would stay there 'til 6, 7, 8. In other words, we worked the American hours in the morning, which were almost useless, except for the internal bit, and then had to stay open to conform with them.

Q: Now, did you have special directives from Washington, as special requests for this or that knowledge?

Adm. M.: Yes, we did.

Q: Well, what did that entail, when you got those things?

Adm. M.: Well, there were two ways that that could be

handled. If we had sent them a document, or plans, or something - I'm speaking of my particular field - they might request drawings referred to in the plans which were not enclosed in the first shipment. In other words, they would request more information on such and such that they wanted and we would get that. We also sent them the ordnance board proceedings, which was sort of a compilation of everything the British were working on, as far as our dealing, and they would have their own references. For instance, we might have come across an exploded DF49, just for example, and so they would ask us to get the ingredients of DF49 or a method of manufacture, or something like that, as a sort of a follow up to a previous report. As a second type of that sort of thing, they would just come out of the blue for something that, maybe we hadn't picked up, or hadn't seen, or hadn't sent to them - "Understand RN is doing this and that, please send available information and detail." We worked it on our own initiative, and on follow up information they wanted, and also new information that we hadn't covered before.

Q: Now, did this entail attendance at meetings of the Ordnance Board - the Royal Navy?

Adm. M.: No. The Ordnance Board was a sort of a closed - in other words, their own people didn't attend that, except the members. Not that it was closed, but I mean nobody particularly wanted to go to the Ordnance Board meetings. We did attend quite a few meetings - I say we, all of us in that field - on various committees over there. Their committees, we were invited to attend. I was lucky to have a Colonel Froggie Reid, a froggy little boy, and he was far senior to me, but he was sort of my Army counterpart, and he and I had a wonderful relationship in that quite a few of the Army things that he thought might be of interest to me, and to the Navy had - I'd go with him, and vice versa. So, we had a good relationship there and probably covered a lot more of the R&D establishment if I hadn't known him that well, and worked together.

Q: Now, when our Navy sent somebody over on some special mission to, say go out on a British submarine, did you query such a man when he came back?

Adm. M.: Yes, we did. The most common instances like that were not so much the operational thing as it was the research or production.

Q: The function of the ordnance then, in particular?

Adm. M.: Yes; and so, one of the things I did quite often was to set up an itinerary. They would suggest an itinerary and ask us to add comments. They were usually groups of five, perhaps, both civilian scientists and engineers, and then, naval officers. And, we would set that up for - make all the preliminary contacts and go with them, very often, not always but often, go with them - depending where they were going, how well we knew the person that was going.

Q: Of course, the man who came on a mission like that was obligated to write a report?

Adm. M.: It was his report.

Q: That was his report.

Adm. M.: That was his report. He'd usually take it home with him rather than transmit it.

Q: Oh, it wasn't transmitted through your agency?

Adm. M.: Could be if asked, yes. We would just send it out as an enclosure with one of our own reports, but usually they took it with them. Then of course, they would let us know what they'd found, whether it was of interest.

Q: Yes, because you'd then have to follow up with some -

Adm. M.: Yes, and then also, if I went with him, of course I was in on whatever they'd discovered. I think it worked pretty well and we had the sort of, you might say security or sureness of the British doing essentially the same thing over here. In other words, what one didn't pick up maybe the other did, because I understand, from my friends over there, that the British even in those days had already called it the British Joint Staff Mission, but whatever it was titled, we had sort of opposite numbers going around the country or going to laboratories and making reports.

Q: Do you want to say a little about the total American delegations over there that you associated with so intimately.

Adm. M.: Well, of course, over in 18, or 20 Grosvenor Square, as we called it, the Admiral and his staff, and the naval attaché, and the air attaché were all over in that building. There was some criticism, I think, that the headquarters were getting really too big. Sometimes we wondered what all those people were doing. In other words, they were shipping control, and they were operational planning, and they were all sorts of things which were out of our scope, although I knew a lot of those people, sometimes I never knew what they were really doing, and if Admiral Kirk felt that he was overshadowed by Admiral Stark, Kirk being the naval attaché, my boss also felt the same sort of thing about being overshadowed, not only by Admiral Stark, but by this huge organization in Grosvenor Square, when his was never more than 15 or 20, at the most, and some of them might be visitors, sort of assigned to us for three months on special projects. It was fairly unweldy, I think too. I got the impression that they really weren't operational, at least in our way of thinking. For instance, all the planning for North Africa and Normandy was done in a totally different place and with a totally different staff. I think they had liaison over here. One of the things that we, sort of middle grade officers, had to do, we had to stand night duty adjacent to Admiral Stark's office, to monitor the communications coming in, deciding who should know what - rarely did we have to call anybody senior at home. But, this was one of the interesting by products of my job there, that as a watch officer we were also briefed pretty thoroughly on what was going to happen. I remember particularly the North African assault.

Q: TORCH Operation.

Adm. M.: TORCH, exactly. We were very, very thoroughly briefed on that, just to get us in the know, so when we saw these messages coming that night, or any night, we'd at least know what they were talking about. We got a thorough briefing on that incident in quite some detail.

Q: You were out from under Admiral King's thumb. What was your understanding of the nature of the Ghormley mission? That was in being when you arrived?

Adm. M.: Yes, that was. He, I think had a different title than they later gave Admiral Stark, and Admiral Ghormley wasn't there - I wasn't there very long with him because, ad I've said several times, my first several months were not in London, they were in Portsmouth and, I don't think I saw Admiral Ghromley more than three or four times, and then when Pearl Harbor came along, and the big buildup came, and Admiral Stark had arrived. I don't really know enough about the previous, much smaller organization because I just wasn't there. I seem to remember that Admiral Ghormley's title was not the same as the one later given to Stark.

Q: No, it wasn't. It was a special mission. He was sent by President Roosevelt on a special mission and it had a special purpose.

Adm. M.: You mentioned Paul Hammond, and I mentioned Kittridge, and so forth. I don't like to name-drop but, the people we worked with over there, or at least, got to know, were quite, quite a well known group. In most cases, reserve officers, John Schiff was there, and I knew him very well. Then we had our quota of movie stars, for instance.

Q: Robert Montgomery.

Adm. M.: Montgomery was there and did very well, later on.

Q: Douglas Fairbanks.

Adm. M.: Doug Fairbanks was there and did very well later on. Fairbanks used to say that his office was his own apartment. I never knew whether that was really true, or not because he had a flat in either 18 or 24.

Q: What was his mission?

Adm. M.: I don't remember. He was the other side of the square and I can't remember. Clark Gable had been there, and the Army and Navy. Fairbanks, I knew pretty well, and Schiff, I knew pretty well. We also had Junius Morgan. You probably knew him.

Q: Yes, he was in our outfit, too.

Adm. M.: He was extremely easy and pleasant to get along with. We liked him a lot. If you pin me down as to what all these people were doing, as I said, I don't really know, in some cases. Even out in one of the air force stations I went where they were working on a low level bomb sight, who should be there from the U.S. Army Air Forces but Gene Raymond. Do you remember Gene Raymond?

Q: Yes.

Interview #3 with Rear Admiral Thomas H. Morton
Place: His residence in Annapolis, Maryland
Date: Thursday morning, 16 October 1975
Interviewer: John T. Mason, Jr.

Q: It's nice to see you this morning.

Adm. M.: I'm glad to see you.

Q: When we broke off you were dealing with that period when you were in London, from 1941 to 1944, on special ordnance duty, and associated with the naval attaché.

Adm. M.: Technical section of the naval attaché; right.

Q: I think that there are many additional points we can add to what you've already said, and you have a few in mind now.

Adm. M.: You want me to go ahead?

Q: Yes.

Adm. M.: Well, I can think of two rather memorable instances.

One was on Thanksgiving Day, or near there - our U.S. Thanksgiving Day.

Q: Of what year?

Adm. M.: '42. The Royal family had an Anglo-American reception at Buckingham Palace - and I've never known how the invitees were selected but it happened that my boss, Captain, later Rear Admiral Solberg, and myself were the two from the technical section who received the invitations. They came with the complete Royal seal on them, and so forth, and came confidential because of the wartime security, I suppose.

To backtrack a bit. At Portsmouth, during my stay at the Radar School, two rather interesting craft were down there. The HMS Victory - Nelson's flagship - is in the harbor, but set in a concrete sort of miniature drydock to minimize the deterioration of the hull.

Q: She doesn't sail any more?

Adm. M.: No, she doesn't sail any more, but she's beautifully preserved, and very much honored down there. And, in the friends I made at the school - students as well as faculty - I had a good tour of HMS Victory. The other one is the then Royal yacht, Victoria and Albert, which was kept at Portsmouth, rarely used at that time by the

Royal family, obviously because of wartime conditions, but in full commission. One of the friends that I met through the <u>Victoria and Albert</u> was her navigator, a Lieutenant Dickens. So I saw quite a bit of him in Portsmouth although, of course, his duties were totally different. He was not a member of the Radar School. Anyway, at this reception when Captain Solberg and I went in to the Palace; as I remember it, the King stood in the center of the long hall. The Queen, now Queen Mother Elizabeth, was at one end and the two daughters, Elizabeth and Margeret, were at the other end, so that they had sort of three groupings where people could pay their respects and chat with the family. The King was so surrounded by top brass - British and American, and I mean political brass as well as military - that I never really had a chance to meet him, and I don't think Captain Solberg did either. I was on my way down to try to see the Queen Mother when I ran into Lieutenant Dickens, my old friend from the <u>Victoria and Albert</u>. And, as the navigator of the Royal yacht, he was sort of, you might say automatically an unofficial aide - sort of ex-officio; and he asked if I'd ever met the Royal family, and I told him I had not. So, thanks to Dickens, I had as much of a chat with the Queen as you could possibly expect; and then he took me down the other end and introduced me to the two daughters, Princess Elizabeth and Princess Margaret. They were most congenial. There's no question about it;

the Royal family is trained for a job and does it well. I felt as much at home with them as anybody I could have possibly met in high position. There was nothing important about the conversations, except for the fact that both the mother and two daughters seemed to encourage the visitor to talk to them. In other words, it wasn't a case of waiting for the Royal family to speak, but they sounded out our ideas in general; Anglo-American relations, America back home, the war, and so forth. Nothing momentous, but really interesting.

Q: There were no awkward moments then?

Adm. M.: None at all. The thing that impressed me was - although, I say, I didn't see the King; I mean I didn't get near the King - was how small they are - all of them were, in height. The two little girls were then, I suppose, 17 and 14 I guess, something like that, but were actually tiny, and as you know, now Elizabeth and Margaret are still nowhere near as big as they look - as tall as they look in their photographs. But, anyway it was an interesting scene. Churchill was there, and any number of American and British wheels. The place was fairly crowded. But, it was an honor to go there. It was an experience that I've not forgotten.

The other one that impresses me a lot is the fact that - I mentioned that the three services of British forces were, specially in the research and development, working very closely in joint organizations under the Ministry of Supply. They had plans for bombing two German dams. One was the Mohne, I think, and the other I've forgotten. They were similar dams, and not too far apart. They'd done a lot of work and we'd been in on it with them, on the fuzing of these things, size, and the type of explosive, and so forth. And a lot of the work, because of the attack on massive concrete, was coordinated by a Dr. Bernal; and we went up there to see him.

Q: Was he an Englishman?

Adm. M.: Englishman? Yes. He was then assigned, because of this concrete being involved, he was assigned to a place that had taken over wartime duties for him called the Road Research Laboratory. It was near Cambridge as I remember, but not connected with the university to my knowledge. And, anyway, the Road Research Laboratory had, as they say, had gone to war. They had these various military duties to perform, particularly in the case of weapon development. They had quite a program on this particular project, whose code name I've forgotten. But, they were not sure of the actual dimensions of these two dams, particularly the underwater part, and they were trying to develop the weapons for the two attacks, to put the bombs out of commission as far as hydroelectric use or -

Q: Put the dams out of commission?

Adm. M.: Yes. Put the dams out of commission. And, yet, without complete devastation. Well, they had thousands and thousands, not necessarily for this project but just as a general intelligence move, which you may remember, of asking people who had been tourists in Europe to send in their pictures, and to send in any postcards they'd got, and that sort of thing - brochures - with the idea of piecing together this tremendous number of photographs and so forth, even if an object might not be of apparent military interest to the tourist, or even if the object was merely something in the background.

Q: It was a broad general appeal.

Adm. M.: Oh, yes. This had been going on since the war broke, I think, with the idea of investigating various targets. Some were never used of course. But anyway, from this multitude of material they deduced that - with engineering expertise involved also- they reconstructed the two dams, and they found one in Wales which was much smaller. I mean a matter of 30 or 40 feet in width - in length, but had almost the same characteristics, in minature, that these German dams had. And they experimented on that with very careful reconstruction. They would collect the debris that was thrown from a bomb on a miniature explosive blast, and they'd correct that for gravity and so forth. By this means they could figure exactly what power weapon they wanted and the type of explosive, which I think was, as I remember - fuze, I should say. I think the fuze was a sort of underwater pressure fuze. It went off at a certain depth. I think that was the idea. But anyway, it was interesting to follow this thing and we went up there several times to watch the progress.

I don't remember exactly when the attacks occurred later. I can't remember whether I was still there or not. But anyway, the operation was very successful against one dam, and only mildly so against the other, as I recall it. I heard about this later, so I can't say whether I was still there when the flight was made. But anyway, it was one of those interesting things that shows how the intelligence comes in and how they pieced all these odd bits together, and really achieved something which was only one of many, many military objectives, but was at least one that got a lot of attention.

Q: In that area Tom, did Washington show any particular interest and ask for the details about the Royal Navy air attack on the Italian Navy at Taranto?

Adm. M.: Yes; we had quite a bit of that. Again, I have to go back. We were on the technical side rather than the operational side, but we went our Navy considerable information, really obtained almost verbatim from the British intelligence and the Admiralty, on this order; the human torpedo, the guided underwater devices, and so forth. We sent them just about everything the British gave us. I think they were holding no secrets from us.

Incidentally, years later in Trieste, I met the Italian commander who had helped to design the devices used at Alexandria, and had led the assault. I'll touch on that when we get to Trieste, a few years later, but he was most interesting about it.

Q: You mean when they damaged the Queen Elizabeth, the battleship?

Adm. M.: Yes. I think Queen Elizabeth and either the Warspite or -

Q: The Warspite, yes.

Adm. M.: Was that the other one? I can't remember the names now. But, they got in there and did the job with these various underwater devices, and I think got out without casualties but, I'm not sure.

Q: They also were a nuisance at Gibraltar?

Adm. M.: They may of been. I just remember, in the case of the information we went, that it was specific but not related to a specific attack. In other words, it was the types of machines that these people used — what we called SCUBAs and that sort of thing nowadays.

Q: Well, there were a number of interesting assaults on continental targets. I wonder if your technical people were involved and interested in the performance of bombs and aerial torpedoes, and that sort of thing? I was thinking of the Ploesti raids on Rumania.

Adm. M.: Yes, on Rumania. I think I'd left by then, Jack. I'm not sure when that was. Wasn't it late '44? I remember the Ploesti raids, but I wasn't in on that. Now, the Air Force people may tell something on that when it happened.

Q: Also, I'm thinking of the constant, and high level bombing of the steel industry in the Ruhr. Were you particularly interested in the effectiveness of our efforts?

Adm. M.: I don't believe we were there because, you might

say, that it was largely non-naval. In other words, our Navy Department wasn't. I suppose the Army/Air Force took care of that.

Q: But, what about commando raids like the one - Lord Lovat on Dieppe?

Adm. M.: Yes, that one; and they also asked considerably about the attack at Saint-Nazaire. The naval part of that was commanded by a Commander Red Ryder, in their combined operations office, and I had several interviews with him. He'd commanded it and came back; and they had gone in there with - I've forgotten all the operational details, but in any case, I know more about that than Dieppe because I was in on this study. They had lashed together - I think it was about, say a couple of dozen - depth charges, just to have an explosive unit to do the damage in the drydock - and I can't remember whether they used one or two of these devices. But, in any case, they had chemical time fuzes which was a part of our report, so that the idea was they could get away and these would explode later, which they did. And, that's the only one of that type that I can remember that we really got into by request of our Navy Department, as I remember, unless we just went down. I was with one of the really big talks with Commander Ryder about it, on several occasions. He was most helpful. He had blueprints and sketches. It seems to me they left some people ashore, per force; and I can't remember whether some of them were hurt in the explosions or not. I don't remember the details on the operations.

Q: It seems to me they used one of the 50 destroyers. They used the Campelltown.

Adm. M.: That's it. They loaded her and took her in there. You're right. As I remember, the sketches of these things being installed in the ship, and I'd forgotten they'd used one of their own. I think it was a four-stacker wasn't it?

Q: It was a four-stacker.

Adm. M.: You're right on that; that's what happened. But, Ryder was the sort of naval escort. I suppose he was in something on the order of a PT boat or something like that. He was quite a character over there. That's the only time I - that week or so after it happened - that's about the only time I saw much of him.

Q: Now, was the technical section interested in the performance of our MTBs against the E-boats in the channel - that kind of thing?

Adm. M.: Well, again, I'm sure they were but, again, the borderline between technical and operational is rather fine, as you know, and we, with the exception of maybe this raid I mentioned, in which we were really interested in the technical end - the ordnance end. Other people were investigating strategy, tactics, operations, and so forth.

Q: And, I suppose that pertained to the whole field of commando raids?

Adm. M.: Yes; right, and they had a group over there which eventually worked with the British - right with them.

Q: Now, go back to November of '42. The TORCH operation, which you touched on briefly. But, certainly a lot of ordnance was used in that. Was there a follow-up? Did you go down to that?

Adm. M.: No, I didn't. I didn't go down to that at all, or anywhere near it. One thing that the British were interested in, rather than ourselves - if you remember the Massachusetts, the new, fast battleship then, was used in the attack on - I think it was Dakar. (Casablanca).

Q: Jean Bart.

Adm. M.: Jean Bart is the one. And, they were extremely interested in the type of shell we had used on the 16-inch gun.

Q: They didn't explode?

Adm. M.: That's right. Meanwhile, Tarawa, in the Pacific, led to the development of the Navy's high-capacity projectile, because so many of the armor-piercing shells which the new and old battleships had were not designed for blanket coverage like they had at Tarawa. And, similarly, the Massachusetts had nothing but the armor-piercing. And so the high-capacity, which was a much lighter shell, but a much greater - relative amount of explosives was used for the future operations, such as lighter ships and area coverage, gun emplacements (When I say that, I mean light gun emplacements). And we reserved the high-capacity for surface engagements against armored ships or heavily armored pillboxes, command posts, and so forth, because the armor-piercing shell was not designed for firing over jungles and palm trees, and had not enough explosive to do a field job.

Q: That particular incident with the Massachusetts caused quite a flap in Washington.

Adm. M.: I imagine so, yes.

Q: Even in the White House.

Adm. M.: Actually, a lot of those shells went through on both sides, as I remember.

Q: But didn't explode.

Adm. M.: That's right. I've forgotten the detail of it, but it seems to me that in underwater hits the projectile was designed to go in through armor and then get inside and explode, and the timed array, which was deliberately built in, was enough so that she'd gone out the other side of the ship before anything happened. That's my recollection.

Q: Admiral King sent over a special emmissary, to London and to North Africa, to be his eyes and ears. Did you have anything to do with him? Bernard Bieri?

Adm. M.: I remember Admiral Bieri, but I don't think I had any direct connection with him; no. I know who you mean. Vice admiral I believe, isn't it?

Early in the war, before Pearl Harbor, and long before I got there - when I say the war, I mean the European war - we had quite a few people who made trips in their carriers and heavier ships, and I'm sure in submarines and that sort of thing. We had one officer who I knew very well at the chase with the <u>Bismarck</u> - and, I've forgotten who that was now, unfortunately, and much senior to me, but he'd been with them, and we had quite a few officers in their carriers in the first year or so of the European war, but not so much shipboard observation after that - that is, in their ships because, after all, we needed our people in our own ships by that time. Admiral Libby, then captain, was one who I think made one of those - say 1940 - operations. I'll think of the officer who was on the scene of the <u>Bismarck</u> later on. There were a number of them, but not so much later in the war - after Pearl Harbor. At least from the London side. Now whether Admiral King or some U.S. Command sent people directly, I don't know.

Q: Do you want to recall some specific visits to R&D Headquarters in various parts of the U. .?

Adm. M.: Briefly, I can, without maybe going into too much detail. I mentioned the HMS _Excellent_ at Whale Island, Portsmouth.

Q: Yes, you did.

Adm. M.: That was one that I frequently went to. I went to Woolwich Arsenal, which was largely Army. I went to their proving ground on the east coast down by the Thames Estuary - Thames mouth. That name slips me. I mentioned going to General McGarth up in Shrewsbury, who was the Chief Superintendent of R&D; his headquarters were outside there. Not so much operational, but I visited the Admiralty in Bath, which was the Director of Naval Ordnance, and his outfit had been moved there from London for both space reasons and safety reasons, I guess, dispersal. I mentioned going on the ship trials at Scapa Flow; several air stations - one Naval Air Station in Yeovilton.

Q: Where?

Adm. M.: Yeovilton is the way I remember it; and Bovington which was an RAF Station. They had a small development outfit down at Weymouth which I visited several times. And then I also went to several of their commercial

factories who were working on a developed item. I
remember one called the Plessey, not far from London
in a place called Ilford. They were mainly working on
fire control - what we now call computers. Not in the
IBM sense but in the machine assembly. And there were
an awful lot of them, but I can't recall any by name
right now.

Q: What was the general attitude of the British worker -
the factory worker - at Ilford?

Adm. M.: Well, we saw a lot of them, and of course,
they were sort of down there on a specific thing which
really involved, not so much the laborers and mechanics,
as it was the idea and the engineering thinking behind
it. Now you mention that, I can tell you one interesting trip that I made with several of our officers. I
think our senior one was then Commander Millis who was our
then BuShips man in the section, later Captain Ray
Millis; and his opposite number as a naval constructor
in the section was Admiral Leahy's son, Bill Leahy,
later Rear Admiral in EDO and Commander of, I think the
Norfolk Shipyard, among others. We went down with a
trip arranged by DNI. I think that's the name they
call it, isn't it?

Q: Yes.

Adm. M.: - with a group of Russian visitors - Russian naval officers. It seems to me this whole trip was Navy. And we went down the Thames in a little - a fairly sized motor launch, and we went to the Ford Plant at Dagenham, ten or fifteen miles down the river - the Thames; and they had a setup corresponding to our places in Detroit, but not nearly as efficient. They were a completely integrated plant. They made their own coke and their own steel; and then went on to manufacturing. We were there sort of as guides with the British officers, I guess you'd call it. The party was really to show these Russians around. And they were fairly high ranking. I think maybe there was one admiral there, several captains. And, not because of the Russian visit but just because of the attitude in Britain regarding Russia's Second Front, the hammer and sickle were all over the factory - painted on chimneys, and sides of building and all that, to show cooperation, companionship. And, you could tell - that's one of the few times I ever really talked to any of the British blue collars - that the Russian attack was very, very welcome as far as they were concerned - the Second Front.

Q: It took some of the pressure off of them?

Adm. M.: Yes.

Q: Were the Russians shown everything in similar fashion to the Americans?

Adm. M.: No, I think not but that trip was really more or less a show trip. In other words, they were not down there looking at any particular piece of equipment or concept. It was just to show them a steel factory, just as you'd show them in Detroit today. Of course they were building trucks, tanks maybe, and that sort of thing, because of the wartime conversion. It was really just a show trip, you might say. Nearly all day long and we had lunch down there.

Those trips, in addition to the factories and the R&D establishments, I occasionally went up, primarily with the underwater man, Fraser, that I've mentioned several times. He and I shared a flat together (as the British call it) and were very close. And, being the two ordnance officers we often went along on each others trips, as a matter of interest. We often went up to Western Approaches - Admiral Guy - I don't know his name. Not Guy Edwards, but a name like that, who was a long time there, based at Liverpool, and we'd go up and see him. Now, this more or less came on, you might say the operational side. But, we were up there just sort of, especially my colleague Fraser, to touch base with him on torpedo performance, mine performance, mine defense and that sort of thing. He had the Western Approaches a good part of the war. I wish I could think of his name. But, that's the sort of thing we did. It was mainly the R&D labs but it was also some of the test stations and, in some cases, either the Government production facility or the commercial.

Q: Was there an early peak in demands from Washington on information? Did it begin to subside a bit as the war progressed inasmuch as the U.S. was also developing so rapidly?

Adm. M.: Right. I can't remember when the actual peak of requests for our reports were in, at least from my point of view. It was fairly steady, I think. We did get in, towards the end of my stay there, we got into General Aurand's office. I guess he was a military Lend-Lease man. There was a very tight monthly report on the amount of 20 mm. ammunition that we'd delivered to Britain from our supply here. Now this didn't involve any trips but just, we worked very closely with the supply in the Admiralty for the Oerlikon Machine Gun which they'd purchased from us in considerable numbers.

An interesting point on that; I don't know whether

I mentioned it in the previous interviews but, when the war came along if you remember, we had a 1.1 antiaircraft machine gun that was not successful.

Q: In spite of Lloyd's efforts.

Adm. M.: Well, Lloyd's efforts to improve the 1.1 led to his conduct of trials to see what we could get to replace it. Speaking of this 20 mm. ammunition reminded me of it. As you know, what turned out to be the two replacements were both built, designed, built - initially built by two of the worlds prominent neutrals. The Oerlikon came from Switzerland and the Bofors 40 mm. came from Sweden. And I've always been impressed by that fact; that when Lloyd and his colleagues finally hit on the replacements they hit on two and they came from the most prominent neutrals in the world at that point.

Q: But these guns were eventually manufactured in the United States?

Adm. M.: Oh yes, indeed. York Safe and Lock built the 40 mm. there, and of course a lot of factories got into the act by then, and of course the design of the mount was predominantly U.S. by then - the fire control. The 40 mms. came in twins and quads - mostly quads in the bigger ships. The single 40 mm. was primarily used by the Army. I don't think we had many ships with a single 40. - at least not of any size. And the Oerlikon, as you remember, started out as a single and then later, in the last year or two of the war, we replaced, wherever possible, especially again, in the bigger ships, with a twin, to give you more fire power.

To go back to your question. I can't remember any particular peak. I can't remember any real significant change in the amount of requests, reports, trips and so forth.

Q: Now, you said, last time, that you were a watch officer and therefore you were cognizant of plans for developing operations. Before you left. Normandy happened after you left London?

Adm. M.: Right.

Q: But, there was a great build up over a long period of time in preparation for Normandy. Were you cognizant of this and were you cognizant of some of the very bizarre, almost, developments on the coast? British ideas that were implemented, such as the Mulberry, that kind of thing?

Adm. M.: Not particularly. We weren't in on that too much. Of course, for the SHAEF operation; that was handled by a large joint staff with their own headquarters in London, and also outside of London, and a totally different group worked on that - the amassing of the material and the landing craft. We knew that was going on. On that TORCH operation that I mentioned, we were briefed specifically on that because it was coming up in about a week, just to give the watch officers some knowledge. We had location, dates, and that sort of thing but Normandy was too much after I left. I imagine the same people were totally briefed on Omaha Beach, Utah Beach and so forth, but not at the time I was there.

Q: Were you at all interested in the early salvage operations off the North African coast and the various ports there?

Adm. M.: No, not especially. Now, where was - was it Commander or Captain Ellsberg? Was that his name? That was in Eritrea or one of those places, wasn't it?

Q: He was there originally, but then he was supplanted by Sullivan.

Adm. M.: That's right, yes. I knew only cursury information on that. We did get very brief periodic reports on the salvage at Pearl Harbor. In other words, "USS so-and-so is 90% completed at Pearl Harbor," or "is being taken somewhere else for repairs," and so forth, but no real, technical information. I think most of that I got as a watch officer in messages that would come in that night and, I think we stood a watch about every eight or ten evenings - nights; and they actually had a watch officers quarters there. You had a bunk and a closet, hand basin.

Q: Well, there was some compensation for being a watch officer then? It was educational.

Adm. M.: Oh, sure it was, yes. It was that indeed. But, I suppose they had to expose us to that much because if we didn't have that information, what good were we doing sitting and sleeping there? They had a miniature war room, I guess, that would show the positions of convoys in the enclosure and the progress of the operations such as TORCH, but we really were keeping an information room through the night hours more than anything else, I think. ComNavEur was not operational.

Q: Do you want to talk about some of the outstanding

personalities who were there at that time? I mean people like Admiral Lockwood.

Adm. M.: Yes. Of course we mentioned him. He was there when I first arrived and, as we agreed, he was taken to command the Pacific submarines when Admiral English was killed, in a plane crash, as I remember. I mentioned Captain Bastido, Admiral Kirk.

Q: Do you want to say something about Kirk? I mean, how did he operate?

Adm. M.: Well, it's like asking a student what he thinks of his principal, because very often you never saw people at his echelon unless you were in trouble - we'll put it that way. It's just like a student going to the principal's office. We didn't see an awful lot of Admiral Stark and Admiral Kirk. They were fine to work with. You knew just where you stood, but I wouldn't say that I would be in a position to give any idea of how efficient they were, or how tough they were, or anything else.

Q: What about some of the foreign governments in exile stationed in London and in the U.K. in various places - De Gaulle, for instance?

Adm. M.: Yes, he was there. Ambassador Biddle - Anthony Biddle - had a sort of exile Embassy - Embassy for Exiles down at Grosvenor Square or Berkeley Square - no, Berkeley Square, and most of their liaison was through that office. And, although you'd see De Gaulle around - there were a lot of people. King Peter of Yugoslavia was there. The King of Greece, George. You'd see them at lunch or something like that in their favorite hotels.

Q: Haakon of Norway?

Adm. M.: I don't remember seeing him. De Gaulle, I did see. Was it Paul or Peter of Yugoslavia?

Q: Peter.

Adm. M.: Yes, the young one. And then there were several of those that you'd sort of see around. I had no business dealing with them at all.

Q: I wondered if they had any occasion to seek out technical information. Most of them had some naval units. The Dutch, for instance. The French certainly did.

Adm. M.: Speaking of the Dutch, Bernard was there too, very much in evidence around. I imagine that for that sort of thing they dealt directly with either Biddle or the British Admiralty. This would be my impression because I rarely remember talking to them or having questions from their junior people or anything like that - very little.

Q: You were telling me about the social life that came your way while you were in London.

Adm. M.: Yes, it was fairly active. In other words, there were visiting people from the States and either the Americans or the British would entertain. I remember one time - Again, Captain Solberg and myself were invited to a reception at the Dorchester for General Campbell who was then Chief of Army Ordnance who of course lives here and is a Naval Academy graduate and since, in spite of the difference in age, he and his wife have been for years, great friends of ours. The Dorchester Hotel is only about three or four blocks from our then Embassy at No. 1 Grosvenor Square, and it was Armistice Day, the World War. I remember it was 11 November, and Captain Solberg and myself were the ones invited to this reception for General Campbell, and I've often talked to him about it in recent years.

It was the heaviest and really last bad London fog. They'd gotten around to controlling the coal and that sort of thing, but not to any great extent like they did after the war, and we knew the way from the American Embassy to the Dorchester Hotel like the backs of our hands, and we literally did not get there. I mean, this was one part of social life which was interesting. We just gave up and came back to the Embassy and waited til things cleared and we could find a subway. He and I both knew it and it was only a three or four block walk. We knew every fence and all that. There were people out with torches leading the buses. It was blackout of course, but to get a bus through the street they had these torches; a man with a torch going down in front of them. It really was a record breaker.

Another thing that I got into which was extremely interesting; there were two or three of us from the American Forces, two or three Navy - there were of course Navy, Army, Air Force - who were invited to join the Anglo-American Dining Club, and that was sponsored by the motor magnet, Lord Nuffield by name, as I recall. And that was a group of about ten middle-ranking officers, like myself and my Army and Air Force counterparts. There may be 20. I suppose we sat about 40 and met once a month at Nuffield House, and they always had an excellent speaker from civilian or military, British cabinet officers, senior British service officers, and an occasional American, and so forth, and that was an interesting thing. It was the first time I'd ever seen Eisenhower. He was there, not as a speaker but his staff, he and the top five or six of his joint staff were there more in a reception and dinner rather than a speaking role. And Air Marshal Tedder who was his Deputy was there, and I'd say five or six of them from the Combined Staff were there on one occasion. You'd have a few cocktails with your British and American colleagues and then go on to the formal dinner. The speaker was introduced by a beautifully garbed flunky who would say, "Pray silence," whatever the British expression is. He'd beat his staff on the floor and say, "Pray silence for His Lordship so-and-so who's going to speak tonight." It was done in real formal, old-fashioned British procedure and was a great deal of fun.

Where I had seen Ike before that was rather interesting. Our office in the Embassy was in the sort of left rear as you faced the building, and to get to the front door you went down a long passage and had a sharp right turn with all this marble walls and marble floor. And, I was going out to lunch I guess, or somewhere, in midday and I made the turn and smashed

into this fellow pedestrian in the Embassy. It was
Eleanor Roosevelt; and I was full of apologies for
bumping into Mrs. Roosevelt, and she was very gracious;
nobody was hurt, but, believe it or not, on the same
corner some months or weeks later, I bumped into
Eisenhower exactly the same way. Knowing both were in
London, on these separate occasions, I picked that corner
in the Embassy to collide with two of our leading
Americans.

Q: They needed a traffic light on that corner.

Adm. M.: Then, of course, going back to social life,
we had - I mean the Americans and some of our British
friends would, especially my opposite numbers in Gunnery Division Admiralty, we would have a small family
dinner at home or at a restaurant or something like
that and, life sort of went on. I mean, the night
clubs were open and the good restaurants were still
serving the best food they could get, and that sort of
thing; and, like they always say, there was a lot of
business done in a sort of way over occasions like
that.

Then I was lucky through my gal Sue, now my wife.
We were invited down to the stately homes of England
on any number of occasions for the weekend of Christmas

leave, something like that.

Q: Where did you go?

Adm. M.: We went to two places primarily. One was that of an Army colonel. I'm not sure if he was still active or not; Colonel Temperley, Clive Temperley. He lived at Rudgewick. These are all south of London and, a beautiful place. And then we went to Farleigh quite often, especially over Christmas. Farleigh, which is near the home of Basinstoke, and he was Gerard Wallop. He was then Viscount Lymington. His father was the Earl of Portsmouth and had bought a ranch in Wyoming and had stayed there, so the Earl of Portsmouth was in Wyoming and this was his oldest son, Gerard Wallop.

During the time I was there, or either when we came back years later, his father had died in Wyoming and Gerard had then become the Earl of Portsmouth, and his son became Viscount Lymington, and that was his secondary title. I remember one either leave or weekend down there - the son was Oliver Wallop, the family name. He was called Noll as a nickname - and I'll never forget going down to the train with him, to go back to London, or else meeting him when he was coming in, and on his baggage were big tags: ORDINARY SEAMAN, THE HONORABLE OLIVER WALLOP. I just thought that was classic, which he loved. Of course he was commissioned. He was going to something corresponding to our OCS, but that Ordinary Seaman, the Honorable really got me. Incidentally, that family named Wallop; they had descended from one of the early British wars, and the term wallop - giving someone a wallop - is derived in a lot of dictionaries as being this ancestor; attacked a port in Belgium, or Holland, or somewhere in the ancient wars, long before this time.

Q: Really gave them a knock-out blow?

Adm. M.: I had a variety of friends; we all did, who we saw quite often and also, in spite of the wartime effort, the theater was going great guns, as the London theater always has done. The only concession they made; they moved up the curtain time from 8:30 to about 7 so that people could get around as much as possible before the blackout, and then it was not getting home too late. There were taxies; there were ways of getting around. I got to love the subway and knew that just like I know the map of the United States, but there were other ways. The subway used to curtail operations after whatever the hour was, and so you had to depend on taxies which were very hard to get because they were so much in demand. And all of this went on in a very heavy blackout. The automobile headlights had a black metal shield with a tiny little cross perforating them. How those people, those taxi drivers, got around; you could see the other cars lights but how they knew to turn right here and turn left there, I've never known.

Q: Instinct, I guess.

Adm. M.: And the stop lights, of course, had these same little crosses in a top shield. Incidentally, the wardens really were strict on that. If you forgot a black curtain, or if you had a space between it, it's your own flap. Comes the knock on the door. They weren't nasty about it but they wanted to be damn sure you'd completed blacking out.

Q: Well, it was real.

Adm. M.: It was real all right.

Q: Quite in contrast to the efforts we made here.

Adm. M.: Yes. Well, of course we didn't have the incentive they did, the reason for it.

Q: They, on the whole, showed a remarkable ability to adapt to very trying circumstances didn't they?

Adm. M.: They did indeed, and the thing that is still true of them, from what I've seen since the war - the American just doesn't have (and I'm not being pro-British - I hope not) doesn't have the makeup to cooperate and - for instance the queues, as they call them, standing and waiting for buses. There was no pushing and shoving. If a guy was at the end of a twenty or thirty person queue waiting for Bus number 17, he was quite content to wait whatever number of buses it took. There was no jamming up at the door; there was single file all the way, and they just accepted that as the best way to make things work, at least in wartime and what I've seen since then. They are much more - have a tendency to be law-abiding than the Americans.

Q: More disciplined then.

Adm. M.: Yes, exactly. Willing to accept, however much of a nuisance it is. The same way with the rationing there. Of course, I guess there was a black market (I wouldn't have been involved in that) but the fact that eggs and milk were only for children, for instance: that was quite acceptable. Nobody expected to get more than their few ounces of meat or cheese a week. They just took it for granted.

Q: In February of 1944 you got orders to come back to the States?

Adm. M.: Yes.

Q: Did you have a relief in your particular job?

Adm. M.: Yes, I did, I had a relief. It was Commander Edwards, nicknamed Doc, who later became a very, very good friend. He was senior to me by about six years, but he took it over, and then Bob Taylor in the Class of '31 later relieved him, and I think that Doc Edwards was there not much more than six months.

And, I went back and after checking in at ONI they sent me over to the Bureau of Ordnance and one of my senior friends got me in. I think he was an administrative or personnel officer, or something. And, he said, "You have thirty days leave and then you have your choice between the cruiser, St. Louis and the battleship, North Carolina, as gunnery officer of one or the other. And, I actually had my choice and actually picked the North Carolina, as a bigger, not a newer ship but, I just picked it on general principle.

Q: Well, she was new with the war anyway.

Adm. M.: She was new with the war; well, so was the St. Louis you see.

Q: What do you recall was ONI interested in?

Adm. M.: As far as I could see it was really just a routine call. They didn't have anyone who wanted to follow up on something, for example, or anything like that. It was just that we were, as people attached to the Embassy, we were under their auspices but, of course, as we were talking of reports we sent to ONI, in my case, they were all sent to BuOrd as of primary interest. Where else they sent them, I don't know.

Q: BuOrd had some questions?

Adm. M.: I can't remember any specific ones. Maybe some of the last reports I'd sent in; some of them had a question on it to clarify it.

But, the visit to the Navy Department, which was in the old Navy Building was simply a check-in, pick-up-your-orders, and you're on your own.

Q: Had you regretted leaving London?

Adm. M.: Well, I wanted to get to sea. I'd loved it in London; I'd loved working with the British, and the work was intensely interesting all the time but, I just went to the staff and told them that whenever I could get a relief I'd appreciate it because I really wanted to go to sea. A lot of my class had been at sea the whole time, as execs and later, skippers of destroyers, and so on. Of course no one knew how long the war would run, obviously we didn't but, at the same time I thought that two and a half years over there was enough.

Q: Now, you were making a drastic change. In effect, you were leaving one theater of operations and going into another, quite different. Did you notice some great contrasts?

Adm. M.: Well again, operationally in London - but, we were very little operation. I can't tell you the differences in fleet operations in two theaters because I just don't know how the Atlantic was working.

Some of our reports went through Admiral King's ASW - Commander, 10th Fleet. Once in a while we'd get a follow up from Commander, 10th Fleet, as opposed to the Bureau. In other words, obviously one of our reports had gone not only to BuOrd but it had gone to Commander 10th Fleet, as well. Again, most of that was on underwater warfare and was mines, torpedoes. In other words, handled by our underwater ordnance complement.

Q: Tell me about the North Carolina.

Adm. M.: Well, I reported to San Francisco Com 12 for transportation and was in the hotel bar, and I can't remember which hotel it was.

Q: Clift, by the way?

Adm. M.: I think it was. I think we were sort of assigned there; and so, one of my Severn colleagues - Severn School colleagues and a classmate, who had unfortuantely scholastically failed to get through the Naval Academy with us but, we had an old home week reunion there, and he asked what I was doing and I told him I was awaiting transportation and he said, "Well, hell, I'm taking my destroyer to Pearl Harbor next Wednesday." I think there were two or three other destroyers involved. And, so he made all the arrangements for me to go with him which probably got me out there two or three weeks earlier than I would have had I'd stood in line.

Q: Where were you joining the North Carolina?

Adm. M.: She happened to be in Majuro. It was right after the Truk operations. As I found out when I arrived in Majuro the Marianas Campaign was coming up. I got there - I can't remember exactly when, probably the 1st of April, something like that.

Q: Who was skipper of the North Carolina?

Adm. M.: The first skipper I had was Captain Frank P. Thomas, Class of '14 at the Academy; and then we had Captain Spike Fahrion was the second one, I believe, and as the years went on, Ossie Colclough, and the last one was Red Hannon. All made admiral except Captain Thomas. Spike Fahrion stayed with us. It was rather interesting. I may have told you but not on the recorder. When the cruiser division commander in the Louisville was killed — I'm talking months later now — in Leyte or Linguayen — one of the operations Fahrion was assigned to be his relief. It was one of those rare cases where — to get there when he could, of course, and he couldn't leave until the end of the then current operation. But he actually — we were lead flagship of the division commander. We had two star collar devices in Ships Service so the heads of departments got him first set and he put them on. We put them on him on the bridge, and for, I'd say, three or four weeks he signed the log as Rear Admiral Commanding, which you don't see very often. I'd never seen it before. So then Colclough was his relief. This was months later; I don't remember exactly what dates. My predecessor in the North Carolina was, as you know, Corky Ward and so I was among friends right there.

Morton #3 - 185

Q: You mean he had been gunnery officer?

Adm. M.: He had been gunnery officer. I was the fourth I believe. Admiral Tom Hill put her in commission, as the gunnery officer and he was on the staff of CinCPacFlt by then.

Q: Admiral Hustvedt was the first skipper.

Adm. M.: I've forgotten who the second gunnery officer was, and then Corky was the third, and I was the fourth.

Q: Well, you must have found the gunnery crew in good condition then?

Adm. M.: They were, in very good shape, and I remember the first time we went out after Corky had left. I guess we were on our way to the Mariannas operation which came off - D Day was somewhere around 15 June and instead of conserving ammunition for their new gun boss, why when the towed sleeve went over everything in the ship got used - every 40 mm., every 20 mm., every 5-inch gun - just to impress the new guy with the power of this thing, which was very impressive I must say. Ordinarily in target practice they fired one barrel per mount and that sort of thing in only selected numbers of mounts in each sector for ammunition conservation.

Q: Well, tell me how you went about preparing for the Mariannas.

Adm. M.: We had already on board, or shortly after I got there, the very fine relief maps, almost as big as this room, or at least half - beautiful jobs that went to each one of the ships and tied in with the operating, or gave you all the altutides and towns -

Q: Were they in plaster, or what?

Adm. M.: Yes, they were a sort of a plastic or plaster.

Q: Must have taken up a considerable amount of space?

Adm. M.: It did. We had them down in the - I think we did most of that briefing down in the - The warrant officer's had a very nice wardroom, or warrant officer's mess, I should say, but as things had come along they moved the warrant officers up to the wardroom to give this space as a sort of conference room, and that's where we kept those models.

Q: That must have been considerably helpful?

Adm. M.: It was tremendously helpful. It was an amazing program because, presumably - I can't speak for the destroyers, but every large ship or any one that was going to be involved in any sort of bombardment had -

Q: Who developed them?

Adm. M.: I don't know that. You mean commercially or in the Navy?

Q: In the Navy.

Adm. M.: I don't know - I mean where we got them from and what staff shipped them out; I don't know that.

Q: This called for a considerable detailed knowledge of the topography of the islands.

Adm. M.: I think they were developed in Pearl Harbor, at the headquarters; either the Amphibious Command, or the Fleet Command itself, or maybe CinCPoA. He had his own intelligence staff. Do you remember the name of that? And a lot of the operations was diagrammed in these things, I think had their label on them - CinCPacific Ocean Areas.

Q: Well, as it worked out, were they accurate?

Adm. M.: Oh yes, extremely so. Of course, your charts were the accurate thing. We'd fix up the charts with assigned targets and so forth, from H-hour plus one on up, and most of this was a very effective visual presentation and didn't actually have to be too accurate. I think they were accurate; but they gave your spotters and your aviation observers - the airborne gunnery spotters, and the gunnery department itself, and the navigator an idea of what this thing was going to look like from North, East, South, and West, and what were the primary landmarks and outstanding features; where the plain turned into mountains, for instance, major towns, and all sorts of things, like in the Mariannas particularly, sugar mills which were a big structure and a very good navigational aid. But, the actual accuracy was not important as much as to give you the impression of what you were going to see and shoot at.

In these operations there was no particular formal training. In other words, when you went out you were given airplanes, utility and towing sleeves from the present fleet base, and you just were assigned enough time to shoot nearly everything, and so the formal training by shooting was done on the way or on the way back. In other words, there was no opportunity to have anything like a refresher training.

Q: Now, the North Carolina was a part of what's known as

the fast battleships?

Adm. M.: Yes. She and the Washington were the first ones. They were absolute sisters and they were the first two, and then the South Dakota I think was next, and then came the Massachusetts, Alabama, Indiana, and one other I think, and then the 32-knot ships - we were theoretically 27 - were the last of the ones built, the Missouri, the Wisconsin, the New Jersey, and, again, another one which I should know.

Q: The Iowa.

Adm. M.: The Iowa, yes. So, she and the Washington were the oldest - that's speaking relatively because they were commissioned in '41 or two; they weren't very old but they had a lot of miles. Generally speaking we were in a carrier task group. The Carrier Task Force was either under Com 5th Fleet or Com 3rd Fleet. They alternated operations, as you remember Halsey and Spruance, and they had a phantom organization under Chink Lee who you mentioned the other day, which was Task Force 34 or 54 depending on the fleet assigned and that was provided for in case of surface action against major Japanese units and then the Carrier Task Forces were 38 and 58 under Admiral Mitscher and Admiral McCain. Which one was with the Third Fleet and which with

Fifth I don't know - so generally speaking we went out with four task groups in the Carrier Task Force and the nucleus of each group was two or three carriers, and then you had the antiaircraft and antisubmarine, and they operated all under the same operation order but the carrier group commander was more-or-less autonomous in these varied operations. In other words, he didn't stay as the full task force; and each group commander had his own ideas on operations around him - minor adjustments in the screening. In other words, he'd have some flexibility.

Not because he became a famous admiral later but, in my experience out there under maybe four or five or six different task group commanders - that is being in different task groups or being in the same one with a different one, Admiral Radford's operation orders and policies were outstanding.

Q: Were you surprised to find the battleship acting as, almost as escort and protection for carriers?

Adm. M.: Not at all because I was aware of it, of course. I mean, if you'd suddenly rung a bell from 1938 to 1944, with my being Rip Van Winkle I might have been surprised but, no, I was not surprised.

Q: And, as the battleships were then engaged primarily,

were they not for bombardment?

Adm. M.: That's right, yes. In addition to this surface action which was, as I say, Task Group 34.

Q: It was always possible that the Japanese battleship would come out slugging?

Adm. M.: Yes. We almost got into that after the Turkey Shoot and Admiral Lee - I remember his message came out. He didn't consider that the night experience of the task force, his ships in the task force 34, were sufficient to risk chasing remnants of the Japanese Fleet. I've often heard that later, and I agree with it; I think one of the officers on Admiral Lee's staff was the one whom I first heard express it: "If Halsey had been at the Marianas he was just the type that would have gone ahead and chased them, whereas if Spruance had been at the Leyte operation he wouldn't have run off to the north to chase the task force as Halsey did and left the jeep carriers there." And, of course, no one knows but, it's rather interesting that with that particular viewpoint, the wrong man was in the wrong place in both cases. Halsey would have swashbuckled along and probably, we hope, sunk heavy ships, whereas Spruance would never have left his little CVEs there off the Philippines to get pummelled.

Q: It's an interesting point of view. Well, take the operations one by one will you?

Adm. M.: Yes. The first - They formed the bombardment outfit and we had a long-range sort of pre-D-Day bombardment. I think this was maybe D-3 - or something like that, as a sort of a softening up which was largely the main batteries from a considerable range.

Q: Standing off how? This was on Saipan?

Adm. M.: Saipan was the first, yes, and, of course, as D-Day came along, or approached, the UDT's had gone in there for their reconnaissance and that sort of thing but there was no close-range bombardment and we were not there at D-Day. In other words, as I recall our preliminary bombardment at Saipan was main battery at, we'll say, 15,000 yards perhaps, and then back to the carrier task force.

Q: Any opposition from the air?

Adm. M.: None. Once the Marines and Army landed at Saipan, then we had a considerable stream of planes, particularly at night; not attacking a group, the task force, but evacuating senior people and that sort of thing; and we had considerable luck at getting them. When I say we; the whole task force. They were using, presumably, transport planes to get top-ranking generals, and so forth from Saipan elsewhere or Saipan to Tinian which hadn't been attacked yet, and so on, and Guam.

Q: And they were flying over our fleet units?

Adm. M.: They happened to fly over. I remember one particularly - Everybody thinks they're flying over them at a time like that, but the one that passed over the North Carolina the closest, I remember seeing him hit. It looked like little cigarette burns. Of course all this tremendous amount of tracer of all calibers goes out from everything, and this little red cigarette glow just - you could just see it spread through the plane. Of course, it damaged the plane. That's the one that I remember. But, no attacks at all. Now, of course, somewhere along the line came the famous Turkey Shoot, and the time sequence I'm not sure of here. Of course that was primarily an air action, a carrier air action, as you know and the antiaircraft protection by the major ships, battleships and cruisers, was for the occasional one that got past the combat air control. I don't remember how many were attributed to gunfire in that thing. It seems to me that the Japanese toll was about 300 wasn't it? This is my recollection - 285, 315. I would say that maybe 15 or 20 of them were by gunfire, not any more than that - and they had not started the kamikazes at that time.

Q: No, no. Well, you were not in the actual landing operation.

Adm. M.: No, not in this particular one. Iwo Jima will come along and I'll tell you.

Q: What about Tinian?

Adm. M.: Tinian? If we had a preliminary bombardment there I don't remember it, Jack. The fast battleships had very little actual bombardment work in the Marianas. And, you've got to remember that with the amphibious task force - the amphibious forces, we had the old battleships, who were ideal for this close-in, post-D-Day work - Tennessee, Pennsylvania, California, New York, Texas, and they did the brunt of the support work once the troops landed. I'm going by memory on this but, that's the way I recall it. And they, of course, were experienced in this. They'd go into three or four thousand yards you see, once the landing was underway; each with his assigned area and assigned targets and so forth.

But the only other action we really would have been

directly connected with - the one I mentioned in night surface action in which I'm almost certain that Admiral Lee had just decided, discretion is the better part of something or other; and so we never formed a task force. Then, in order, Tinian and Guam came along and I, as I say, unless we had some preliminary bombardment, we had no particular part in the land operation.

Q: And no bombardment of Guam in preparation -

Adm. M.: This I don't remember; I say unless we had pre-D-Day bombardment which was really area bombardment on any - We were primarily with the first area task force the whole time.

Following the Marianas operation the North Carolina had had a long scheduled Bremerton overhaul, or had one coming up; and we got to Bremerton about the First of August for an exactly two month overhaul - not at Pearl, but at Bremerton. While we were there, it seems to me the Philippine operations had started.

Q: Yes, they had.

Adm. M.: And, I'm positive we were not there when the light carriers were beaten up so much, and exactly what phase we joined up, I don't remember. But, anyway, it was a Third

Fleet operation and we were brought back and joined them in October. And, along about that time, I'm sure it was the famous typhoon in the South China Sea, and we were very much in that.

Q: Well, tell me about that.

Adm. M.: It really was an impressive storm, I must say. Of course the thing that highlighted it - it didn't really interfere with fleet operations, with the exception of those three destroyers that were lost. I think it was three. And of course they had deballasted for fueling, and I think three were lost with fairly heavy casualties. It didn't affect the big ships too much. It was a violent storm, there's no question but, it was not the violent one that I told you, as a Midshipman we witnessed with Captain Dutton.

Q: In the North Atlantic.

Adm. M.: There was no roll to the -

Q: Danger of capsizing. No danger of capsizing?

Adm. M.: No, none, except for these three little fellows, and I think that they were all destroyers. They might have been one of them a DE but I'm not sure. But, the Philippine operation was just about over. The only thing that was impressive to us in the North Carolina was that we saw our first kamikaze attack in that operation. Now, whether these were the initial ones or whether they'd had a few in the weeks we were away, I'm not sure. But, I remember distinctly seeing these birds come in, just keep on going.

Q: Had you had intelligence about such attacks?

Adm. M.: I think so. I seem to remember that. The thing that made them difficult for us to protect our ships against was the carrier was almost always the target, and as you know, in any type of gunfire, hunting or anything else, the bird coming at you is the easiest one to hit. And the screen had the problem - the CAP either getting these people before they got in on the task force, or the heavier support ships getting them before they started to dive. The dive on the gunships was a rarity. They were going for the carriers and that's what they did, and they make an awful difficult target for anybody on the support ring because of the fact you've got to think about the ceasefire, or that you're going to hit someone else. And, of course, they intensified, from that date on which I would say was maybe the first of November, something like that. But, this was our first view of those boys.

I think the Nevada was hit, in another task force. Either the Missouri or the Indiana had a very close miss. There's a well-known picture of that, and you see 'em more-or-less hitting the ships side, but the carrier was the prime target, and quite rightly from the Japanese point of view.

Q: Did the North Carolina go into Manus at any time?

Adm. M.: No, we were ordered to Manus for some reason. I can't remember whether it was repairs, or what, and while on the way the orders were cancelled. Now we had some damage and we went back to Pearl to get that fixed, repaired. And, whether that was the same occasion, I don't know. So I've never crossed the equator. I missed it by less than a hundred miles, I guess, so I'm still a polliwog.

Q: But, in wartime these special operations in crossing the equator were dispensed with weren't they?

Adm. M.: I think it depended on the — on what was going on around the ship and what you were doing. I think for instance, on the way to Manus, I think we had one or two destroyers with us as our escort; and I think we had plans for one because it was in a quiet zone and there was no particular operations. The sole reason for going down there was, whatever it was, repair maybe, and I think we'd had something like that. We certainly were making plans for it.

Q: You want to say something about the fueling operations at sea?

Adm. M.: Well, of course the logistics of the Service Force, under Admiral Calhoun at the time, had developed this operation to a very high degree. Fueling at sea was no longer an experiemental thing. It was sort of automatic. I wouldn't say it was not a very big event, but it was something you sort of took for granted. You would fuel the destroyers, and the tankers would fuel you, and so on. And, of course this was always done as much as possible in a more-or-less backwater. Now the heavy - heavier replenishment was usually done in the atolls - I mean ammunition, food, stores, and so forth.

Q: Places like Ulithi?

Adm. M.: Ulithi. As the war went along it was Ulithi and then Kwajalein - I can't remember the order here; but, as we moved up a particular atoll would become a new fleet base; and the heavy stuff was usually done in port. The operations were planned so that, in theory, you had enough ammunition of all types; enough food - the only thing you worried about was the oil, so that this worked all right.

Q: Now, you say the North Carolina had an interesting experience at Iwo Jima?

Adm. M.: Yes. As I told you, the prime use of the fast battleships was protection of the carriers, and the secondary was the (leaving out any possibility of surface action which had almost disappeared by then) long-range area early bombardment. Now, in the Iwo operation, while we were preparing for that the old New York had a serious breakdown. I can't remember whether she lost a propeller or hit the turbine or what it was. But, anyway, the New York was deleted from the operation and, arbitrarily they picked the North Carolina to take her place, which for the first time made the North Carolina assigned the same as the old battleships.

Q: A close-in bombardment?

Adm. M.: A close-in bombardment, right. And, so that completely changed the operation over there; we got the same operation the old battleships and cruisers had. We did whatever the New York had been assigned. In other words, "Where New York appears, insert North Carolina," and we were, as I recall, the anchor ship of the first units, and so we were really in there about 4,000 yards, and, there again we employed for the first time, to my knowledge of the bombardment, all of our batteries, particularly the 40s and the 5-inch. I don't think we tried the 20 mms. for that work, but anyway, in addition to the main batteries 16-inch, we had targets assigned to the other batteries.

Q: Did you have a relief map on board of Iwo Jima?

Adm. M.: We had that anyway. Yes, we did have that, and we had had it - as I say, that went to any ship that might be involved in this. What our function was going to be in the new orders, we hadn't touched the New York. I'm not sure but I imagine it was a preliminary -

Q: Softening up -

Adm. M.: Yes. We were in there about four days and, as you might say, saw the whole show from beginning to end.

Q: It was a pretty hot contest wasn't it?

Adm. M.: It certainly was, and also the fact that that volcanic earth and, as I understood it later, very deep excavations.

Q: The caves.

Adm. M.: The caves made it extremely difficult, in spite of the tremendous firepower we had there - extremely difficult to really do an effective job. They'd just sort of wait us out. In the whole operation the North Carolina's total tonnage fire was the second highest in the operation. The old battleship, Tennessee, I guess because of her size, she fired the greatest tonnage of ammunition and the North Carolina was a close second. As the invasion went on and things began to slowly improve the North Carolina was sent around to, I guess it was the west shore; I think we landed on the east shore. Anyway, we went around to the opposite side where our Marines were beginning to advance up the coast towards the remainder of the Japanese troops. And we had the, again, first experience for the ship of blind fire with a five-inch, with a Marine spotter on the ground. We fired out of sight and to pave the way for the advancing Marines by then. The way they would do it; we had no air spotter at that time. The Marine ground spotter would give us a safety distance. Now, we'll say we would fire 1,500 yards beyond - where he wanted. In other words, if he wanted the fire a thousand yards ahead of his troops, we'd fire at 2,500. We fired entirely on his orders; and then when he saw that we were in the right position, then he would walk us back a couple of hundred yards each minute, something like that. So that finally, not seeing anything we finally had it where he wanted it and then it was easy to keep it there. The five inch pattern of bombardment was pretty good. In other words, all the projectiles were more or less where he wanted them. And of course, there still was a safety zone there, but the initial salvos were always two or three times the safety zone just to be sure we were in on the right navigation and fire control, and that was really one of the highlights of our experience there because it was the first time the ship had done that.

Q: It was a very exacting routine wasn't it?

Adm. M.: Yes. It was for several hours. It was all daylight.

Q: Well, what about Japanese air attack?

Adm. M.: None. We were always manned for it but I don't recall any. A few, I think the Pensacola - cruiser, or possibly the Pennsylvania; a few of them were hit by ground fire from the beach but air opposition was almost nil. You see the carriers still had their operation going as cover and provided combat air patrol and so forth. I recall nothing at either Iwo, or later Okinawa where, during the bombardment, there was a serious air threat. There might have been a threat but there were no attacks.

Q: Well, that was a rigorous four days. And then what?

Adm. M.: Then after this five-inch blind bombardment - that's about the last thing of moment that the ship was involved in and the Marines, and then later, the Army, as I recall, were then beginning to make progress. Of course, it took a long time, and I've forgotten how long the operation lasted on the ground, but I think shortly after that particular bombardment of ours, I think we were released and sent back to our regular assignment.

Q: Was there any danger from Japanese submarines in that operation?

Adm. M.: No. As a matter of fact, the whole time I was in the North Carolina I don't think we had as much as even a submarine alert. The attrition of Jap subs had been pretty heavy for one thing, and we had one miniature sub brought into one of the harbors where we were which got a tanker about six o'clock in the morning - just daylight, and she burned fiercely, and so forth, but of those two - they think it was two of them - but in the sea operations I can't recall any serious submarine threat.

Q: Did you say that the attrition was great, but also the Japanese submarines were used so much for supplying?

Adm. M.: That's right, yes. Then the next - unless you have any questions on that. The time spent in the atoll between the operations is no different than it was at any of the others so I don't need to go into that. The only thing is, by this time they had a whole host of complete commercial vessels with a complete commercial crew, operating under the Fleet Commander - Fifth Fleet. A lot of our ammunition, between operations, came from them - Waterman Line, and any number of others, which augmented the relatively few ammunition ships we had. I think there were also some commercial tankers.

Q: Yes, there were. Did the crews, as you observed them on these commercial ships, operate in much the same manner as Navy crews?

Adm. M.: Pretty much so, yes. It's the same sort of rigging and the same sort of loads. In other words; I remember one of our biggest loads in preparation for either Iwo or Okinawa - it was from the Waterman Line, that's why I mentioned the Waterman. And we got along famously with the officers and their crew.

Q: You ran into no problem then. I have heard others say that in some isolated instances that they ran into the problem of work hours and that sort of thing.

Adm. M.: Yes, I think I remember hearing that. We had no trouble that I recall. They were just as good workers, probably better really because they'd probably had more experience in that line - handling heavy loads and cranes, but we were just as happy to resupply from one of them. And there were so many of them that you nearly always did towards the end of the war.

Q: Well, we come up then to what? Okinawa?

Adm. M.: Okinawa, yes. Okinawa was, as I recall, Easter Sunday; the first of April, I think it was. Does it sound right? And the primary mission of my particular ship and the fast battleships, besides the usual carrier task force work, was to do a diversionary bombardment on; we'll say the landings along on the south coast. We had a diversionary bombardment with no particular target at all, just as a ruse to make the Japs think the first landing would be there.

Q: What, on the opposite side of the island?

Adm. M.: On the opposite side, yes. I don't remember how Okinawa is now, is oriented. But, we'll say that the landings were here, this was up here. And that picture that Lloyd got taken from our flagship, that is during that bombardment. How much that ruse worked, I don't know.

Q: How much in advance was it that the -

Adm. M.: I'd say three or four days. That is the North Carolina firing but the thing that makes it interesting; up there you could see six of the shells on their way - beautiful picture. Do you see them moving? Six out of nine.

Q: Looks like planes.

Adm. M.: Yes. I wouldn't know whether it was two days or seven days, something in that range.

Q: Well, having completed that mission, that false bombardment without any specific target, you came around the end of the island again to -

Adm. M.: No, we didn't get in on the close bombardment phase. You're remembering we were there only in place of the New York at Iwo. So, we rejoined the carrier task force and, I think it was during this time, in mid-April; I believe my date is right, when the Franklin was hit, if you remember the Franklin. We lost six or seven, and that, we felt very much connected with, and I'll expand a little bit on it.

The carrier planes were returning from a strike - possibly Okinawa or possibly the mainland. This, I don't recall because we later went into the mainland operation. But, we had a whole fire arm, the whole carrier task force and we'd stopped zig-zagging to allow our planes to return and the Franklin was right bang ahead of the North Carolina at this time - two, three thousand yards, whatever it was. My boy, Vallentine, I'll never forget his name, Ted Vallentine was what we call Sky One. He had the four antiaircraft directors for the five-inch were arranged in diamond form forward, and two amidships and the one aft and he had the four going more-or-less above the bridge. I think our air warning system had reported a Bogie, and so we put Vallentine's director in this direction, and I remember him hollering on the phone. He said, "I have a bogie; it's a red Judy", or whatever the code name was. I don't remember; we'll say Judy. He said, "That's a Judy, and he's coming in." And, my CIC people down in the plotting room tried to report this to the flagship, the group flagship. Admiral Bogan and Admiral Davidson were turning over in the carrier. I can't remember which was relieving which but they were both aboard; and we got the absolute emphasis "Hold Fire". This boy had seen it in his magnified glass - range finder. We couldn't get a release. What conversations went on with the North Carolina and the carrier flagship, I don't know except my people told me they'd gotten the word over and then they were told, "Hold Fire" which we did. That bird came right down with the - with our own planes. My Sky One director had literally had us tracking them all the way and he did not kamikaze-attack; he dropped three or four bombs that went through the flight deck down below, and the planes later got him in his retreat because none of us could shoot, because of our own ships and in order to protect our own returning planes. But they got him somewhere away from the formation. But the thing happened in absolutely no time at all. The Franklin was a huge mass of explosions, flames and a tremendous column of smoke. And we were right behind her and had to actually steer off to one side, and I don't remember which way the captain went, and there must have been hundreds of her crew in the water, which we passed on both sides. Some had jumped, some had been blown over, and some were badly injured - all in life jackets, as we all were. But, the formation carried on. You couldn't do anything else really, and the destroyers fell out, a couple of them fell out to pick up what survivors they could. And that went on for a long time. She dropped out, and I believe it was the St. Paul or one of the cruisers pulled alongside for assistance - fire fighting and that kind of thing. But, I still look back on that as something - It may not have been anything to do with it, but when you think of six or eight hundred men and one man in one ship had done his best to just let one ship shoot at this fellow. We might have gotten a couple of our own fighters in there in the course of time but, on the other hand it wouldn't have been eight hundred people.

Q: Well, in analyzing it was that the primary reason why they said "Hold Fire", because they were fearful that you'd shoot down some of our -

Adm. M.: Either that or because they didn't have a bogie and they didn't believe us. We'll never know. I used to write the action reports, particularly from the gunnery side. In fact, I was responsible for preparing it for the exec and the captain, and I put more time on that than anyone because I was trying to get over the specific times, messages, and so forth, and the fact that we weren't depending on radar or IFF. This boy saw the plane and was trying to describe it as coming, and then probably 10,000 yards away, because they picked up the radar and things around it at 15,000 yards. And he had that bird all the way but, these things happen. I'm not blaming the carrier task group commander. I merely mentioned there were two admirals there, and one turning over, and which one, or the staff of which one made the decision to insist on cease fire, I don't know because that North Carolina action report has, from our point of view, the complete story, times, etc. And, I said this was April. It may not have been. It was somewhere along in there. During our Okinawa battle, or on the way to the mainland.-

I believe you asked what we did after the initial stopping at Okinawa. I belive that the carrier task force, including the Carolina, had the first strikes on the mainland, and believe this is when it happened because something makes me think the Franklin room was hit very, very close to Japan.

Q: When you were making that false attack on the opposite side of the island, were the kamikazes in evidence, because they were very much so at Okinawa?

Adm. M.: Yes, that's right. No, they weren't as far as we were concerned because again, we were away from the carriers which were always their prime target. In one of the atolls - I've forgotten which two operations it was between - we had one kamikaze come down about 9 o'clock at night, without warning, and simply hit a mess hall. We don't know what he thought he was hitting, and he crashed into the mess hall but he was the only one. I mean, the boys on the ships were not even at general quarters. We had normal gunnery watch in port. So he just completely surprised everybody, and yet, as far as his Japanese cause was - really to no avail at all. It was too bad, we lost some troops from the Marines in the mess hall but he would probably have done his cause more good if he'd just hit one ship, we'll say. That's the only time - and that minature submarine attack on the tanker were the only two times that I recall anything like that in port.

Q: Now, was it during or immediately after the Okinawa operation there was another typhoon?

Adm. M.: You've got me on that, Jack. I don't really recall. It must not have been as severe as the South China Sea.

Going back to the Carolina. During one of these attacks on the carrier task force one of our own support ships hit the Carolina in what we call Sky Two, which was amidships port side director, tower. It was a five-inch - I still have the base plug around here somewhere. It was a five-inch antiaircraft shell from, presumably a ship that crossed the formation. Nobodys fault. They didn't cease fire in time. There couldn't have been worse circumstances because the velocity of the shell at that time, and the thickness of the director towers armor - I mean tube - it would have been better if it had been thicker or thinner. What it did was wiped-out the machine-gun barrier, 40-mm. there. Fortunately, only about three or four, or five were killed, but a whole lot wounded; and then had enough blast left to go in and completely demolish the director wiring. It was completely inoperable. It was just one of these things, and the yard confirmed this when we got there at Pearl. We went back to Pearl and they fixed it in no time - remarkable that they did. But which operation this was, I can't remember. But, we went up and they gave us a complete re-wiring job, and whatever else the director had. I think the roller path and the director itself, and we rejoined in almost no time. I mean as long as it took to get to Pearl and get back. In the yard - we stayed a week or ten days, something on that order, but whether that was between Iwo and Okinawa, or Okinawa and the mainland, I can't remember. She was luckier on that. She'd had - in other words, her battle casualties were, fatalities, were not more than about ten. When she was first out in the Pacific, a submarine got her. The torpedo must have been almost past the bow, and they got her in the - you know, the forward structure - chain locker, the bos'un locker, and three men were forward down there. This was not during any action. It was just one of those firings out of the blue by a submarine. There were three poor guys down there conducting an air test, a routine air test to see if each compartment was tight, and of course, they caught the full blast of it. But that, and this U.S. shell were the only serious hits we had.

Q: Of course I mean to ask about damage control on the North Carolina. How developed was it?

Adm. M.: Well, the damage control was excellent. The crews were experienced, well trained. The markings were highly developed over the time I mentioned in the mid-Thirties and condition Baker - I guess they call it Bravo now. Condition Baker and Condition Abel and all that were just automatically set. In other words, the damage control complement in wartime had been so augmented that you didn't worry about damage control. These guys were highly trained on closures and the different types of conditions, and fire fighting so that your damage control organization really was the reliable and excellent thing. It was no problem at all. When they wanted to go to general quarters and button up the whole ship it was done right away. Run around and check on it.

One little sidelight on the Carolina, and this was towards the end. We didn't have the racial set up we have now. In other words, with the exception of some engineers, most of the blacks were stewards - or Chamorros; we got a lot of Chamorros from Guam - really excellent. But anyway, these few firemen, and so forth got ahold of a Marine sergeant who had one sector of our 20-mm. battery - Clyde Gallagher. And, believe it or not Sergeant Gallagher was - he was multi-chevron, sort of, for a first sergeant, and he had, we'll say, a sector amounting to one quarter of a machine gun - the 20s, not the 40s the 20s. Somehow he got the idea, and the remarkable thing was he was from Atlanta. He came to me one day and said, "Some of these boys who are down passing ammunition, and that sort of thing, in the bow of the ship want to get up and fight." So he got himself two 20 mm. crews. That was two 20 mm. twin crews, and what the complement of each one is I've forgotten. But, anyway he built up two black crews from the bowels of the ship - the ammunition passers and whatnot. Of course it was just a small part of the gunnery department, but he always claimed that these two mounts were the best ones he had, and it was completely his idea, and they stayed, assigned to that the rest of the war. But I always thought, a real tough Marine sergeant from Georgia did this.

Q: Because these black boys had expressed their belligerency?

Adm. M.: Well, they'd said that - I don't know how they happened to come to him; I guess because he had one of these 20 mm. commands. They just said, "Is there any chance in us getting up to do a non-passive part and get a piece of the action?" as they say nowadays. And, he arranged it, and he arranged it very, very successfully. I've always remembered that, complimented him many times. I think the skipper did too.

Q: Very interesting. A forerunner of other times.

Adm. M.: That's right. Then our last operation was the first bombardment of the mainland.

Q: Honshu, wasn't it?

Adm. M.: Yes, I believe so. Hitachi and some of those places. I think it was. And that was interesting in the fact that we had one or two British battleships with us in the same -

Q: KG-5

Adm. M.: KG-5 I'm sure was one of them, and may have been

the only one. KG-5 was the one and whether there was a second -

Q: How did they perform in conjunction with ours?

Adm. M.: Perfectly well. I mean we used the same procedures. The procedure had been made joint for several years by then. We had their carriers out in the Pacific early in the war you remember when we didn't have enough.

Q: Had they been schooled in refueling at sea then?

Adm. M.: Yes, they had. And, that was the last one; that was a night one and I think there must have been some air action, kamikaze or whatnot. And I think that was probably our last firing in anger. There wasn't anything momentous after that.

Q: That was instrument firing wasn't it on target. Your targets were factories?

Adm. M.: Yes. It was area, yes. Hitachi is still quite an electronic factory center and it was just a sort of late version of a General Doolittle raid. It was just letting the mainland populace know that, we're out here buddy, we're that close.

Q: It had a psychological factor?

Adm. M.: I imagine it did. I think that was the whole purpose of it; plus the fact that these were big manufacturing plants. But, I think it was a psychological thing. And then of course, as you know, OLYMPIC was cancelled - I mean cancelled by the Japs surrender. Some of the surrender things I remember.

Somewhere along the line here in April, one morning early, and I think there was almost no action, we got the word that FDR had died. Our time, it must have been seven in the morning, something like that. We were at general quarters. And again, like I said a few days ago, whatever you or anyone else personally thinks of FDR as a President, as a man, the impact in that Carolina was really something. I mean, the skipper made the announcement, or the exec, on the PA system. And the chaplain gave quite a nice prayer. But those boys, all of us - it was like losing a father, something like that. I mean, that was the general impression. Disbelief!

Q: Well, for the younger men on board ship, he'd been President most of their adult lives.

Adm. M.: Yes, from '33 to '45, yes. But that was most impressive. Didn't make any difference who you talked to, a JO or a bosun mate first, or a seaman, fireman, they were just - The wardroom for several meals was just sort of hushed, and the whole ship was just like someone, as I said, that every one of them had lost their father, some similar impact. I guess that was April -

Q: Yes, it was.

Adm. M.: I should have mentioned that in sequence but I wanted to let you know about that. Of course, I suppose that every ship had the same experience at that time, naturally. We couldn't believe it in the first place.

Then in the aftermath we, I remember when they had surrendered we were still at sea and Admiral Halsey's message came out to all ships. The exact wording I don't know but this is sort of, "We think they'll behave but if not shoot them down in a friendly way." I know friendly way was in there somewhere. And then between the capitulation and the surrender in the Missouri we went in with a whole bunch, and we still kept the alert.

Q: Went in to take troops?

Adm. M.: No, just. We went in there just like it was going to be our own base.

Q: Tokyo Bay? What precautions did you take as you went?

Adm. M.: Well, we kept everything in the way of the - Standby gunnery watches were on. In other words, we had enough people to get going.

Q: Did you have a Japanese officer come on board - a pilot - to show you the minefields and that?

Adm. M.: We had a pilot -

Q: Because there were minefields?

Adm. M.: Yes. We had a pilot who, I guess, was a naval officer, but this I've forgotten. But, as we stayed there two or three days and nights, the confidence in the Japanese sincerity, of their somehow getting the word to these thousands of people, particularly the kamikazes. There was no incident that involved us. In fact, our senior aviator in his little spotting plane - he would take people in and fly them around to see the area, etc.

Q: Sightseeing?

Adm. M.: Yes, sightseeing. He wanted me to go and I said, "No, I'd rather not." So then we - before the actual surrender in the Missouri, we pulled out of there with, I'd say six, or eight, or ten ships, to head for homecoming in New York City.

Q: Before the surrender ceremony? Were you also standby in a sense?

Adm. M.: Yes, we still were and the first message we got out when we got clear of the harbor and formed up - I think there was a cruiser and carriers but whatever the New York contingent was, and the admiral was in a cruiser. But anyway, the word came out, either from Halsey or from our group commander, and he said, "Secure all gun watches. Do not darken ship." Then we knew it was really over.

Q: As I understand it, Admiral Spruance was not at the surrender ceremony but was at sea. Was he with your contingent?

Adm. M.: Let's see. It seems to me that - I'm almost certain that - I'm almost certain that that shooting down in a friendly sort of way was Halsey.

Q: Yes, it was.

Adm. M.: So that meant that Spruance was not in the operation. Maybe Spruance was getting ready for Operation OLYMPIC. Would that of been his fleet maybe? That's probably the way it was.

Q: You and the North Carolina missed the surrender ceremony.

Adm. M.: That's right. And then of course the trip home was completely uneventful except that the Carolina was changed from New York to Boston as homecoming port. Going through Panama was just the same as it had been in the Thirties. The bars and joints were still open. I don't think I ever played so much bridge in my life. The chief engineer and the damage control officer and a couple of my assistants and a couple of their assistants had two or three tables of bridge in the wardroom every night. You know, no watches to stand, or anything. Lieutenant commanders and up - their watch days were over in that war. There wasn't a command duty officer needed on the bridge. We must have played 'til three in the morning every day.

Q: You must have constituted one of the early contingents of the MAGIC CARPET did you?

Adm. M.: Yes, we did, as a matter of fact. Our MAGIC CARPET was all Navy. No soldiers, and I think no Marines. We took the short time. Somebody in the fleet picked them, and we took, I don't know how many hundred - a few hundred people whose enlistment was imminently up.

Q: Well, what about the crew members on the North Carolina itself? Were some of them due to be released?

Adm. M.: Yes, I think so, yes. But we did have a form of Navy MAGIC CARPET you might call it.

Q: What was the atmosphere on board as you returned home?

Adm. M.: Well, I would say it was the same as it was in the wardroom. Great relief, as I say, by that message - secure gun watches. Do not darken ship. Those two things were welcome because the gun watches included everybody because if anything happened everybody went to general quarters whatever his station was, and the idea of being able to sleep at night and no G.Q. a half an hour before dawn every morning of the year.

Q: Tell me about your reception when you reached the States.

Adm. M.: Well, that's really one of my, I hope, interesting stories. We had one that involved Governor Curley.

Q: Massachusetts.

Adm. M.: He had seven or eight children and two of them in the Navy. One whom I met in Norfolk. One was a lighter than air pilot, and in our communications gang we had a Lieutenant George Curley. I had nothing to do with him as far as the organization went, but whether it was just the friendship that developed in the trip home or whether he maybe was one of the bridge players. But, anyway, George Curley, when we got to Boston, Jamaica Plains was out. Why they singled Sue and me out, he did, I don't know, but we were wined and dined and entertained by the Curley family, including His Honor, the Governor.

Q: Now, Sue had been notified that you were returning, and had come to Boston?

Adm. M.: Yes. To come to Boston and she did.

Q: You had married by that time?

Adm. M.: Yes, we were married during the Bremerton overhaul. She had come over from England.

On this occasion in Boston through some old friends of Sue's - a sixty year old batchelor, Wally Balknap, and his 85 year old mother - it was arranged for us to stay at the Somerset Club. The Somerset Club only had about three suites that during the war they'd allowed members to put up guests who were in the services, and their wives. And the ship's chaplain and I shared a taxi, and he told me where he was going. He was a Bostonian, and I said, "I'm going to the Somerset Club on Beacon Hill, and he said, "Oh, gee, I thought your wife was here, I'm sorry she didn't make it." I said, "She is here. She's at the Somerset Club," which being a Bostonian he couldn't believe that a woman could be upstairs, or anywhere else besides the Ladies Lounge at the side door. So, anyway, that was our homecoming, and we stayed there the whole time, very happily. And through these friends, old Mrs. Belknap and her son, we really had Beacon Hill and had an awful lot of fun, and met a lot of their very good and old friends, and again dined and wined. And then the Curleys picked us up, so we would alternate between Jamaica Plains, and I'll never forget his shamrock carved in his shattered heart. And, down there at Jamaica Plains the family would say, or he would say, "What are those SOB's on Beacon Hill saying about me?" He knew where we were. We'd go back to Beacon Hill the next night and, "What's that old bastard Curley up to now?" It was a fascinating time, and one of the real highlights of that. We loved Boston. We went to all the good restaurants and stuff. John of course, was some years later. But, we got to know old Jim Curley very, very well. Everybody still called him Governor but he was running for Mayor. This was October of '45 and his battle for Mayor against a man named Hanes or Hayes was coming up at the usual first week in November, and they invited us down - one of the many times we went, and this was just Sue and myself, none of the others. They didn't have the wardroom. I think they had a few in the wardroom at one time. So we were invited down there to hear the election returns; of course pre-TV and most of that, and he sat at the dining room table at the head of it, and he must have had about four or five of these little tables, each with a telephone on it, and this would ring and ring and then that one would ring and he'd say, "Get that Joe, get that." And all of these were precinct reports, you see. And some of them came in by messenger. Somebody would drive out and push off this precinct leader and report. Well, it was pretty obvious early in the evening that he was way ahead by quite a margin. But, all sorts of things happened that night. The thing that impressed us a lot - all these henchmen, a lot of these henchmen who were not there for dinner but just for the election, kept their hats on. Nobody bothered to take off their hats. Just like "The Front Page" or something like that. And, they'd come rushing in, "Hey Governor, you've won the eighteenth handily," and all this stuff was going on and the phones were ringing and they were cheering and, if you remember old Curley's history of jail, you know way back. One guy came in, with his hat on and Sue turned to old Curley and said, "Guvernor, he looks like he just got out of jail," and the Governor said, "Sshh, he did, last week." And he was speaking of his henchman. Well, finally, his opponent conceded and there was nothing to do but to have us go down with a big motorcade to the local radio station, somewhere in Boston, for his victory speech on the radio. So, we piled into these limousines, and of course, they had motorcycle cops. Every limousine had a neon sign with Curley flashing on it - "Curley, Curley." We rode up with George and whoever the other Navy son was, and we got to this square where the radio station was and we piled out of these into this absolute loud mob, and of course, all these fishwives and hangers on would see the two Curley boys in their lieutenants uniforms, and me in my lieutenant - no, I guess I was a commander by then I think. But anyway, they'd lean over, "Hey George, you won the war didn't you, hey Dave, you won the war." And they'd even hit me. As far as they were concerned, I was a Curley too. And it was really something. We went in and heard the old boy in his victory speech. And it was fascinating to see those two aspects of Boston, both of them aware we were seeing them -

Q: The fact that you were going from one to the other.

Adm. M.: And, I think both factions envied us. Curley and his outfit would have loved to get to Beacon Hill. And the Beacon Hill people, they'd never heard anything firsthand about Curley's pull; just what had been in all the investigations and newspapers. It was really an experience.

Q: It must have been an eye-opener to Sue, as an Englishwoman, to witness American politics.

Adm. M.: Oh yes, right. Well, we got along very well. His wife, who was a stepmother to the children was a wonderful pianist and she would occasionally give us these pop concerts down there in the old house. But it was one experience. It really made Boston for us. Both Beacon Hill and Jamaica Plains. And we saw them in times when we went back.

Q: The Curleys?

Adm. M.: I'll get to that later because it comes in a different year. Unfortunately, all of that family (as I say, Mrs. Curley was not the mother of these seven or eight) all of that familys children had a very serious blood disease of some sort, and it was open knowledge. A couple of them had already died.

Q: It was a congenital thing?

Adm. M.: Apparently, although, whether it was from the mother or from the old boy - the old boy lived quite a while longer and we saw him later. But, by the time we got back to Boston, which I'll cover later, which was seven years later, the only ones left were George and his father, and the stepmother. All these other kids, including the other Navy one, had died of the same thing. It wasn't hemophilia but it was some congenital thing that got them at the age of 30 or 40. But, while we're talking about the Curley's: One time in our next visit to Boston, in a '52 trip, we had George at our cocktail party. Again, we were on Beacon Hill but in an apartment that the Belknap's had arranged to sublet for us, and George was fascinated by our shipmates and they were fascinated by him. He took us down - John was along by then about five-years-old - and we went down to Scituate where the family had a beach cottage for generations, I guess. And there were a couple of young Catholic priests there, and they sat at the feet of old Governor Curley - still called him Governor, whatever jobs he'd had. They sat at the feet of him like he was a king, just in awe listening to him. And he had the gift of gab; he reminds you, in that scene he reminds you a little bit of FDR. He was just a charmer from way back, and these young Catholic priests would just look up at him like he was the King of England. They were glad to sit at his feet and just listen to him. He couldn't have been nicer to us, I'll sure hand it to him. We used to get all kinds of cracks like, as I say, "Why is that bunch of Curley's staying there," and then other people would say, "Well, you don't admit that you go to the Curley's house, do you?" It would all depend on the person. I often wondered if George Curley is still alive. The old man died.

    Well, shall we have a drink?

Interview #4 with Rear Admiral Thomas H. Morton
Place: His residence in Annapolis, Maryland
Date: Tuesday morning, 25 November 1975
Interviewer: John T. Mason, Jr.

Q: Well, Tom, last time you told me the very interesting story of the battleship North Carolina and her exploits in the Pacific, and then you had returned with her to Boston after the end of the war, and you had a social whirl there which included two elements in the city - Jamaica Plains and the Somerset Club - or Beacon Hill. Now, do you want to resume?

Adm. M.: Yes, I think that just about covers our Boston stay. Of course it was, besides all the social whirl, it was a chance for all of the families to finally get together after us North Carolinians had been stag for so long. At the end of the stay, which I would say was about the first of December, I should say, the North Carolina and a few other ships shifted to the Hudson in New York which, as you remember, was where we were originally to stage our homecoming. My assistant gunnery officer, Bob Lowell, had taken the first month's leave and I was scheduled for

Morton #3 - 232

the second month, which would probably have been about mid-December to mid-January roughly; and, so I took off on leave to Annapolis, and Sue and I had an apartment on Murray Hill briefly, as a matter of fact in Jack Chew's mother's home there on Southgate Avenue. We'd been home probably two weeks when I suddenly got telegraphic orders to go and report to CNO and consequently, I never saw the North Carolina again. My gang packed me, I suppose, and shifted everything to Annapolis. It was a Sunday, and I went up to Washington to report in at the Old Navy Department and of course on Sunday nobody knew anything, as usual; but anyway, in compliance with this telegraphic order I did check in with the CNO duty officer who, as I remember might have been a WAVE. I think it was a WAVE, and we went through all the formalities of checking in on time, and so forth, but she hadn't the faintest idea what part of CNO I was to go to, and the only thing was to come back Monday. Well, meanwhile - Sue was up there with me - and we decided to go to one of the fancy restaurants for Sunday luncheon - LaSalle de Bois, if you remember it in those days?

Q: I remember it very well. I'm sorry it isn't there now.

Adm. M.: Me too. And, while we were enjoying our very fancy meal, a classmate of mine, Bill Mott, who had served a good part of the war with Admiral Turner in the Pacific said, "Hey, I hear you're going with Admiral Turner." Bill was no longer on the staff; and I said, "Am I?" Well, then he briefly told me the story that the Joint Chiefs of Staff had organized, or were organizing, their delegation to the United Nations Military Staff Committee, and Admiral Turner, as CNOs representative, was also the senior officer in the delegation, and I was to report to him for his staff. Then I found out, through Bill, that we were going to London in about three days for the initial meetings over there, which made things quite hectic; and further, Bill said, "By the way, whether or not you know Admiral Turner, I don't know but, we're having a cocktail party at our Chevy Chase home and he will be there and it will be a great chance for you to meet him." So, that afternoon we went out to the Motts, and sure enough, we met Admiral Turner and, as typical of him, he was there in a comfortable tweed suit when everybody else was still in uniform, and would be for months or years after the war. But, that was just his way of enjoying life and being comfortable.

By way of background, we found out that none of the wives of the military delegation and, in fact, very few of the senior delegates wives, would be able to go to London, for various reasons. The housing shortage in London, post-war, and the food shortage. When Sue met Admiral Turner he said, "I understand you're British, and if you still have a British passport, I want you to try to get to London, and I can use you," as he said, "as the official hostess of the U.S. Military Delegation." So, with his encouragement, we flailed around. Sue did have her U.K. passport, and about the 28 December '45 the U.S. Delegation sailed from New York. We all went up on the train together, and Sue followed along in the next Queen. I can't remember whether I went on the Queen Mary and she went on the Elizabeth or vice versa, but anyway, she followed over and got to Britain about the say, fifth of January, or something like that, on the next Queen. Well, that started a very interesting almost two years. It was a fascinating job and it was something quite different from what the average service officer comes in contact with. Going over in the Queen we had all the senior U.S. people, and the people were fascinating and they got to be people that we not only met aboard ship but saw a great deal of later in London and in New York.

Q: Who were some of the others in the delegation?

Adm. M.: Well, let's see. Stettinius was the senior member of the delegation, and the others that, mind you, I saw a lot at meetings where the military was involved, and also at the social functions in London and New York: Adlai Stevenson was one; Eleanor Roosevelt and, to cite some of the senior wives who were able to go: Senator and Mrs. Tom Connolly, and Senator and Mrs. Vandenberg. John Foster Dulles was another member who, as it turned out specialized in trusteeship when we once got going over there. The delegation was small in those days - the initial delegation - and so you really did get to know these wonderful people and, as it turned out, later we were on speaking terms with, for instance, Gromyko, and the Frenchman, Parodi, and others.

We were in London for about two months. The Security Council met at one place over there and the Military Staff met at another, and the General Assembly another. I've forgotten the name. One was called Church Hall, and what the others were, offhand, I don't remember.

Q: This was a temporary arrangement? They hadn't determined where their headquarters would be, or what?

Adm. M.: No, they were scheduled to come back to New York. Just exactly why the two months in London; it apparently had been decided at the preliminary conference in San Francisco in that July that they'd agreed to meet in London and then come back to New York. The plans, as I remember, were all laid on. There were places ready in London, and ready when we came back to New York. The reason for this two months over there, I don't know. I've forgotten.

But, as I say, it was a fascinating time and of course the Military Staff Committee commenced their meetings right away, then meeting about twice a week, as I recall.

Q: Well, what was their overriding purpose?

Adm. M.: They were the military advisors and military staff of the Security Council, and they had as one of their objectives, the formation of what was in the charter called, "Armed Forces made available to the Security Council," which we later sort of abbreviated in our minutes as the United Nations Armed Forces.

Q: This was to be an international armed force?

Adm. M.: It was to be an international armed force, originally consisting of forces of the five permanent members of the Security Council which, as you know, were U.S., U.K., France, Nationalist China, and Russia. Well, we realized, right from the word "go" that the Russians were going to stymie practically everything that came up. It was a good indication of what was going to happen in the future. They were going to stay in the United Nations, drag their feet as much as they could, and delay everything on what seems now, plain nitpicking.

By way of background, the Military Staff Committee

consisted of senior officers - flag and general officers of each of the three services of each of the five permament members. On the U.S. side, there was Admiral Turner as the senior member and the Navy representative, General George Kenny who had commanded Air Force in the Pacific, or South Pacific. He was the Air Force general, and then Lieutenant General Matthew Ridgway who was a wonderful man to serve with, was the Army man. He was three-star; the others were four-star. The other four nations had similar organizations. In a few cases they were not flag general officers. You remember the RAF commander. I mean the RAF officer from Britain was Group Captain Harry Eiles. The British delegation we knew very well, through language and Sue's connections in England, and so forth. Admiral Sir Henry Moore, four-star admiral, was their senior officer, and then Lieutenant General Morris was the Army representative, and so on down the line. The Chinese Navy representative was a Captain Chou, and their senior officer was again a four-star general in the Army, Shang Chen. And then, of course, we had the French. The Russian senior officer was - they were all three-star, as I remember; Lieutenant General Vasiliev was their senior. The Air Force Lieutenant General was Shaparov, and the Vice Admiral was Admiral Bogdenyko. Now, each delegation also had a secretary who was responsible for the usual drawing up the minutes of the agenda, and they did this jointly outside of the staff committee's meetings, before and after in each case. Our secretary was Captain Dennis Knoll who had long time experience in Russia and was quite fluent in the Russian language, which was a great help because of his ability to translate the Russians. This was of course, long before the days of simultaneous interpretation and everything that went on in the Security Council and the General Assembly, and the Military Staff Committee were broadcast to the meeting in the delegates own language and then, invariably two others to make up a complete and successive translation in English, French, and Russian.

Q: It was a very slow process?

Adm. M.: Very slow, and it continued in the U.N. for at least a year. In fact, I think when I left in September of '47, I don't think they'd come to simultaneous interpretation.

Q: The frustration of these multiple translations, plus the actions of the Russians must have been unbearable.

Adm. M.: It was; and them Gromyko, and also - the one who was in the Security Council; I'll think of it in a minute.

Q: Vishinsky, wasn't it?

Adm. M.: Yes, right. Vishinsky it was. They all had enough understanding of English, they refused to speak in any language but their own, and most of the delegates were this way. But, they would correct an interpreter right off the bat, if they found, to their ear, a mistake in the English or French translation. It was kind of funny. Gromyko was particularly careful.

Well, anyway, among other things we decided over there was to set up two committees in the military staff. One was, of course, the usual Rules of Procedure in the Military Staff Committee, and the one to follow was the composition of the Armed Forces made available to the Security Council which was, as I say informally abbreviated to UNAF. Admiral Turner and his senior officers had the policy that one officer out of the delegation would attend the meetings of the Security Council, as a spectator sitting with the U.S. delegation and, consequently I was able to see quite a few of the initial meetings of the council, as well as taking my wife along. They were always scheduled at a time different from the Military Staff Committee's so there was no conflict. As Admiral Turner's - I was sort of - I wasn't officially an aide but, I suppose I was. I was the junior member of the Navy, and besides Captain Knoll, the secretary, we had then Captain Elliot Strauss, who was sort of s senior assistant. The rear admiral Chief of Staff was not to be assigned until we got back to

New York so that Turner had Captain Strauss, Captain Knoll, and myself, as his staff, and the Army and Air Force had roughly the same. Of course, as I say, the closeness of the individuals involved was much more than it was later because of the smallness of the delegation and of the political delegation, and, as a matter of fact, of the U.N. as a whole. There were only 51 nations in the initial assembly and, of course, the Security Council at that time was only 11. It's now been expanded to 15, I believe. Other than that, on about the 26 February, we'll say, we all sailed together in the Queen back to New York to pick up the meetings of all three - well, the Assembly, the Security Council, and MSC, Military Staff Committee - in the New York sites.

Q: Perhaps at this point Tom, it would be well to ask you to say something about the prevailing spirit among the delegates at these initial sessions of the United Nations.

Adm. M.: Right. Well, the Security Council was the one that I saw the most of, and really was the most active, because they were to have the absolute, sort of executive power over security matters, and of course, most of London, just as it was in the Military Staff Committee, were organizational meetings; the election of vice presidents and the presidents and rules of procedure, which took up most of our time. Being small that way there were a lot of, you might call security council parties. One nation - one member of the Security Council, would entertain the others, without trying to include the whole assembly of 51 nations. As a matter of fact, Admiral Turner arranged a party which was held at Sue's aunt's house in London, where we had the entire Military Staff Committee, including their aides. And, then the larger Security Council parties were at places like Claridge Hotel, the Ritz-Savoy, and so forth. It was a round of good fun and it was a round of very optimistic hopes for the United Nations, except that the thing that each unit ran into was the attitude of the Russians. They were friendly but they were obviously, whether we realized it at the time, they were obviously going to obstruct as much as they could without destroying the organization. It was quite noticeable, even in those early weeks.

Q: This wasn't a normal way for human beings to act?

Adm. M.: No, and it was not the way that anyone else acted. Of course, in the General Assembly now, there were six committees who were, sort of - You might say committees of all because all 51 members were members of each - or 51 states had membership, but not necessarily the senior delegate. For instance, as I remember the Assembly Committees then, there was a political one, and then there was the overall steering committee, and then there was the Economic and Social Committee, the Trusteeship Committee, the Legal Committee, and the Administration and Budget. I think that's the number. Well, each one of these had 51 members and were rather unwieldy, but I think still are being continued in that form, to this day.

Q: With 160-some members?

Adm. M.: No, 51. Yes, yes, yes, present members. And as far as I know that's not - the only change I'm really familiar with is the Security Council, which I think has gone to 15.

One of the things that was rather interesting in England. Of course we knew the Charter like the back of our hand in those days, and there was quite a long chapter of the Charter on the Security Council, and a reasonably extensive one of Military Staff Committee but, one of the things which was to come up later, in New York, were the abstention votes in the Security Council. Now, to my knowledge this still has not been changed. The Charter specifically said, at least seven votes in the Security Council, including the concurring votes of the five current members. Now, even there in London, in those early days, they had already started an unwritten rule, which to my knowledge it still hasn't been put into the charter, that an abstention on absent permanent member did not constitute a veto. In other words, in some of these hassles in the Security Council, they did not require the concurrence of all five members; by a sort of Gentlemen's Agreement, I guess you'd call it, the thing could pass, provided it had the majority of the whole council, if no permanent member actually vetoed it. This is not the way the Charter is written, and still isn't, I don't think.

Q: But that was an act of survival, wasn't it, or then they couldn't have gotten anything done?

Adm. M.: Well, this is true but, I think - It's a small point except that you see in the Security Council to this day you'll see that, for instance, France abstained and you'll see China abstained, but because the U.S., the U.S.S.R., and the U.K. voted affirmatively the thing was not vetoed. In other words, by this unwritten rule you have to, as a permanent member say, "I abstain" or, "I veto." This has come up at a lot of times and it's interesting to me because we saw it in the early days. Some of Gromyko's walkouts, for instance, were not considered veto. The Council just went ahead without him and his absence was not taken as a veto.

Morton #4 - 244

That just about covers the London scene I think; but we saw a lot of Admiral Turner.

Q: Was Mrs. Turner with him?

Adm. M.: No, she was not. No, as I say, Sue was the only military wife there, and the very few exceptions otherwise. I mentioned Mrs. Vandenberg and Mrs. Connolly. And, I don't think there were any others.

So, we got back to New York, and the initial arrangements were that the General Assembly and the Security Council, I believe it was, met at Hunter College in New York, then an all-woman college; and I know the Security Council met there and I'm almost certain that the General Assembly also did, and we still continued having a representative there.

Q: New York was the permanent site designated?

Adm. M.: Right. Yes. New York was designated as the site without any actual physical site having been chosen. The Military Staff Committee met at the conference rooms in the Henry Hudson Hotel there on 57th or 59th Street, for a long, long time. Towards the Spring or Summer of '47 the whole operation was moved to the Sperry Plant at Lake Success where, as I recall, the Assembly, the Council, and ourselves all met there in different rooms. As a matter of fact, it's interesting to go ahead a little bit.

The last General Assembly meeting that I attended, and I think Sue was there with me, was when the Assembly accepted the Rockefeller proposal to use property which is now the U.N. Headquarters. They had just gotten around to voting the acceptance of this, which later became the U.N. as we know it now.

The struggles of the Military Staff Committee continued and we reported in the State Department's nightly cable. One of the jobs was to go and review for the State Department delegation the material of what had happened at that days Military Staff Committee meeting. Incidentally, Senator Warren Austin was the head of the delegation upon our return to New York.

Q: Yes, he became the permanent representative.

Adm. M.: He became the permanent representative whereas Stettinius had led them to London. I think Senator Austin was still there when I left.

Q: He was there for a number of years.

Adm. M.: Yes. He was there the whole time. Any real important thing coming up, and particularly the Security

Council meetings during the General Assembly sessions, which were about two months once a year, the Secretary of State would come up, and sort of take over. Jimmy Byrnes was the first one I remember. He must have relieved Stettinius somewhere along the line of '46. I mentioned that Gromyko walked out. I happened to be at the Security Council meeting where this occurred. At least, for the first time it occurred. The argument was concerning Iran, and concerning Mossadegh, and the whole Council was obviously against the Soviet delegation - such points as had come up and Gromyko, their Council member then, apparently chose not to veto but to simply walk out of the chamber, and I'll never forget that day. The Chinese delegation was the President of the Council that month. They rotated alphabetically month by month to establish a Chairman of the Council, and Byrnes was in the U.S. seat and, as I told you, we went through all this translation. Gromyko had stated, in Russian, his intention to leave the Council and refused to take any part in that discussion - of that point. Then he sat down and waited very calmly for the French and English translations, whichever came next; I don't know. But, in any case, as soon as the last translation was finished and the audience, as a whole, then realized what was going to happen, he simply stood up, and I remember he took off his glasses and put them in his breast pocket, and turned on his heel and walked out behind the Chairman. I suppose

the door was the far side from the Russian seat. The little
Chinese Chairman didn't bat an eye and didn't look around.
I remember Jimmy Byrnes very much looked around and watched
the whole thing. It was rather impressive because with
Gromyko's standing up very calmly getting himself all ready
to go, his assistants did the same and the few military who
were sitting behind him, so we had a Soviet parade out of
there; and, one of those things that you don't forget.
Of course, later on there were other Soviet walkouts,
but that's the one that probably was the most famous one
because it was the first, and I was fortunate enough to
be there to see it.

Meanwhile, in the Military Staff Committee the work
going on was finished on the Rules of Procedure, after a
lot of hassling and nitpicking, particularly by the Russians.
All of these reports went to the Security Council as our
supervisory body. And then we commenced work on the Composition of the United Nations' Armed Forces, and this is
where we ran into real difficulty. It wasn't a case of
dotting Is and commas and things but, this is where the
Russians really wanted to obstruct, and they did. Incidentally, by this time we had gotten Admiral Ballentine, Rear
Admiral Ballentine - then Rear Admiral - the famous carrier
leader, as the Chief of Staff to Admiral Turner; and the
U.S. service delegation had built up to, probably ten of
us in each service. Dennie Knoll, the secretary, had gone,

and he was relieved by Colonel Truman, later Lieutenant General Truman of the Army, who became a fast friend of mine; and I was assigned as the Navy assistant secretary to Truman. Each delegation, each of the five nations on these subcommittees appointed a secretary, not the senior one but one of the assistants. That's how I happened to be the U.S. secretary on the two committees. And, again, the three services of each country were represented but were not the senior members on these subcommittees. The five secretaries would then meet, and we had professional interpreters - civilians hired by the U.N. - who assisted in the wrestling out of the minutes which would be very complicated because there was a case of interpretation there. But each day we would stay there in the Henry Hudson Hotel for an hour or so to get the minutes ready for writing up for submission to the members and then at the next meeting the members would approve or amend, and you'd get amendments in one language and not in another.

The general idea there was that the Russians were looking after themselves. For instance, there was a great argument as to how many carriers would be in the naval part.

Q: Did carriers under the control of the Security -

Adm. M.: Well, as the words said, "Made available to the Security Council." And, I think we got that down to something. It settled on the number of divisions and the number of aircraft wings and squadrons, and so forth; but, we could never get anywhere on that because the four other delegations would be somewhere near the thing. For instance, the Russians never wanted any carriers, and the reason they didn't want any carriers was that they didn't have any. They knew that certainly the U.S. and Britain, and to some extent, France would be able to contribute carriers. The idea was that the forces would be earmarked. This was the theory. Foreign divisions: so many aircraft wings, so many destroyers, so many carriers, and so on; but would not be assigned except on call.

Q: Like the Strike force?

Adm. M.: And also like the Gaza strip. In other words, when the time came we would, in theory, have the number of various units involved and then the Military Staff group maybe would call up and say, "We'd like you to send one carrier, and you send another." That was the theory. But, as I say, one big obstacle was the fact that, of course the Chinese had no carrier, but the Russians didn't want anybody to have a carrier because they knew that carrier, or carriers in the outfit would be non-Russian – and they were very, very sticky on this. So this went on for months and finally – I'd say in the middle of '47 – we finally submitted a report to the Security Council which was strictly a divided one. The other four had pretty much agreed on it, with some minor exceptions; and then the Russian minority view was set forth so that at that time, at least, we never did have a final organization on this thing.

Q: During this period, Tom - this several years - was there a call upon these forces that were earmarked for the United Nations?

Adm. M.: No, not that I recall. If there were events that required, as I say, something like the Gaza strip, it was not handled through the Security Council.

Q: This was indeed high idealism, wasn't it?

Adm. M.: It was; it was high, and pretty much supported by most of the 51 nations. You see, you have to remember that one of the compromises at San Francisco, in July of '45, involved the Russians, in effect having three representatives in the Assembly.

Q: Belorussia -

Adm. M.: Belorussia and Ukraine as well as the Soviet Union

itself, and this was one of the things that enabled the Charter to go because, having Russia with three seats in the Assembly didn't really make a great deal of difference. It was just the idea of it. Of course then they could also have one of these other two states on the Security Council.

Q: As a non-permanent member.

Adm. M.: As a non-permanent member with no veto, so called but, at least Russia had two votes right there.

Q: Tom, if Russia had not been so obstreperous - or if she hadn't been there at all and this plan was formulated and the forces were available, in your opinion would it have been a workable thing for the nations of the world?

Adm. M.: Well, I think it would of. I think that, for instance, the direction of the emergency forces now are actually done by the U.N. I mean the Norwegians and the Swedes, and the others involved in these various operations, and it seems to work; and they're not getting orders from their national government, to my knowledge. They're coming right from New York.

Q: But, the major powers have not been involved in this?

Adm. M.: No, the thinking, long since the time I was there - the original forces were going to be of the major powers, with the idea of spreading out to the others as time went on. Now, I think the feeling is, and has been for years, just from what I see in the press, there's been a deliberate attempt to omit the major powers; and, as you know, the Scandinavians have done a lot - I think some South Americans - Bolivians, Brazilians. I can't name the countries that have been involved, but by-and-large there have been none of the major powers involved deliberately.

The way I remember it, in seeing it work, were particularly in the Military Staff. The ones who were really willing to stand up and shout down the Russians, if you want to call it that, were the British, and that General Morris, their number two, he didn't care whether the Russian generals and admiral got mad or not; he called a spade a spade. Admiral Turner and Generals Ridgway and Kenny were almost as adamant, particularly Turner, but they had a little more kid glove effect on them. The Russians were impossible; the Chinese were almost - God bless 'em - almost, I wouldn't say useless; but powerless. They usually went along with the U.S. They usually had nothing much to say. They were nice guys but, that was it. And, the French, because the French admiral was a known Communist, which was something we couldn't do anything about; the French had nominated him - and so the French, although not as obstructionist as the Russians, they tended to side with the Russians on several points, not always. But, it was really a case of the British and the Americans against the Russians the whole way through, where there was disagreement.

The personnel in the U.S. delegation, as a matter of interest, changed in the year and three quarters I was there. Admiral Hewitt relieved Admiral Turner, General McNarney relieved General Kenny, and I think General Ridgway was there the whole time. This was before he went on to Panama and NATO and Chief of Staff, of course. Incidentally, the Army system being what it is, a lot of Ridgway's colonels and lieutenant colonels had been with him for a long time and went on with him to these successive senior jobs he had.

The general was squiring Penny, I think her name was - at the time.

Q: Very, very attractive -

Adm. M.: Yes, she was and they were about to get married. But, about every two months we'd put out a new telephone directory in the Staff Committee, with changes and home addresses, and so forth, and General Ridgway had put - I've forgotten which way around but we'll say he put an asterisk or something to show that, "Married, but out of town," or maybe he said, "not married." I guess that was it and, I think in editing this damn thing I put, "Married; wife not in New York;" and, of course the rough went around to the old boy - he raised hell about that. He said I had no business to change it and I shouldn't have changed it, that's the way he wanted it, and that's the way it would be; and I think it was towards the middle or end of '47 that he was married to her. I think she was a WAC, wasn't she? Yes.

Q: Was Catherine Ballentine there?

Adm. M.: Oh, yes. We saw a lot of her - very much so and they were tremendously good to us. The Ballentine's, I believe, were at one of the big hotels. Admiral Turner lived over in Summit, New Jersey. He had a beautiful house or big apartment over there, and we were often asked over there, and Mrs. Turner - Harriet, I think it was, was fond of these two little white dogs that invariably got all over the chairs and all over Admiral Turner's blue uniform. He used to jokingly beef about this, by the hour.

We had allowances in the Navy contingent for getting our own quarters. In other words, we were reimbursed for it. Fort Totten was turned over as official government quarters to the U.S. Army and U.S. Air Force, then called the U.S. Army Air Forces, I believe. I don't think the

the Air Force came along 'til the year later. At Fort Totten they had a big club hall out there, and our delegation gave the Military Staff delegation a reception, a cocktail party, at which, of course, all the wives of all ranks were invited - strictly a military party; there were no State Department or others, and one of the commander's chores was to help arrange this thing, and I remember being out there; it was, we'll say six to eight, and at six o'clock by the clock's stroke in came the Russians in about six or eight cars. They were there absolutely on time and when, later on in the party - they didn't wait 'til eight but, Chairman Vasiliev gave some signal and cars came up to get them and everyone of them went out together.

But, it was an interesting time. It's one of those things that not many people would be lucky enough to go through. I don't know how many people would like it but I loved it, so did Sue. We took some of the British to night baseball at Yankee Stadium, and they were thrilled in seeing a new game, and so forth.

The Russian delegation had a party at their headquarters in New York. I don't know whether it was the old Russian Consul-General's quarters or whether they just acquired one -

Q: It was on Park Avenue, wasn't it?

Adm. M.: I don't remember now. We moved from 57th Street to Park Avenue, as far as the office went, later in my stay. It could have been on Park Avenue. Anyway, we had our child, who turned out to be John Morton, coming along any day then, and we went to the Red Army Day at the Russian delegation's - I wouldn't call it a home but, anyway, to their quarters, and the Russian Air Force general's wife had taken a good shine to Sue, and so, in typical Russian fashion, Mrs. Shaparov sneaked Sue into the private room where straight Vodka was being served. Sue told Mrs. Shaparov that (her English was fair, by the way) she was afraid to have straight Vodka, that she was becoming a mother in about three weeks - it was dangerous; and Mrs. Shaparov, she, typical of the way they can be, laughed and said, "Well, if you have enough Vodka, you'll have it here and we can give it Russian citizenship." It was the sort of way they were.

But, to go back to Mrs. Ballentine which got me off on that. She was wonderful to everybody, and so was Mrs. Turner, but the Ballentines were far more active; being younger than Admiral and Mrs. Turner, they were more active on the scene. It turned out beautifully because later on in this interview I'll tell you about the times in the Mediterranean - 6th Fleet -

Q: When Bally was there.

Adm. M.: When Bally was there. And Sue and Mrs. Ballentine traveled a lot of those countries together, largely through our knowing them through the United Nations.

The only other thing up there which was of some interest and importance: Bernard Baruch, who was to present the Atomic Energy Control International to the U.N., set up a unit under the U.S. delegation, and again, some of us in the military were asked to sit in and advise him on it. He had people like Jouett Shouse, Mr. Hancock. He had a very young Air Force general - Ludecke, who was with them as a military advisor, permanently; and the sessions of that group were extremely interesting, internal in the delegation; and I was fortunate enough to go out when Mr. Baruch presented his proposal to the Security Council.

Q: Now, was this to use - the proposal to use atomic energy for peaceful purposes?

Adm. M.: Yes, it was. That was the whole idea. It was based on our own AEC, then called. It was International Atomic Energy Authority, or some name. But, what he did in his presentation - he stressed atomic energy, but he particularly was for control and abolition of all weapons of what he called mass destruction, and there was provision for control for peaceful use.

Q: The result of this was this International Atomic Commission that was set up?

Adm. M.: As far as I know that was the follow up to it, and the U.S. was the first nation to submit this proposal. Of course, the Russians didn't get their weapons until a couple of years later so we were the only ones that were in a position to make any proposal, I suppose.

In these meetings - I remember, this was '47, we'll say - early '47 or maybe '46. The best judgment of all of these experts with Mr. Baruch's group was that the Russians would not have anything for five to seven years. I remember that distinctly - would not be able to even conduct a test. Well, that would be, if we'll call it early '47, that would be '52 to '54 whereas actually, I remember I was in Norfolk when the first tests were made in mid-'49, so our estimates of the Russian progress capability were much too optimistic.

Q: When you were there, did the issue of Kashmir and a plebiscite come up.

Adm. M.: Yes, it did -

Q: Was Nimitz' named?

Adm. M.: - and I think Admiral Nimitz was maybe appointed to that. Would that be about the same time?

Q: Yes.

Adm. M.: Yes, he did. And, in this nightly report to the State Department that I mentioned that one of my jobs was to fill in what the Military Staff - that was a wonderful summary of everything that went on in the U.N. that day, and in the military we got a copy of it from the people that were there. Kashmir was very much in there. Iran also - and worldwide quotes of newspapers like the French, and they'd indicate that the press was Liberal, Conservative, Communist, and so forth. They would all be in there too, and you were able to keep up, just in a little thumbnail capsule of the information. Meanwhile, of course there were bigger and longer reports of what the Security Council did and the General Assembly had been in session. Ours was just a really very small part but, in reading the whole report every day, if you got to it, it gave you a pretty good idea of what the U.N. was doing and what was happening to the world.

Q: Now, Mrs. Roosevelt, at that time was our representative on the Human Rights Commission, was she not?

Adm. M.: I believe so. I think she must have been; I'm pretty sure she was. She was awfully nice to work with. The ones I knew best of that group were Stevenson and Dulles, because I happened to meet with them more often than the others.

Q: What was your impression of Stevenson?

Adm. M.: Very well thought of, and very smart.

Q: Did he have an understanding of the military role?

Adm. M.: Well, I don't think that that came up as much as we were sitting in at his meetings. When I say "we", it would be myself or one of the two others. See, they would let Admiral Turner know when they wanted someone from the military present - what the discussion was - except when they would ask us advice. This was largely in the early stages of procedure - we'd give them advice, but there was never anything in their particular line that very much involved the military.

Q: What was your impression of John Foster Dulles?

Adm. M.: No real way that I could judge it on that, Jack. The whole interest of his was Trusteeship that largely involved the final settlement of the small islands in the Pacific - Marianas, Truk, and others.

Q: Was there any thought, at any time, that the Navy would have a role in the trusteeship of these islands, inasmuch as the Navy had had a role after World War I?

Adm. M.: Yes, in Samoa and Guam. No, I don't think that had ever come up. I think we were there largely because - I mean that was not the only area in the world that was involved in this - but, we were familiar with the islands and their relationship, and so forth.

To go back to your question on Stevenson. In later years, I think you have to give him almost full credit for the test ban. I'm almost positive of that - I'm talking now of late '50s or early '60s. The atomic above ground test ban I think was his idea, and pushed by him. That's my recollection. Of course it was years later.

I don't know whether that covers all the U.N. you want, but it's about all I can think of at the moment, unless you've got questions in connection with this continual and continuing U.N. obstruction -

Q: On the part of the Russians?

Adm. M.: Yes. The Military Staff, although still functioning to my knowledge, is muchly downgraded. For instance, some years after I left the - either the Commandant of the Third Naval District or the Eastern Sea Frontier, also had additional duties, where Admiral Turner and Admiral Hewitt had been. As a matter of fact, even in their early days, the British did this. Sir Henry Moore, the senior British officer - four-star admiral - he was, even in those early days, doing this as part-time. He was the head of the British Joint Services Mission at the time, in Washington, and that was his primary duty, and when the meetings got down to routine, twice a week, or whatever, he'd simply come to New York for that and go back.

Q: Perhaps the British were more realistic about the success of this whole operation?

Adm. M.: That's right. On the other hand, the Air Force Air Marshall and the Army lieutenant general were, as I remember, full-time there, just as our people were.

Q: Well, Tom, your sojourn at Lake Success came to an end in '47?

Adm. M.: Yes. Then I was ordered - in September or October of '47, after almost two years with the delegation, to command the destroyer, Compton, DD-705, as designated, who was the flagship of Destroyer Squadron 12 - at least in those days.

Q: She was a part of the Atlantic Fleet?

Adm. M.: The Atlantic Fleet, yes - homeported in Newport. At that time we did not have the facility at Mayport, Jacksonville, but we had most of the destroyer types in either Newport or Norfolk, and that squadron happened to be Newport-based.

Q: Newport was something less than ideal for a destroyer base, was it not?

Adm. M.: Of course, the destroyer piers, and that sort of thing had not been built at that time. The winter weather was a little rough but, Norfolk in the winter can be just as bad, or almost as bad. Without the destroyer piers, which were built later at Newport, we all nested at the buoys in the harbor which was somewhat different from Norfolk where they invariably went along to the destroyer piers at the Naval Base. But, that meant boating could be a little rough, a little difficult, particularly at night but, I liked Newport, and most of us did. As a matter of fact, I think for destroyer life I would prefer it - I liked it better than I would had it been at Norfolk.

Q: The families were able to be there?

Adm. M.: The families were there, yes. Sue moved up. I went to the usual assignment of about a month at Key West with the Sonar School, which was almost mandatory for a destroyer skipper or unit commander, and in that period, which we will say was, October I guess, Sue moved up to Newport and found herself, and us, a nice little house up there. John was then about six months old. And so, things started with the Sonar School at Key West, and then the rest of the operations that winter were pretty much routine, I'll say. Then the squadron, or the division, and I'm not sure whether it was the whole squadron or not, yes, the whole suqadron was sent to Philadelphia Navy Yard for routine overhaul and eventual deployment to the Mediterranean. We went from the Norfolk overhaul to the usual business of Earl, New Jersey for ammunition - no, I guess it was Fort Mifflin at Philadelphia in those days. Mifflin was the Naval Magazine and Ammunition Depot, and then we went to Guantanamo for the usual four, five, six weeks, coming back from there in about July or August, and then deployed for the Mediterranean Sixth Fleet assignment in September.

Q: Was that a six-month assignment?

Adm. M.: It was about five in those days. It was a triple rotation. In other words, three times a year but with the overlap of turning over to your relief, ships, and that sort of thing, it amounted to about five months. Five months away. The whole squadron went, and you mentioned the other day, Josh Cooper. My first commodore, so called, was Captain W. R. Headden, and before we went to the Philadelphia Yard the squadron was taken over by then Captain Cooper, and he had the squadron for the good part of a year.

The Mediterranean is always, in my opinion, the high point of a ship's operations. Meanwhile, we'd had all the gunnery and engineering and navigation/seamanship at Guantanamo under their expert instructors and ship riders, as they call them, and bombardment at Culebra was a part, and then we deployed in September to proceed to the Mediterranean. The turnover on that particular tour was at Gibraltar, and Admiral Forrest Sherman was the Sixth Fleet Commander and Admiral Ballentine, who I mentioned had gone from the U.N. to the Carrier Division and at that particular rotation he was the Carrier Division Commander for the Sixth Fleet. On the personal level, I was particularly lucky on the later three deployments that I made to Sixth Fleet because Sue had a home base in England and was able to get over there and then, as we found out when you went to the more eastern ports - areas such as Turkey, Greece - it was a little far to go, and so she could pick the countries that she could visit handily and then go back and spend the rest of the time in England, either before or after. John was then about two years old, I guess, and was left behind with family and friends in England so Sue could make the trip with me; so we were able to do France and Italy together. Incidentally, in two later trips, in the Sixth Fleet as a destroyer division commander, and later as an AKA skipper, John was old enough to come down and see the world with us.

There were interesting operations over there and nothing out of the ordinary really, but we were very much involved in the Trieste situation, as I was again five years later. In that late '48 period the Anglo-American Military Government was still controlling Trieste, and they invariably had a cruiser or a destroyer, or both ready, in theory, to bombard if anything happened with the Yugoslavs at the border. It was still very much divided into Zone A, which was Italian owned, and Zone B was the Yugoslav. We, of course called on the American authorities there, as well as the British. They had at least three-star generals in Joint Command, possibly four. We visited the Yugoslav border, and particularly that time, in 1948, the Yugoslav border guards obviously meant business and you didn't get too close to them. You could take pictures but you took them from a discreet distance. There never was any real trouble there while we were there. Incidentally, Trieste and Venice were always combined as a visit. You went to one for say, a week and then the other for a week so that the Adriatic swing always included both ports. Of course, Venice was an equally attractive place to go. One of the other assignments during our last few months over there was, you might say, to carry the mail for the U.N. presence in Palestine - I'm trying to think when Israel was declared independent. In any case, the U.N. was represented by the Peace Truce Commission, Peace Commission, which had been headed by Count Bernadotte, who was assassinated there some months before my particular ship was sent. I think he was always called Acting Truce Administrator - and that was Ralph Bunche - and he was there, and had been moved to Rhodes. The U.N. delegation largely, at least the American contingent was in Haifa, which was the seaport, and the mail would come into Nicosia in Cyprus, and then the assigned destroyer would go up to Famagusta, Cyprus, and bring the mail and documents back. Planes were not flying in, although the antiaircraft fire had ceased between the Arabs and Israelis at that time, yet they still felt that this destroyer mail system was the safest, and so that was our job for, I'd say, almost a month. We were fully accredited, at least visibly, as a U.N. unit. The ship flew a large United Nations ensign - the blue with the white globe on it and directly under the Stars and Stripes, and anyone that had business ashore, which usually was only the skipper, and in our case, Commodore Cooper, wore U.N. bands here, just as the group did ashore. There wasn't much to do there; one thing of interest - he and I were invited to the Rotary Club luncheon there in Haifa and, although the actual fighting was pretty much over, there were in a group of say 50 or 60 Rotarians there were several Arabs who were citizens of Israel - residents, citizens of Israel, and business men presumably - professional. And, it was rather interesting that when they often talk about the civic clubs like Civitan and Rotarian, and so forth. It was a good example of how, at least once a week, the Jews and Arabs would sit down together and be perfectly normal and enjoy life, no matter what was going on around them. They encouraged the skipper to go ashore as sort of "liaison with our group. Among others I met was a Jewish Israel Army major - Shuman by name, I think, and he arranged for one or two of my officers and myself to go up through Nazareth to the Sea of Galilee, which was a beautiful and interesting place. The note he gave us was in Hebrew and, of course, I never knew what I was passing to these sentries, but whatever he had written worked. It was one chance to have a few of us, at least, to see something besides Haifa dockyard. Another Israeli, an older man, was the honorary Swedish Consul there at Haifa. Like so many nations do, they designated a local citizen to be their honorary consul;

and he was extremely helpful in giving us advice and so forth. The headquarters were at the - I was going to say King David Hotel in Haifa, but I'm not sure of that. The ones we saw were largely American. We discussed before whether these peace-keeping forces used the -

Q: Major powers.

Adm. M.: In this case you might say it was a Truce Commission, and with Bernadotte killed and Bunche in charge it was largely American. There may have been others in it but I don't honestly remember. The others may have been in places other than Haifa. I saw a few of the people that I'd known in the U.N. there, incidentally, usually civilian, State Department part of the delegation. I never actually saw Bunche, although I'd met him in New York. He was largely headquartered at Rhodes in those days. We went in there too, but I never met him.

Q: What was your relationship with the Royal Navy in the Mediterranean?

Adm. M.: Very close. We went into Malta to bombard at one of their offshore islands and then went in and saw the Combined Staff at Malta.

Q: Mountbatten was there, wasn't he?

Adm. M.: I don't remember. If it had been Mountbatten I'd probably remember it. I'm not sure whether it was - I don't remember who the British admiral was. Then, fortunately, Admiral Troubridge was the staff senior naval aviator, and on his staff was Sue's Navy brother-in-law, so I had the good fortune to have a relative by marriage there to show me around Malta and -

Q: What was his name?

Adm. M.: His name was Brian Logan - Navy captain aviator.

Q: Did we have access to the facilities at Malta for repair jobs?

Adm. M.: At Valletta? Yes, we did although we didn't need to use them. We also had them at Gibraltar. I'll discourse a little bit on Admiral Forrest Sherman. One of his brand new regulations, it turned out, over there in the Sixth Fleet, was that every officer of every ship had to wear a hat ashore, and I didn't have a hat and didn't own one, and I went into, in Malta there, with my brother-in-law, and also Admiral Ballentine was there in the carrier at the same time and, I think I went over to meet Admiral Ballentine and was riding with him, or something and, I said, "Admiral is Admiral Sherman serious about this headgear thing?" and he said, "You bet your life he's serious." So, one of my efforts in Malta was to go to Gieves, or one of those big stores and buy myself a hat which I then wore the rest of my time in the Mediterranean.

Admiral Sherman was really a stickler on a lot of things. He was absolutely insistent, whether you were destroyer, or minesweeper, or what you were, that you stayed in blues at sea, and that was really a hassle because there are a lot of things in which you just can't run a ship, particularly at sea, other than dungarees. So, we would always be careful when we were fueling from a bigger ship, or something like that, and we got into blues in plenty of time.

Q: For fear he might be aboard the big ship?

Adm. M.: Yes, or maybe one of the other flag officers would be. The Columbus was a big cruiser, flagship, up in Britain for ComNavAir. I'm trying to think what Sherman's flagship was. Albany was his flag, and I remember we fueled from the Albany one time, at sea, underway, and a lot of my boys had been inspired to grow beards before the beard became so famous with hippies and so forth. But, anyway, I was fueling alongside, and rather busy, as the fueling skipper has to be, and the signal came over from Admiral Sherman and said - the words were somewhat like this: "The efforts of some members of your crew to grow beards is as ridiculous as their appearance. Get them off." And, needless to say, after we broke away one of the first things the crew of the Compton did was break out the razor.

I met him only once on that trip. We were in Augusta Bay, Sicily, and we were fueling at anchor from one of our Navy tankers - Shemong, I think it was, but no matter, and the tanker skipper was one of Josh Cooper's closest friends, classmates, who also happened to be a cousin of mine, G. W. Wilcox by name. So, with the destroyer commodore, so called, and the tanker skipper there together - the whole fleet was in Augusta - so those two invited Admiral Sherman over to lunch, after some discussion. It was held in Compton rather than in the alongside tanker. So, Wash Wilcox, Josh Cooper, and Admiral Sherman, and me, as what you might call flag skipper, had lunch together. He was very nice but he really, in my opinion, was an absolute cold fish. I mean, to be Chief of Naval Operations, and command the Sixth Fleet before that, he must have been good but I can't give him anything on personality. I hate to say that. He was just a cold fish. No sense of humor, no congeniality or anything else.

Then let's see, there was of course the visits to other places, Cannes, Naples.

Q: You had access to North African ports too, didn't you?

Adm. M.: Yes, we did. We were not allowed to go into Alexandria because, at that time the naval attaché, military attachés had been booted out, I believe. In any case, the ambassador had been stoned and they'd thrown rocks at his automobile, and that sort of thing, a few months before, so Egypt was off-limits, but the others were available. We went into Tunis, for instance, and Wheelus Field was then very much going as a U.S. Air Force Base. Beirut, Rhodes, I mentioned. On that particular cruise, Tunis was the only one that we got into.

Q: That was Bizerte?

Adm. M.: Yes. Yes, it was. I said Tunis was the site of Wheelus Field. It wasn't, it was —

Q: Libya —

Adm. M.: Yes, Tripoli. We went there. You asked about the relations with the British. I tend to get my three Sixth Fleet cruises confused as far as time goes but, in any case, certainly, if not by then, in later tours there the NATO signalbook and the NATO tactical book and so forth, worked extremely well. They were, if anything better than our own signal book because it was newer and prepared jointly. Whether we had joint maneuvers on that cruise with other nations, I can't say. I don't remember, but in any case, in one, or both of my destroyer tours over there we had excellent maneuvers with the French, British, Italians, Turkish, and Greeks. I'm talking now when we were operating at sea together. Incidentally, a lot of the Navy that I met up in Venice - the Italian Navy - were extremely friendly and high in their praise of the United States. It's surprising how many of them were prisoners in Key West or California and such places during the war, and very much made a point of learning English while they were there, and apparently were very well treated and consequently they were very nice to us you might say.

Q: As yet there was no evidence of any Russian presence there?

Adm. M.: No, none at all. As a matter of fact, my last tour over there was in the AKA which ended in '57, 1957, and I think, even then - I have no recollection of seeing a Russian or there being very much of a stew about the presence like there was in later years.

Q: And, in this early tour of duty there was no indication of the eventual pullout of the British, was there?

Adm. M.: Pullout of the British, or the French?

Q: British - reduction in British forces?

Adm. M.: Oh, no, not at least in this stage, no. You're right. And, of course the French were very active, either in this tour, or the next, before they stopped playing NATO games with us.

Q: In this tour, did you go into any Spanish ports?

Adm. M.: No, I didn't get to Spain until the mid-fifties. That is if you don't count Gibraltar, of course. There was a shift in later years to Oran, as the place to turn over to and from reliefs over there but this particular trip it was Gibraltar.

Q: At this stage, the Sixth Fleet didn't have a land base at all, did it?

Adm. M.: Well, no they didn't, only to the extent that the fleet flagship was homeported at Villefranche, near Nice; and therefore, being that one ship, the <u>Albany</u> I think it was, was the only one homeported there, and actually it was really just an anchorage for them but it did give the families transportation over and back and quarters allowance ashore, and PX, commissary and whatnot. Incidentally, a good many of the wives of our squadron made the trip over there, particularly skippers and execs wives if they had the money to do it, and all of that was completely at our own expense, as you know. The flagship was the only one whose families had transportation paid to and from, and quarters allowance. That was one of the reasons, in those days, why they held the rotation to four or five months because, as I remember, the rules were then, if you were over there more than six months you qualified for the things that I mentioned, and so they were very careful that the ships got home in four or five months to avoid what was then a legal problem and a pay problem.

Q: When you went into a foreign port over there in the Mediterranean, what kind of preparation did you give your crew members? After all they were, in a sense, minor diplomatic agents of the United States.

Adm. M.: I'm glad you asked that because I intended to cover it. The Sixth Fleet then, and through the last of my three tours over there, had an excellent publication called The Sixth Fleet Directory. The Sixth Fleet Directory was an alphabetical listing of chapters by name of port, regardless how big or how small and, each ship was given one or more of these, largely for indoctrination of the crew and advice as to amusements and no-can-dos, and that sort of thing, and the publication was really excellent.

Every senior officer of a group of ships that went into port was required to send in a report to ComServFor 6th Fleet, who was responsible for this directory, and you'd go down the directory paragraph by paragraph and send him recommended or necessary changes, so that periodically Commander, Service Force could rewrite pages and edit them and bring them up to date, and that book was kept up to date and was extremely useful. It covered just about anything you can think of in a port. I mean, it gave a smattering of history of the place, the population, and so forth, but furthermore they listed the best areas and the worst areas. They listed the hotels and restaurants. They listed amusements of various types; any possible area that might be out of bounds. It was extremely useful and, as I say, we used that for briefing; prior to getting to a port, we used that for notes in what we call the plan of the day which is on all the bulletin boards in the ship, so that these people could pick the tours they wanted to make, if any and, that was our medium for indoctrinating the crew on, besides the business of American ambassadors and behaving ashore, and so forth, to give them some idea of where they were going, what would be pleasant and interesting to do, and then, any taboos, if any. Sometimes this backfired to some extent - humorous. In going into Athens, one of the things that was highly stressed in the <u>Sixth Fleet Directory</u> was the danger of ouzo, the anise drink of the Greeks, which I think in the Middle East, Turkey and so forth, they call raki, but anyway, we duly warned the crew against ouzo and, of course there was no real great harm in this happening but, invariably the ships found out that the more they told them to stay away from ouzo, the more ouzo they'd drink. And ouzo mixed with plain water and ice, if you like it, is not a bad drink if you like the anisething, but the trouble was these boys - especially the young segment - I don't know whether they drank it straight, or too much, or what but, it had the most disastrous effect, which I saw in later cruises over there. These kids would come back, perfectly on time, say midnight, or whenever the liberty was up. They would come up and salute the petty officer of the watch and then they'd fall flat on their face, and they'd be out for as much as 18-24 hours, just out cold from this ouzo. To my knowledge, it never did anybody any real harm, but it was that after effect that was so notable. The guys would get back perfectly alright, as I say, on time, salute the petty officer of the watch and all that, and then they couldn't move until late the next day.

Talking about tours, and what the sailors can do over there, when we were in Naples - I don't know whether it was the Embassy or the Consul, or maybe American Express -

some unit, organization, arranged an audience with the Pope for either my ship or, maybe two or three of them, and that was most fascinating. I did not go on the trip but, I'd say about twenty or thirty of our people, including a couple of officers, went along. He was then Pius XII, I believe. Would that be right? And they brought back these marvellous photographs that either the Navy or the embassy had taken, in their joint audience with the Pope and, the impression, in talking with these young men, most of whom were petty officers, because they had the money to make the trip, I guess. Seamen didn't. The public relations and the genuine feeling of the Pope himself were tremendously interesting. I am not a Catholic, but I always admire the Pope's stature in the world.

Anyway, they would say, for instance, he would come down the line, in his audience, which was only Navy, and he'd pluck at a mans sleeve and say, "I see you're a second class bosun's mate" or "You're a machinists mate first," or "You're a storekeeper third," and he knew every one of these. He'd either been terribly well briefed or just knew them. And, he'd say, "Where are you from?" And these young men would say, "I'm from, " we'll say, "Chicago, Indianapolis, St. Louis," and he'd say, "Oh, I know it well. I was there in 1937."

In other words, he, somewhat like I mentioned at the Roosevelt graduation in '33, he just had that touch of having every one of those people think that he's the one that the Pope wanted to see, and he knew a lot about him. It was fascinating, and any number of them told me that.

Q: Maybe that was an American way that he learned. He was a Papal Nuncio -

Adm. M.: Yes, that's why he knew so many American cities, you see. I said 1937. I don't know what his dates were over here but, that was the reason he knew the States so well.

Then of course, they had places to go like Capri, Pompeii, and then Rome I mentioned. I had a marvellous chief gunner's mate named Harkness - Charles Harkness, and he was with me the whole time over there, and a humorous story, if I can fit it in. A whole bunch of the chiefs went over together to Capri, and the finicula there - Each one of them had one of these young Italian girls with them, just for the trip and the day. Whether they'd come from Naples, or whether they lived in Capri, I don't know. And, Harkness was from, well, say Des Moines, Illinois, or somewhere like that and he was getting the girls aboard this car to go up the hill, and he either patted the little girl on her bottom or goosed her a bit to help her up the steps, or something, and to his horror, this elderly woman said, "Why, Charles Harkness what are you doing?" - and it was his mother's best friend from his home town, who had witnessed this little episode, and he told that story on himself a lot. He was quite a guy. A bachelor, I might add.

Q: Did you have any problems with men ashore?

Adm. M.: Not to any extent. I know Josh Cooper told you that incident with the boy in Trieste -

Q: With the broken glasses?

Adm. M.: We had to furnish our own shore patrol, of course. Fleet units visiting all did and I don't remember anything really serious in the way of our own people or in the way of any difficulty with the natives. I think the Sixth Fleet's reputation on behavior ashore was then, probably still is, pretty damned good.

Q: Well, there was very little hostility toward Americans in the ports where you visited?

Adm. M.: That's right. The only place you really had to be careful and obey the rules, because of the international situation, was Trieste. The Yugoslavs were not, at that time, friendly to us or the Italians, and, do what you want but don't fool around near that border. Of course, very few of them did because it was quite far out in the country.

The organization of the Sixth Fleet, and we'll have to credit Admiral Sherman, at that time, but it was true of it through the years, to my knowledge. The organization and the preparation given to the ships in the way of documentation and operation orders and plan given to us before we sailed, so we could absorb it on the way over was quite remarkable when you think that there was only one ship over there - the Albany, who was permanent, and yet you could bring a couple of carriers in, and a squadron or two of destroyers, and a tanker or two, and that sort of thing. The amphibious forces, minesweepers -

Q: And they functioned as a fleet?

Adm. M.: They certainly did. During my time, I would say that the operation of the Sixth Fleet was the most efficient that I ever participated in, not counting World War II, but, I mean in the peacetime Navy. Whether the Seventh Fleet and the Asiatic had the same, I don't know. But, it was quite remarkable that she could take twenty, or thirty, or forty, whatever the total was, and have a turnover of that many ships and types and then just go out, and really do the job in every way - in gunnery, in tactics, in fueling, replenishing, that sort of thing. I have to give them credit for that; and that was true of every tour.

Q: Could you say, in part, this was due to the advanced training? I mean you were all trained in the same fashion.

Adm. M.: Yes. It probably was.

Q: There was a common denominator?

Adm. M.: Yes. I think you're right on that, and I think it was the idea that the people, by and large, didn't like to be away from home even that long - four or five months - married or not. You know, it was a long time away. But, on the other hand you felt it was a prestigious fleet, and it had a purpose, and it just worked together remarkably well. No question in my mind, it was an excellent outfit.

Q: Well, now when you left the Sixth Fleet did you leave the Compton?

Adm. M.: No, we left right from Haifa, as I recall. We left from Haifa, and the Haifa diversion had delayed us a little bit so the squadron came home together, the other ships having left ahead because of our somewhat extra time in Israel and also the distance from one end of the Mediterranean to the other. Anyway, we went back to Newport, and this would have been February '49 and then in about May or June, after the normal Newport operations, that squadron was given the assignment on a sort of rotational basis - just like we did in the Sixth Fleet - to be based in New Orleans to carry Reserve cruises.

Q: In New Orleans?

Adm. M.: Yes, and we were at the Algiers Naval Station, as they called the New Orleans Base then; and all eight of us were sent down there and, just as we did in the Sixth Fleet, we relieved previous squadrons who went back to Norfolk or Newport.

Q: Then, how many reservists would you take on board the Compton?

Adm. M.: Well, what they did, they somewhat reduced the crew, not extensively but to get enough space. We could take care of the officers without any trouble. As I remember, we had ten officers and each ship could take about six more maybe, something like that; and they would make these on a two or three week basis. Of course going up and down the river was an interesting thing in the first place. But anyway, we would take them to a recreation port, you might say, to give some idea you were going somewhere. Once, I remember we went to Kingston, Jamaica. On another cruise we went to Tampico, Mexico, and I think we also went to - I was going to say we went to Key West, But I've been there so many times I'm really not sure. But, in any case, we were down there until October and again, as I've mentioned, it concerned the Sixth Fleet. When you've made reserve cruises after reserve cruises, as a squadron, you get to be pretty good at it. I mean, I say that modestly, because we all did. You knew the form and you knew what to expect, you knew what to give them - officer and enlisted. And the exact number of enlisted men we took on each ship, I don't remember.

Q: What did you attempt to give these reservists in particular?

Adm. M.: What we did; we put them in their specialty. If a man was a boilerman, he worked right with our boiler crews. If a man was a signalman you gave him as much - no extra watches, but as much chance to actually do the signalling as you could. Same way with quartermasters, machinists mates, gunners mates, and so forth; and it was just one of their active duty cruises.

Q: Now this put an extra burden on the skipper and the

exec, did it not, to see that they were in the proper slots?

Adm. M.: Oh, yes. There was a lot of planning on this.

Q: Then supervising?

Adm. M.: Right; but most of them, of course the kids - the seaman and firemen - they were learning. In other words, you just made sure that our senior petty officers gave them as much training as they could, on the job. On the other hand, most of the officers and most of the petty officers were fairly well experienced, and all it was to them was a refresher on their specialty.

Q: Is this a disruptive influence in the fleet?

Adm. M.: No, I don't think it is really because the squadron only got that once in many, many years I think. But each one has done it in turn and, of course, your maneuvers were somewhat restricted. I mean, you had nothing else with you in the way of carriers or tankers. I mean you were strictly squadron and division maneuvers but, I think we had considerable enthusiasm in our crews, and in all of them.

Q: You said that the crew itself, as you went to the port

called Algiers, was somewhat reduced. The men who were removed were reassigned?

Adm. M.: Yes, yes they were. And it wasn't a great number. Really, it was a case of berth and messing space more than anything else, but it wasn't a significant number. As I say, we didn't offload any officers; and the Navy knew from experience about how many you should need. We went down there with reduced enlisted crews, but not to any great extent, and, as I say, how many reserve enlisted we carried in each ship, I just don't know. It was an interesting time and I think we all enjoyed it, and the reserves were given a chance to, like so many procedures like that, to give a thorough critique of what they learned - suggestions, criticisms, so forth, and the results were pretty good because, no thanks to us particularly, but thanks to the reserve organization in the Atlantic Fleet organization, the destroyer command, and so forth, they had it down where you could do a good job without a great deal of strain.

Q: How long would a reserve have to be on board before he could function as a regular seaman, or what have you?

Adm. M.: Well, it all depends on his background and experience and, of course, you have to remember this was only '49 - four years after the war and most of them, particularly the petty officers, were World War II veterans, whether they'd been in the Navy one year, or all four years of that war but, the first and second class petty officer knew what he was doing. I don't remember that they were specially destroyer people but some of them must have had preference for destroyers because that was their previous assignment; and, as I say, the senior petty officer you could use just as if you got a new regular petty officer on board. He got to know the people and the ship and then he's tending the throttle or acting as helmsman or whatever else you can name.

Q: Now, when you got to sea you had gunnery practice and that kind of thing?

Adm. M.: We had that and we had antiaircraft. They'd send the target planes out to us from wherever they could reach us. I don't remember whether we got them from Guantanamo or Key West, or somewhere like that. We didn't have a great deal of actual gunnery, but we had enough; and there again, they were just filling in here, and then you had your own gun crews.

Q: In order to make it more interesting did you have competitions with other fleet units who were also carrying reserves?

Adm. M.: No, we rarely saw them. We only had our eight ships and, I've forgotten exactly how we did. Seems to me four of us went out at one time and then the other half of the squadron went out the next time so that she had a slight overlap. I don't think we had the eight together all the time.

One of the interesting things that I'd like to mention. Going back to Newport, say in March, April, somewhere along there. Admiral Felix Johnson had been a great friend of my family - I don't know whether you know him or not. He's a great person.

Q: I know him very well.

Adm. M.: And he was then ComDesLant. I don't think they'd gotten around to calling him ComCruDesLant, but, anyway he was in his flagship in Newport. This was just after, I imagine, or just before we went to New Orleans and we were alongside - I guess we were having a tender overhaul, with his flagship as tender, and he sent to Commodore Cooper and he said, "Admiral Johnson is sending over someone to see the skipper." There was no indication of what it was or anything else, and I don't know why they picked the Compton, but they did. A man named James Kenworthy, who was on the White House or Pentagon Commission to Study Minorities in the Armed Forces. I think he was a Baltimore Sun reporter, but, in any case he was there in his capacity. So Mr. Kenworthy told me in the cabin - He said, "Admiral Johnson told you I was coming but you don't know why, do you?" And I said, "No sir." And he said, "Well, I want to just look around with you and see what your black crew members are doing." And, we couldn't have been luckier on this thing. I remember some of the instances. There were either one or two colored boys in the gangway watch. We went up to the signal bridge and the boy on either the semaphore or the searchlight, talking to the ship down the bay, was colored. We went down to the boiler room, or engine room, one or the other where they were doing some major overhaul on a pump, or blower, and two of the three people were black. In other words, it couldn't have been better. He was very complimentary to the ship, and me for that matter, and when we had our little debriefing in the cabin he said, "By the way, how many colored men are in your crew?" and I told him I hadn't the faintest idea, and he said, "Well, that's the finest answer you've given me all day long. If you don't know, it can't be a problem." And I still don't know how many there were there. Out of 320 it might have been - I have no idea, twenty? Anyway, months later he wrote that as a front page article in the New York Times Magazine - Kenworthy himself. And he went through all this, more-or-less just as I've told you. Of course, he'd been to a lot of other ships but, I mean the Compton episode was pretty much the way I told you; and he ended up his paragraph or two saying, "These people had been working, that he'd found with no warning to the ship; that blacks were doing key jobs," and that sort of thing, and then said, "The most remarkable thing is that I asked the skipper how many colored boys he had, and he didn't know."

Well, that about ends the Compton, I think.

Q: You then left the Compton after a tour of two years?

Adm. M.: Yes, exactly two.

Q: And came back to Washington?

Adm. M.: And, I was relieved by Captain Robert C. Morton, so the Compton had a Morton for four years, as it turned out. Very good friend of mine.

Q: But, no relation?

Adm. M.: No relation, no. I mentioned two of my commodores. Just before we went to Norfolk, while we were down there, Josh Cooper was relieved by Captain McIllany, who we were very fond of, but I was only within a very few months before I was detached. So, I served under three squadron commanders, as the skipper of their flagship.

Then, I was off to my first tour at the Bureau of Ordnance, largely a result of having been to the ordnance PG course, and I was assigned as a Special Program Director, they call it. I don't think there's any need to go into details of the BuOrd organization.

Q: No, but tell me about that particular division.

Adm. M.: Yes. The system has changed, long since but, the system at that time, the organization of BuOrd - They had the Chief and Assistant Chief, and then they had the major divisions, who were Research, Production, which included maintenance. They'd had Research, Production, and Maintenance and then they combined those two, so that you had the item of hardware going through Research and then into Production, and then through Production to finished delivery, distribution. Now, sort of sitting on top there were others, such as Quality Control, Shore Establishments, and so forth. But, the main ones that the Planning Division had to deal with were these two - you might say, hardware producers, and development. The Planning Division had five or six officers under the Director of Planning who were assigned such fields as underwater weapons and undersea warfare. Another one was gunnery and fire control; another one was missiles, which were coming along then. Another was ammunition, and another was - well, they were the main ones - and they were sort of the ones who monitored their respective programs through RE: Research, and down through. In other words, they were the monitors, if you would call it. Sort of overall planners is what they were.

Q: Then, they'd follow a particular piece of ordnance through?

Adm. M.: Right through. Decide to go ahead with research or not, decide when to go into prototype development; decide, with the help of the R&D boys -

Q: Those planners sound like little czars.

Adm. M.: Well, that's about what they were. They represented the Chief, as a czar in their program. They were very senior.

Q: What about the input to the planners? They didn't generate all these ideas themselves?

Adm. M.: No. It was their decision, with the advice of

Research, for instance, of whether to go ahead with development at all on the particular thing. And then, once decided to move that through and decide when to go in production.

Q: They worked out the time schedule?

Adm. M.: Yes. And then another group in the Planning Division, which was not czar, they were the ones who decided on the peacetime and mobilization schedule. In other words, we're going to produce this. How many do we need in peacetime, and how many do we need (in a separate document) in mobilization - wartime conditions.

Q: Now, this took their interests outside of the Bureau of Ordnance, did it not?

Adm. M.: Oh, yes. Well, they worked with the Ships' Characteristic Board, for instance, and they worked with any of their corresponding branches in CNO. They were more-or-less a sort of liaison between Bureau and Undersea Warfare or whatever.

Q: Well, they had to be in touch with the intelligence people too, didn't they?

Adm. M.: Yes, they were. Right. And, as we were saying, a lot of the attachés' reports that we were talking about in wartime days. Of course, they had tailed way off once peacetime, but, we still got them in the Planning Division. For instance, the information that - the British are working on such-and-such; - and then the decision was made with, in this case planning and research and development. And, they were a small group. There were two or three officers in each field -

Q: But you say senior officers?

Adm. M.: Yes, they were senior. They were captains, I would say probably senior to anybody in the Bureau, except the Chief and Deputy; in some years and not in others, the head of Research and Development was an admiral - rear admiral. He could be either a captain or a rear admiral. But, other than the chief and deputy, and possibly research, at least a captain, senior; and their word was go.

Q: It sounds like a pretty effective system?

Adm. M.: Yes, and I don't know why they changed it. I'm not completely familiar with the then BuOrd, and now BuWeps, and now Ship System Command, or whatever they call it.

Q: Seems to me I recall that Admiral Burke had something to do with this system, as it developed.

Adm. M.: Well, he had been head of Research and Development, I think, before my time. But, the system worked as well as any Washington system works. I mean there's a lot of red tape, and a lot of flailing around.

Q: Now, what was your particular job? What was your particular interest?

Adm. M.: My particular job as a special planning director - I really had two. In one case, my office, which was only three people, prepared what they called directive summaries. They were actually prepared by the program director whose responsibility it was, say gunnery and fire control. And my office kept the files on all of these inputs and sent them out to research or shore establishment, or production. In other words, we were the central funnel for the five program directors. We also, by the way, had a sixth one, who was the land-type ordnance, and he was always a Marine colonel because he took care of the Marines. Then, the other job I had was sort of the assistant to the director, I guess you'd call it, sort of "George", you know, odd jobs, something that no one else wanted to do, I did it.

Q: Now, what happened to a particular bit of ordnance that had been begun in research and was progressing along the line, and suddenly, the Congress decides they don't want to appropriate funds for it, its further development. What happens then?

Adm. M.: Well, in that case, first of all the CNO people, and the BuOrd people would probably do the best they could to reverse this thing, in Congressional Committee or in the Bureau of the Budget, as far as that goes. The preliminary hassles with the CNO's budget screwed me. The Bureau of the Budget, now called Office of Management and Budget - all of that was thrashed out before it went to Congress, then if the Congressional Committee wanted to axe out something, then it was up to the Chief and CNO support to try to get it back. Of course, if you didn't get it back, production just stopped, or was never commenced. Is that what you mean?

Q: Yes. Now, where did some of the ideas generate that got put in the lap of research people?

Adm. M.: Well, a lot of our ideas, the Bureau's ideas, could come from almost any source. For instance, just like you see in aircraft production, a commercial firm would come up with an idea and submit it as a possibility. Maybe they had developed it. Or, it could come from any number of the weapons laboratories, such as White Oak, Dahlgren, Inyokern, China Lake, where the preliminary research had been done and, under Bureau auspices, but then it was up to them to tell you, "well, now I think we can go into production on this"; and then it was the responsibility of the Research Division to decide yes, it is producible and we'll do it. So that you had the ideas coming from the field, I mean especially the research laboratories, and you had them coming from commercial producers, or you had them coming from England, as far as that goes - in some cases.

Q: Was there any effort at consulation with fleet commanders? I mean, before something got too far along?

Adm. M.: No. I would say the main outfit in the fleet was what they call the - it used to be called OpDevFor and that was for evaluation and development.

Q: And then it became OpTevFor. Testing?

Adm. M.: Yes, right; for testing and evaluation as to whether this can do the job it thinks it will. The biggest hassles with Congress were over large programs. Shall we build X nuclear carriers or not? and, shall we build the <u>John Paul Jones</u> - class destroyer? Can we build twenty-five of them? The Congress would take things like ammunition and that sort of thing - after all the internal studies, mobilization studies, production studies and then - as I say, the hassle with CNO, the OpNavs and Navy control and the Bureau of the Budget. By that time it would be just a case of, "Well, we don't think you need five million five-inch shells. We think you can get by with three." So, that in most hardware item cases, it was a question of quantity rather than telling the plant, "Well, don't make any more of them."

Q: Has that practice, on the part of Congress, changed somewhat? It seems to me, in recent months and years they have sometimes singled out a particular thing and said, "We don't want that."

Adm. M.: Well, I just don't know, Jack; I really don't. As I say, I can think in those days, and in later days in BuWeps that they did tackle the bigger programs whether on policy or on expense, and even feasibility but when you're talking about minor - small - items which support a big program - Now, I don't say they didn't cut back - they would. But, it's only when you get up into the grand weapons system that Congress says, "No, we'll not do it." Just like they've done in the space programs - some large, multimillion dollar thing like a submarine type.

Q: You mentioned the Ship's Characteristics Board.

Adm. M.: I'm not sure that that's even in existence now, but it was then, very much so.

Q: Well, how could you anticipate, within BuOrd, what the Ship's Characteristics Board might decide to include on a particular type of destroyer.

Adm. M.: Well, as each bureau, and as each material bureau - Bureau of Ships, Bureau of Aeronautics, Bureau of Ordnance had representatives that met with the Board. In other words, the ship's characteristics board was, in theory, a group of OpNav people who were the nucleus in the record keeping, minutes, studies, and all that, but they had, you might say, opposite number inputs - opposite number officers - to give the bureau input. Now, because in the case of a new ship, the BuOrd program director for gunnery and fire control was a BuOrd member of the Ship's Characteristics Board, because he was much more likely to be involved than, for instance, the ammunition officer, or the undersea warfare officer. Now that didn't mean he couldn't take those with him, and they also took research people. He was the man who was the contact for the Ship's Characteristics

Board. And, of course, just like in any organization, the minutes are circulated and proposals are exchanged and hassled over, sometimes outside of the meeting.

Q: Well, you were in this job for what, two years?

Adm. M.: Yes.

Q: That was hardly sufficient time to follow a project through from its inception in research to production.

Adm. M.: That's right. In other words, it was strictly overlapping. We used to think in those days, and I don't know why its any different today, that depending on the complexity or the cost of anything, that the so-called lead-time from inception to fleet supply was five to seven years, depending on whether it was a torpedo or a bomb, or what, so that I saw ends of some programs and beginnings of others; neither the beginning nor the end of another.

Q: What percentage of the programs that were under way at that time would you say had been improved and inspired by experience in World War II?

Adm. M.: Well, of course it's hard to say exactly whether it was World War II experience, or whether it was, you might say, scientific advance. In other words, the missiles were coming in very heavily then - the earlier so-called T-missiles. There was the Terrier, and the Talos.

Q: Tartar.

Adm. M.: Tartar. Tartar was a little later, I think, but they were all surface to air missiles and they were very much in the development stage then and, it's hard to say which was most important - experience or ability/capability - because they were always trying to get, for instance, in the case of gun mounts; they were always trying to get a faster rate of fire, or a lighter amount, or more accurate fire control and, in other words, you can't put your finger on exactly what inspired this particular thing. Then there were other things, like in the ammunition field there were developments in the commercial factories of improvements in - I mean sort of things like centrifugal casting, cold working, hot working, that could improve either the performance, or at least the production of a particular thing.

Q: So, you did then have, somewhere along the line you had many contacts with industry?

Adm. M.: Yes. Again, I'm getting my BuOrd tours mixed.

I visited several of them - several laboratories. I went to American Machine & Foundry, and Westinghouse, and - I've forgotten a lot of them now. Mostly though, the production people did that.

Q: The production people did that? And were the production people the ones concerned with the contracts then, too?

Adm. M.: Well, we had a contract branch. I mentioned the other shore staff and quality control; contract branch was another one. Production people were really the technical input on that, but the contract branch, with the help of a legal section, which was also a small, but powerful, one. They were the ones who actually executed the contracts, did the negotiating, if any, and prepared them really, and then monitored them. But, of course, your professional input, your technical input was not in the contract branch. They worked pretty much together.

Q: Was there anything comparable to the SP which we identify with the Polaris?

Adm. M.: Yes. I'm trying to think when SP came along. Of course, the father of all that was Admiral Red Raborn.

Q: I think it came along with him - with the Polaris.

Adm. M.: Yes, it did, and I think my first tour in BuOrd he was the deputy to Research for Aircraft Armament, so that I know he hadn't taken over the SP then.

Q: Well, that didn't come until about '55.

Adm. M.: Which was my second tour at BuOrd. That was it, yes. Because the reason I remember Red Raborn was that as a captain, he lived down here and I was in the same driving pool with him; that's how I got to know him so well. So he was in the Bureau of Ordnance then, having no idea he'd ever be SP in this, as far as I know.

Q: Well, my question was based on the knowledge that there was an SP under Raborn, but, in this earlier period was there anything that might have been construed as comparable? Any project - ordnance project that was termed a "crash" program sort of thing that had to be rushed along and that some special effort was made to do so?

Adm. M.: I can't pinpoint that, but I'll have to say I just don't know because I can't recall any now, and I also, as you say, until Raborn established his Special Projects ofice, I don't know what started it. In other words, I really don't know how much had been done in preliminary in the Bureau of Ordnance.

Incidentally, in your question as to whether the the two years was enough to see a thing start from inception to delivery in the fleet, the normal tour in the bureau, or in any shore job in those days, was three years. But, at the end of my two years I was selected for the Industrial College of the Armed Forces and had the option of whether to go or not, and I chose that. So, unless we have other things to cover in BuOrd, the next chapter will be on Industrial College.

Q: All right, fine.

Interview #5 with Rear Admiral Thomas H. Morton
Place: His residence in Annapolis, Maryland
Date: Thursday morning, 11 December 1975
Interviewer: John T. Mason, Jr.

Q: Well, Tom, before we begin in sequence this morning with this chapter, you have several items that you want to include.

Adm. M.: Yes. I thought the fact that it was, you might say, a romance and marriage in the middle of World War II, that meeting my wife, Sue, might be of some interest from the family point of view.

One of the key people in - I'm going back to the time in the American Embassy in London, as an observer - was then Captain Flanagan, later Rear Admiral Pat Flanagan. He had been retired and come back as a retired officer, and later did make admiral on the retired list. He was a great friend of my family's and had known me since I was a little boy, and he asked me if I was going to the Ligonard's cocktail party, one day in London. Ligonard was also a retired officer called back. And, I told him I was not because I hadn't been invited; and he said,

"Well, I know Ligonard well enough, and you do, too, so let's go to the yard party." So, he took me to the yard party. Well, there I met Susan Fass, and that led to a courtship and later, marriage.

Q: What was Susan doing at that time?

Adm. M.: She was in the Air Ministry as the Number Two in what they call the RAF Comforts Committee. She was not in uniform, she was a civil servant. Their job was to set up plans, procurement, and shipment of recreation material to the RAF bases as the war moved along. Such things as ping pong or billiard tables, checkers, radios, record players, that sort of thing. I don't know what our exact counterpart to this is.

Q: Ours would be more nearly the USO, wouldn't it?

Adm. M.: Except that the USO was really, you might say, quasi-government, you see, whereas this was actually a part of the Air Ministry. And of course, she, in her section knew pretty much how the war was progressing and what was going to happen, as much as secrecy would permit them, because they had to make plans; that the RAF would eventually have a base, or was planning to have one, in some captured territory, such as in North Africa, so they pretty much knew what was going on; and this was her job.

Well, when I left London for the USS North Carolina, the Carolina came back to Bremerton in August and September of '44, on the Pacific, and to go back. This was not a damage occasion, this was just a routine, scheduled overhaul; and then we started the wheels turning. Well, of course, in wartime, with priorities in shipping and aircraft, it wasn't easy, and except for the fact that she had been a fairly key person in the Air Ministry she probably would never have gotten there. As it was she didn't get there until about the 19th or so of September, with the help of her friends in the Air Force. And then she was able to get aboard one of the Queens, and then flew from New York to Seattle. I'm not sure whether it was New York or Washington or Baltimore, but anyway, my family met her here, and then she was on the way as soon as she could, and she got to Bremerton and we were married there, and the ship gave us quite a nice reception. It happened to be one of the ships cheduled wardroom parties anyway, which meant they had it for the two sections.

Q: What was the date of your marriage?

Adm. M.: 19 September, she having arrived at Boeing Field that morning.

Q: And the year was?

Adm. M.: '44. So, as it turned out, we only had about ten days there before the Carolina sailed, having waited six weeks to get her there.

One of her interesting experiences was flying back to Washington; she was bumped in Billings, Montana - bumped under the wartime priority list. And Northwest Airlines, or whoever the line was, of course, paid for her to stay there, which turned out to be two or three days. Of course, I found all this out later. She found herself in a hotel room with venetian blinds, which she'd never seen before and didn't know how to work, so, at least during darkness, when she was dressing or undressing she'd have to go close herself in her bathroom because she didn't know how to shut out the outside view. The other thing that impressed her very, very much was the great number of real cowboys on the street - real Westerns with their hats and their fancy studded boots, and that sort of thing. That's her memory of Billings, and then she finally got back to Washington where she took a job, which had been arranged for her, in the Combined Resources Board, I believe it was called. It was an Anglo-American-Canadian, really Allied - procurement outfit, and she stayed with them the rest of the war. And then, as I told you, years later when we were in the UN in New York, John was born up in Manhattan - our son - in 1947. And, John is named for her only brother. Sue had two sisters and one brother. I knew him fairly well from London days. He was a colonel in the Armoured Brigade of Guards and was killed about D+30 or 40, in Normandy, while he was with his troops. And he, being her only brother, John Fass, that's what we named our son.

Just a little background: We mentioned the Boston homecoming in late '45, and John's birth.

Now, the other thing that I have to put on record: the pride we felt in New Orleans when I was down there with the Compton in that Reserve Squadron; there we received the battle efficiency E and pennant for the Compton and the squadron. We thought we were pretty much up in the league to get the E and the pennant, but we weren't sure, and the news came to us in New Orleans in '49, including letters of commendation, which are automatic in that case, from ComDesLant and the CNO. Now, that's about it. I just wanted to get that on the record, and then we can go on from there, if you want.

Q: All right. Then we'll go to the year 1951 when you went for ayear of study at the Industrial College of the Armed Forces in Washington.

Adm. M.: Well, before we leave BuOrd entirely - BuWeps

now called - it strikes me worth mentioning that this was back in 1950 in the Bureau or Ordnance. The interesting thing was the Korean war hadn't started, which was June 1950, as I remember, and, of course we'd wound the war machine down from World War II, and Louis Johnson was a very embattled Secretary of Defense - a difficult one, I think - and, just in contrast to today, it's worth mentioning that the armed services then each had roughly three and a half billion dollars in their budgets; very close to being evenly divided - Army, Navy, Air Force, making something like, maybe like 11 billion total defense budget, and now, as you know, we're now talking 75 and 80, and sometimes more than 100 billion dollars total defense.

Q: Twenty five years later?

Adm. M.: Right. Of course Johnson got into trouble when the Korean thing broke out, and when he was actually relieved I don't know, but I think part of his being relieved might have been his very tight and very small budget which left us completely unprepared for something like Korea.

All right; now down to the Industrial College.

The Industrial College is a great institution, I think, and it was an interesting year. The year was from we'll say, August or September '51 until we graduated in

June '52, and, it was not only an excellent course, which I'll come to later, but, as I found out in the UN, dealing with the other services is an extremely interesting and valuable experience. As I remember, we were about 30 or 40 of each service. That is somewhere between 30 and 40 Air Force officers, Army officers, and a combined Navy and Marine. I'd say the Navy must have been maybe 25 naval officers, or 35, and five or six Marine officers. They were practically all colonels or Navy captains. There were about six or eight of us in both Navy and other services who went there as commanders but, since I made my number after selection to captain in October of '51, I'd only been there a month or two.

In addition to this 120-odd service officers, we had a variety of civilians from the various government departments, not necessarily Defense. Probably one of each from the departments that I recall. Internal Revenue had a very fine man there taking the course. The Labor Department had one, and there were various -

Q: CIA people?

Adm. M.: I don't remember CIA particularly; but, I'd say there were ten or twelve Commerce. Commerce, Labor, Internal Revenue and, maybe five or six or eight others.

Q: Was there any common denominator, Tom, of interests among these men from the various branches of the government? Were you all interested in ordnance type things, or what?

Adm. M.: Not particularly. I'll get to the lectures later. They'd divide us up each semester, which I think were three or four of them down there. They'd divide us up into panels, or committees, and under the general subject being discussed that, we'll say a month or two, each committee was assigned a subheading under that. For instance, we'd spend time on manpower, and on industrial production, and raw materials; transportation, sort of, you name it. And where the various interests came in - invariably each committee might have someone in it who was extremely experienced in this particular subhead; and of course, each committee had its own faculty advisor and instructor who stuck right with it, through that part of the course, so that your various people, including the civilians, at least once had an opportunity to give his opinions and his knowledge which no one else had, so it was a good exchange that way.

Besides the staff paperwork, theses, whatever you want to call each one of these, we had a wonderful series of lectures. People who lectured at the Industrial College were always topnotch, and you had sometimes two, or even three a day. They could be almost anybody - Senators, congressmen, ambassadors, top military people, top industrial people, bankers, shipping line people, and that sort of thing. Now, in addition to that, once a day, nearly every weekday, the Industrial College attended the National War College lecture, as a joint one. In other words, this was almost routine and, of course, there we had the same caliber of people, probably more important people than the Industrial College, but not below the Industrial speakers. The only difference in the lectures: we were quite free to question the speaker at our own lectures but we left the questioning in the National War College lectures to the students of that college. There was always a question period, and it depended on the speaker, but you always had at least a half an hour if questions didn't run out.

I mentioned the fact that practically by the end of the school year, all of us were colonels or captains. The National War College was considerably senior to us but had the same setup of the three services and the civilian students.

Q: They, as I understand it, included, and do include a fair segment of State Department people. Did you have State Department people?

Adm. M.: Yes, they do. We had one or two, yes, we did. I forgot that. But, the National War College had a considerably bigger proportion of people from State. For instance, one of the deputy commanders, or Commandants of the National War College is a State Department one, usually I think with the rank of Ambassador and at that time had quarters in Fort McNair. You had the Commandants of both colleges quartered there, and the deputies. Both schools had two deputies of the services not represented by the commandant, and in addition to the National War College, you had the State Department Deputy Commandant. Our faculty's were - I can't tell you what the proportions were. We both had excellent libraries, and we had complete use of the National War College library for our research reading; and it was just a good opportunity to study some extremely interesting facets of the economy and to be able to do a lot of research. You had the time. They gave you ample time for what an ordinary school would call study period.

Q: Quite a different routine from what you'd known in the Navy?

Adm. M.: Yes, you were completely on your own when you were not in lectures or in other words, the committees set their own time very often. Most of the afternoon was set for this, and so you were either at one of the libraries or in some committee meeting, or on your own doing your part of the report, that sort of thing.

Morton #5 - 316

Q: One of the things that men have mentioned; men who were enrolled in National War College or the Industrial College, is the value of being in a car pool. Were you in a car pool with other members of it?

Adm. M.: Yes; only one other because I lived here, and there was one other neighbor who was a classmate - a Naval Academy classmate as well as an Industrial College Classmate. But, I also found that in commuting to the Navy Department or the Pentagon that we had four or five people, each one in a totally different job. For instance, BuShips, personnel, and that sort of thing. I agree with that but, as I say, I only had one driving partner that whole year.

Q: Did the class at the Industrial College go on a so-called "Cook's Tour"? Did they do anything of that sort?

Adm. M.: Yes, they did. I'm talking about 1952 now. I don't know what the routine is now. The National War College went to, we'll say, European Headquarters or Far Eastern Headquarters, that sort of thing. In May we had a whole week - we were divided up by our preferences; first, second, and third choice - to industrial centers, such as Houston, Los Angeles, Seattle. I happened to be in the Detroit team by choice, and I'll come to that. But, places like that; major industrial centers with a variety of industries involved. Prior to that we had made one-day field trips to such places as Fort Eustis in Virginia, which is the Army Transportation Research and Development Center. We had a full day at Aberdeen Proving Ground. I'm sure there must have been others but those two come to mind.

Now the Detroit trip: there were about ten of us I think, and all services were represented. We had an interesting week. Not only was it the automotive industry, but it was related ones. All of those teams were given the red carpet treatment by their hosts. We went to Ford's complete plant - River Rouge; and we went to Chrysler's trucking plant. Then, aside from straight automobiles, we went to U.S. Rubber, now, I believe called Uniroyal. And then we went to a company called Excello, which was a fascinating smaller company, but fascinating.

Q: Machine tools, aren't they?

Adm. M.: Well, that particular plant was the one that made the machines that make things like milk cartons. I mean, the machines are almost human to watch. That sort of thing - whether it was a cheese box or a milk carton, or anything that needed a cardboard or paraffined, or plastic container, Excello's machines could do it. Now, in addition to seeing all these plants and getting a complete guided tour through all of them, they always had a sort of a luncheon meeting where they were available for questions.

Q: The executives?

Adm. M.: Right. At Ford we went to their Dearborn Inn, I believe it was called. It was in Dearborn, in any case. And, each one of these companies had a sort of informal, but business luncheon meeting where we were able to sit next to our various hosts, and they were open to questions, and sometimes had a brief summary of what we'd seen, or were going to see, whichever the case may be. But, it was a very fine week and, as I say, the field trips, so called, were a highlight.

Q: Well, I suppose it was a certain implementation of some of the things you'd been learning?

Adm. M.: That's right. It fitted in very well, and particularly the timing; there in May we were almost finished, you see, and had done these three or four - semesters is the only word I think of.

Then, at the end there were selected students who gave their presentations to the student body.

Q: This was a particular project you'd worked on during

the year? A particular subject you had chosen?

Adm. M.: That's right, yes. That's true; and everybody got a crack at that -

Q: Did you give one?

Adm. M.: No, I didn't. One amusing story on that. I have a Naval Academy classmate named Ed Metzger, who was rear admiral later. Rear admiral in the Supply corps. And Ed was the chairman of one of the student committees who was giving this presentation, and we had a very likeable, but loquacious Air Force colonel named, as I remember, Shumski, and I would say that two out of three of the lectures during the year, whoever they might be - visiting lecturers, invariably Shumski would arise and, going through the procedure would say, "Shumski, Air Force," and then he'd go on to some long-winded question.

Q: A speech on his own?

Adm. M.: More or less. And of course, he'd always get his answer. But, he was one of these people that just couldn't get out of the habit of having a question at nearly every lecture, and, one of these long-winded questions. So, when Ed Metzger was giving his presentation, as a student chairman, sooner or later at the end of the thing Shumski got up: "Shumski, Air Force." And then he went into a long harangue about almost as much time as the main speaker was given, and finally, in exasperation Ed Metzger reached under the rostrum and got a blank pistol and shot Colonel Shumski. I don't know whether it was put-up; I guess it was, but anyway, Shumski went along with it.

Q: What was the subject you chose for your particular interest?

Adm. M.: As I remember, it was part of the raw material thing. It wasn't that particular interest as much as I was assigned it. It was on the copper industry of the United States, or the copper situation in the world at that time. The raw material countries, the pricing - and as I remember then, it was about 24 cents a pound. I don't know what it is now. And, a little background on Anaconda and Phelps-Dodge. These were actually assigned.

Q: In order to have full coverage?

Adm. M.: Right. I guess it was for graduation; we went up to the Departmental Auditorium on Constitution Avenue and our particular class was given diplomas, or certificates, by Mr. William Foster, who was then Deputy Secretary of Defense and later was the head of the U.S. Disarmament Agency.

It was a happy year. It was relaxed; it was interesting, and it was very helpful. I can't specify any particular thing now but it was just a broadening education and a broadening experience. I wouldn't have missed it for anything. In general, you went to either one of the service war colleges, or the National War College, or the Industrial College. There were very few that had been to more than one.

I think that covers it, unless you've got some questions on it.

The physical program (athletics, if you will) was fairly well encouraged in both schools down there. We had intra-school softball teams, for instance.

Q: That is with the National War College?

Adm. M.: And then picked a school team that would play the similar team from the National War College, and that included such things as bowling, and golf, and tennis. But the softball - so-called World Series' - which were held twice in the early fall and late spring, were the sort of key feature and really brought out quite a gang of spectators. You were encouraged to use that hour or so before lunch to get some form of exercise. The sports I've mentioned were the ones that were feasible.

Q: They didn't want you to think of it as too much of a sedentary period?

Adm. M.: In those years, the Industrial College used to sweep the National War College. I don't know whether it was a difference in age, or what, but the softball World Series would usually end up something like four to one, Industrial College. I still get the Alumni Bulletin and I notice this year that the National War College won the World Series - at least won the fall series, in softball.

Q: Now, having completed that year of mental exercise, as well as physical, you were given a very interesting assignment as commander of a destroyer division - 122. That was in the year 1952. Is this something that you were seeking?

Adm. M.: Yes. I'd put in for first choice on it. Of course, I had no say over which division I might have gotten, but I had put in for a destroyer division because that was another one of the steps up the sea-going line.

Before we get to the destroyer division though, one of the things that I remember occupying my home time with, at the Industrial College, because we didn't have a great deal of homework. You had some, but you could cover it in the study period. Then Congressman John F. Kennedy had written a front-page article in the New York Times magazine on the lack of correlation, he claimed, between the scholastic standing at the Naval Academy and the performance in the Navy career later. And, he'd taken the Naval Academy classes - say '25 or '26, which were then captains, most of them; and he and his staff had pretty much indicated that performance at Annapolis bore no bearing on how the officer performed for the next twenty or thirty years.

So, just without any real research, I got out my Register of Alumni and dreamed up all of the three and four-star admirals that I could think of that had performed in key position in World War II, without actually making any attempt to get all of them. Some names were more familiar than others. And so, I found out that, at least in that group of flag officers which Kennedy had not studied, the correlation was very, very high in their performance at Annapolis. This must have been, maybe thirty flag officers - twenty-five or thirty. In each case I figured out the percentile standing in his class, regardless of what his actual standing was, and what the size of his class was. I don't remember the exact figures but, I did write a letter to Shipmate, as a matter of general interest, I thought, giving my findings. Now, the great bulk of those senior officers were in the second quarter of their class, and a lesser number was in the top quarter, and a far lesser number was in the third quarter, and only two, possibly, were in the lowest quarter of their class, which certainly was in contrast to Kennedy's finding. Oddly enough, the ones that I remember now who were in the low quarter, and I think they were the only ones, were Admiral Halsey and Admiral Jonas Ingram. The others were very much in the first half of their class, at least. I wish I had that still. I don't know where it is. Shipmate published it sometime during that '51-'52 period.

Q: What was back of Kennedy's article?

Adm. M.: I don't remember what prompted it. He was then congressman, before he became senator - just before. He wrote it as an interesting survey that he and his staff had made. As far as I know, no axe to grind, but just what he put forward as fact, and which I found in the case of at least the World War II very senior officers, didn't bear this out at all. I've forgotten exactly how much of a lack of correlation he'd discovered, but he as much as indicated that it didn't make any difference what you did down here, and that if you did well there wasn't any guarantee you'd do well in the Navy.

Speaking of Jack Kennedy; I think in my dissertation on Boston in late 1945 that I might of omitted mentioning that

we had met him up there, again through our friend George
Curley, who I described at length. One evening I had the
command duty in the North Carolina and had my wife down
for dinner, and George Curley may have had the duty too,
but in any case, he brought John F. Kennedy aboard for
dinner, and he was very, very congenial and nice to
everybody. In other words, we felt we'd more than met
the gentleman. And, my recollection is that in the same
election or whatever, so-called Governor Curley was running
for mayor, as I described previously. I think Jack Kennedy
was running for his first term in Congress. I believe this
is correct.

Well, anyway, coming to ComDesDiv 122. I needn't
describe again that, as usual, in case of taking over the
Compton, we had the four or five-week course in Key West,
which was standard for commanders and unit commanders.
The whole division happened to be in the Boston Yard at
that time, and that's where I took over the division.
I relieved Bill Groveden, later quite prominent in the
ASW field in the Pentagon, and an old Mississippi shipmate
of mine. We fortunately, through our, again Beacon Street
friends, got a very nice sublet apartment on Arlington
Street, just above the Ritz Hotel there, which was a
wonderful place to stay. We had only a summer rental, with
the regular tenants having gone to Europe, or gone somewhere;
but we had a very happy couple of months before the overhauls

were finished.

One of the things I remember was that August or September was one of the hottest periods I've ever been through temperature-wise. I thought Panama and New Orleans in that time of year were hot but, there's no exaggeration that, in going to - by subway that is - in going down to the Navy Yard, to the flagship, which happened to be the Hyman - 732; that by the time you got there, you were completely soaked, and changed into the khaki uniform, and by the time the day was over you were completely soaked and had to put on a new outfit of civilian clothes to get home. This went on for about five or six days and was one of the warmest periods I could possibly remember.

The other ships in that division, by the way, were Hyman - DD-732, Purdy - 734, Bristol - 857, and Beatty - 734, it might have been. Oddly enough, the Compton had been flagship of Squadron 12 when I had the Compton, and this division I took over was always known by us then as the other division. So, I ended up in the same squadron that I had been in as, now as the Division Commander.

Some amusing things happened there. The skippers of the Bristol and Beatty were due for relief, in the Yard, before we sailed, and the new skipper of the Beatty happened to be Chris Jennette, who had been my exec in the Compton; and the second skipper to be routinely relieved, in the Bristol, was relieved by

Commander D. K. O'Connor, who had been a Naval Academy classmate of mine, and was the skipper of destroyer escort that took me to Pearl Harbor on the way to join the North Carolina. I covered meeting him at the Clift. So then, the skipper of the Purdy came to me jokingly, or half-jokingly, and said, "Now, look, if you're going to fill up this squadron with your old buddies and classmates, when do you think I'll have to go?" Well, of course, Jim Coleman of the Purdy was not due to go so he had no worries, but, it was a sort of a coincidence that two of the new skippers turned up at a place and a time where the whole gang might have thought, "Well, he's really loading us up with his best buddies." Of course I had nothing to do with it, and neither one of them did I know was coming.

Incidentally, George Curley was one of the few Curley's left, and we saw him quite often. I think I remember mentioning before that we went down with George to see his father at Scituate, and this was the case of where the young priests were gathered, paying him homage in his cottage on the beach. I mentioned this before, but it was this period where that happened.

Anyway, when the overhaul was completed, I think, I'm positive that our next scheduled period was the refresher training at Guantanamo, and no need really to go into that. Of course, I was the unit commander at Guantanamo. We really had very little to do except ride the flagship, and the usual administration of a division, because the refresher training is strictly an individual ship affair, and there is no refresher training for a unit commander of any type ship. In other words, as a unit commander I attended the critiques and made an effort to - in fact, did ride each ship one time or another, probably more than once so that I wasn't confined in my observations of the Hyman only. In fact, it was a chance to ride the other ships which, in normal operation you're unable to do. Nothing particularly exciting or significant that I can recall about the warships at Guantanamo. They did well; some better than others.

Q: What was the overriding duty of destroyers in the Atlantic at that point?

Adm. M.: When organized, they were part of the Second Fleet and they were screen ships for the, usually carrier, carrier task force. They were, what we used to call plane guards. Each operating carrier always had two plane guards assigned.

Q: In case of accident, or something like that?

Adm. M.: To pick up downed personnel, and that sort of thing. And every sortie after Guantanamo - every sortie from Newport was a so-called opposed sortie. In other words, you either had submarines off Newport, or they were simulated, and the squadron commanders - not the division commanders, but the squadron commanders in every sortie Monday morning, no matter who was going out, how many ships, or what type, if a squadron was also going out on exercises for that week or for more, the squadron commanders, in rotation, set up the sortie plan.

Of course, the basic sortie was usually set up by either the senior officer sortieing or the senior officer present afloat. But, in the case of the screen and the plans for protecting the sortie, the squadron commander had fairly considerable leeway in the type of screen he used, the station of his ships, and that sort of thing, around certain sortie points in time. Incidentally, if more than one squadron was sortieing - more than one squadron of destroyers; for that particular exercise, the senior squadron commander was not necessarily the screen commander, but whichever squadron commander through rotation took his turn at it. He included every destroyer that was sortieing, regardless of their squadron assignment or seniority. But division commanders didn't get in on this too much, except in their usual capacity.

I'm trying to think when we deployed for the Sixth Fleet. It was December or January, I believe. We got back from Guantanamo in November, and then after a few exercises, and so forth, we sailed with the Sixth Fleet deployment ships.

Q: Was this for a six-month deployment?

Adm. M.: Four to five. I think our turnover in this case was in Oran, and there we conferred with Commander Service Force, Sixth Fleet who happened to be in port, and conferred with our predecessors. In other words, the division which we were relieving.

Some of the experiences over there were somewhat interesting. As a division commander I found that, very often, I was not operating with the squadron commander of that division. In other words, not operating in the same vicinity as 121, which was the squadron of course. So, I had considerable experience in being a screen commander in the fleet exercises. Sometimes, for instance, the squadron commander's division was off at recreation ports. Or, maybe he was in another unit of the fleet at that time. But, in any case, I got a lot of experience with maneuvering a screen, and so forth, all of which we had rehearsed in our own exercises off Newport. But, the interesting thing here was the NATO Tactical Instructions and Signal Book were now fully in effect. I mentioned this last time, but I wasn't sure how far along those publications were in the 1948-49 days. But by 1952 and '53, these publications were very much the Bible of the Sixth Fleet, and very often I would have French ships in the screen, or British, or Italian. Almost anybody was liable to be in the screen. For instance, the signal flags meant the same thing to everybody. And they had a system of, when using the tactical radio circuits, they used a sort of phonetic - it was in English, but it was the best English they could do. For instance, the French invariably said, "Rojere" for Roger. But, the thoroughness of the signal book, and the thoroughness of these screen diagrams and that sort of thing that were in the tactical publications made it very easy for you to operate a screen like that, or for the screen to operate under the screen commander because the amount of English required was almost minimal. In other words, if they could pronounce the international code alphabet and the numerals, and then the various other pennants like the repeaters and the designated pennant, it didn't make any difference whether they didn't know any other English, and it worked surprisingly well. It really did.

Q: Now, tell me about the line of demarcation between Sixth Fleet units and NATO units.

Adm. M.: Well, what happened here, in those days: the Sixth Fleet was there as a U.S. command, usually deployed in the Mediterranean - almost wholly in the Mediterranean. Now, when a NATO exercise came along, which would be planned in, for instance headquarters at Naples, I suppose well in advance, the Sixth Fleet, through the fleet commander, would be asked to commit his whole fleet or just his destroyers, or just his amphibious ships, or whatever. In other words, just as the other navies did, when a NATO exercise did come off, whether it was amphibious or fleet exercise - at sea exercise, each nation, including the U.S., was either asked to assign such and such, or else volunteered them, well in advance, so the outlines could be drawn up. So, in those exercises you became a U.S. unit assigned to whatever command NATO had set up, and you might say, borrowed from the Sixth Fleet. We were only NATO as such, during these specific exercises, although the NATO publications that I mentioned were used across the board.

Q: That's understandable, and less confusing that way.

Adm. M.: That's right. And, incidentally, back in the Atlantic Fleet, the Second Fleet - the Newport and Norfolk ships; they were using these too. In other words, that became a U.S. Navy standard.

Q: Because those units had to go and relieve the Mediterranean units?

Morton #5 - 333

Adm. M.: That's right. In other words, that signal book, the NATO Signal Book became the U.S. Navy's signal book.

Q: We were moving into one-world Navy, were we not?

Adm. M.: It worked surprisingly well. Of course, you had the same goof-ups by one or more ships that you'd get in your own exercise, as you'd get off Long Beach or Norfolk. But, at least there was a damned good start.

Q: Can you recall an exercise or two of some interest?

Adm. M.: None particularly. Most of them were routine. In the case of amphibious exercises, I think we had a landing at Arzeu, which I believe is either Tripoli or Tunisia, and the destroyers then were mainly to screen the force going in and screen them after they got in. Some of the ports might have had some interest. I mentioned the ports that we went to in Compton days. They were pretty much the same this time, as I remember; Naples, Trieste, Venice, and we did go to Istanbul. One of the real interesting visits was in Tunis. Tunis was having an Anglo-American-French, and Greek celebration in honor of the Tenth Anniversary of the Liberation of Tunis and the Hyman, my division flagship, was assigned there as the U.S. naval representative. The British had a destroyer there and the French had a destroyer, both of which, I think had unit commanders aboard, such as we did; and then the Army was also represented by much more senior people in this week's celebration. General Gruenther was our U.S. Army senior representative. Marshall Juin was the French representative, and General Anderson was the British representative, all of who had been key military people, on the Army side, in the liberation of Tunis.

Q: This celebration took place in Bizerte, or where?

Adm. M.: Well, really Tunis itself. We did visit Bizerte but the celebration was in Tunis, the capital itself. That was quite a week of the usual ceremonies which Hyman's people participated in, such as visits to the military cemeteries and laying wreaths on the monuments in town; all the typical celebration of a historical event.

As the USN senior officer, I saw a lot of General Gruenther who was marvellous to be with and fortunately, and quite rightly, the flagship skipper, my flagship skipper, was also included in all of these things, and in some of the bigger functions, several of the ship's officers, or even a contingent of enlisted men took part. I mentioned the Greeks. My memory's a little hazy. The Greek's had a batallion, or a regiment which happened to be in the operation that threw the Germans out of Tunis, and they had a Greek general present, but no Navy representative, as I remember it; but it was in theory a four-nation celebration. And, of course, we happened to visit the palace. I guess you'd call him the Bey of Tunis, I believe he was -

Q: Was he still on his throne?

Adm. M.: Well, he was the senior executive of Tunisia.

Q: Yes. Well, he was the King of Tunis and the Bey of Tunis.

Adm. M.: I'm sure he was. He gave a very elaborate and enjoyable luncheon at the palace. That was one of the highlights because it was an unusual thing and I was rather fortunate, I think, to be the U.S. Navy representative there.

I'm trying to go around the Mediterranean countries now, and see if there was anything like that. All the other ports visited were pretty much as they had been before. I mean Athens, Paris really, and Cannes - the usual recreation ports were just as enjoyable and no different than they'd been five years before.

Q: Do you want to talk a little about the morale on board

among the men. How was it in those days?

Adm. M.: I would say it was good. I don't remember any ship, or ships having any serious morale problems. I think the fact that the family man perhaps did not care for this four or five months - well, usually five, and even six - away from home and parted from the family. I think in the ships that were in the deployment rotation to the Med that this was expected. It's as short as possible that the Navy can make it. It's gotta be done, and so it's just par for the course. I think the morale was probably a little bit better than in the Compton days because in '47, '49, and '49 you see, we were still coming downhill from this demobilization period, and whereas by 1953 we had a more stable Navy, I'll put it that way, and, of course, it had grown a little bit because of the Korean situation - from '53. But, I would say that morale was probably a little bit better because we had a younger Navy, at least had a more nearly career Navy, in both the cases of officers and enlisted men.

Q: And this was before the time when we began to talk so much about minorities?

Adm. M.: Yes it was, except I mentioned they were talking minorities when I had the Compton, and I did mention the

member of that committee coming aboard. We had none of
the troubles that, for instance, the carriers had three or
four years ago. Do you remember? Nothing like that; no
racial activists and no racial conflict - I mean of any
significance. If an individual didn't get along with the
opposite color why - we had no problem, as a skipper of a
unit commander, in those days.

I would say that we probably had more colored aboard,
because of the gradual getting away from the stewards
branch business but, they bunked together in the same
compartment. I mean all of the old-time segregation of
separate compartments for the race, and that sort of thing;
that had gone. We had chiefs, and chief petty officers
and that sort of thing - twenty - who were black, and this
was new. I mean they had just gotten to where they'd
reached the rank of chief, whereas before they'd only become a chief steward.

Q: Then there was no polarization, I mean in terms of when
they went on shore leave or anything?

Adm. M.: None whatsoever. I think in general they went
with whom they wanted to go. If a couple of whites and a
couple of colored wanted to go together, that was it. You
naturally had the tendency to go with your own people,
whether you're talking race or not. There were no black

officers at this time; at least not that I recall. Neither had there been on the Compton. There may have been some black officers in the carriers and cruisers by then but there were none in the destroyers that I recall. In other words, they weren't as numerous as they are now. I think that any racial, serious racial conflict, in the mid-50s was due for just what we were talking about off the record. That the civil rights movement had not gotten underway. In fact, it wouldn't get underway for ten years, or more, and the fact that the Korean War was over, or nearly so, and we didn't have the violent feeling, such as all Americans, or some Americans had regarding the Vietnamese War. That of course, wasn't to come up for another 10 to 12 years. So, I think it was a case of the time and the circumstances just didn't spawn a serious racial conflict we had later, in the bigger ships in the Seventies.

Q: Well, you were there before the Suez Crisis?

Adm. M.: Yes.

Q: You'd been deployed in the Mediterranean for a series of months and then you came back to the States?

Adm. M.: Yes. We came back in May, having gone over in early January. We came back towards the end of May; I'd

say the 25th, which would have been four months. And
incidentally, the return trip was of interest, to me
particularly, because we came back as a unit. The last
port having been Istanbul, we came back a totally different
outfit from the returning deployed ships. So I was the
senior officer and OTC for the whole transit back to Newport,
and we had a chance to try all the maneuvers and fancy
formations, and so forth, that we could, and for safety
we assigned them well spaced night cruising. In other
words, the ships were a mile or more apart because there
was no reason to be any closer. One of the reports of
that transit that I had occasion to make - not instigated
by a higher command - we found that the coverage of radio
Washington, in the so-called FOX schedule, the fleet
broadcast, did not come through. We found this particularly
coming back, but I think we noticed it going over too.
Coming back we had to stay on Port Lyautey's broadcast,
much beyond the longitude as to where we were supposed to
automatically shift to Washington. Washington, whether it
was the time of year, or what it was, was just not carrying
as far as the theory called for and we stayed with Port
Lyautey, then in Morocco, to catch the fleet broadcast
much longer. In other words, we were never out of communication on the fleet broadcast, but we found that the
longitutde for automatic shift was well west of what had
been prescribed. That was the only thing of any moment.

Many miles off Cape Cod and Martha's Vineyard, we arrived in a dense fog which made our arrival a lot less pleasant than it might of been because for hours and hours we were at reduced speed. I remember I had them slow to seven or eight knots, and one skipper was continually on the radio, "Can't we go faster than this?" It was a dense fog, there is no question. We had radar and all that. I remembered in my studies of seamanship, in various places, in the Naval Academy, PG School, and even lectures by a Captain Farwell. Do you remember him? He was an expert on collision law and had written several books. Sort of the caliber of what Captain Dutton was to navigation. Farwell was with the University of Washington, I believe. He was the expert on it. Among other summaries he made was the fact that the records show that the tendency to go too fast in a fog was too prevalent, and if you had the case of two ships - different formations, or two independent ships - both going too fast, you'd really be in trouble; and, of course, this has been proved out. But anyway, one of Farwell's points in his summary was the fact that no ship had been held to blame that had been going seven knots or less, so I took that as my best doctrine, from years back. I think we did go eight, but, I felt pretty assured that if a collision would be occurring, or imminent, that at least none of my ships would be to blame. That's all I was thinking about. They were in a loose, and quite distant formation, but, naturally had the ability to maneuver independently, if necessary. But, one of the skippers; he insisted that we ought to be going at 12 or 15 knots, and I was just adamant.

Q: He was the impatient type?

Adm. M.: Yes. The other thing that I did on my own there, which I thought was very good training; except for radio checks on the various circuits, everything we did was visual. We used signal flags, semaphore, light blinker and, except for transmissions to ComDesLant or ComSixthFlt or wherever, from us, no radio was used the whole transit, until we got into this fog. So that meant for seven or eight days - except for tests - we were in complete radio silence, which is a great relief when you're used to being on destroyers and this damned radio going all day and all night. Of course that's easy to do in a perfectly normal, uneventful little cruise, but it was an exercise I enjoyed.

Q: You were coming back to join the Second Fleet were you?

Adm. M.: Well, the Second Fleet was only set up for certain maneuvers. We were coming back to really join DesLant is what it was. It was all scheduled. Just a very few weeks after we were home in Newport, and in fact the squadron was in there for recreation and rest, and so forth, I was routinely relieved by Draper Kauffman, whom you probably know, a classmate of mine at the Naval Academy, and he relieved me in, I would say, June, July, something like that. I think that's about anything of interest on 122.

Q: You had an accident at this point?

Adm. M.: Yes. You mentioned that I'd got to the Bureau of Ordnance for my second tour there in December '53. The delay here between having been relieved in the destroyer division and the reporting in Washington was due to the fact that, in a fall I had broken my right leg.

Q: This was on board ship?

Adm. M.: No, this was actually at the Officer's Club. So, I had the leg four months in a cast and then, perhaps a month or so therapy up there before I was able to report to Washington.

Q: That, in effect was enforced vacation wasn't it?

Adm. M.: Yes, I got lots of kidding messages from Bureau of Ordnance; old friends who said to me, "It's a rather drastic way of avoiding coming to Washington isn't it?"

and that sort of thing.

Q: Well, were you happy to come back to the Bureau of Ordnance?

Adm. M.: Yes, I was, because I knew the people there, and knew the Bureau, and so forth but, I never really liked shore duty. We'll put it that way - or to the extent that I liked sea operations. I'm not trying to sound like an old salt but, Washington, as it turned out, was getting more and more frustrating as time went on, and so forth and I don't think anybody looked forward to going back to Washington - only very few.

Q: Well, when you came back to the Bureau of Ordnance did you continue to live in Annapolis?

Adm. M.: Yes. We had lived in Annapolis from the end of the Compton tour, which was '49. We lived in Annapolis all through the fifties.

Q: In this house?

Adm. M.: No, in the house across Ferry Point. About a mile away. I've forgotten exactly what the arrangements were when we were in Boston. I suppose we just shut up the house or sub-let it; but we lived down here the whole time. It wasn't until '61 when I was promoted to the exalted rank of rear admiral that I found out that commuting and car-pooling was not feasible because of my own hours. A group of three, or four, or five commanders and captains can usually pretty well say, "Well, we'll be ready to go at 5," but once you've got up in somewhat higher rank in the Pentagon that's when we decided to live in Arlington.

Q: Flag rank carries it's own responsibilities and limitations.

Adm. M.: Well, I just didn't think it was either feasible or fair to the others and I certainly didn't want to be riding the bus too many evenings. So, the fact that in 1961 I just decided, well I'll have to drive my own car, and I'll have to drive it a much shorter distance than from down here.

Q: Well now, when you came back to the Bureau of Ordnance in December of that year - 1953, your job was known as a Special Program Director. What is that?

Adm. M.: Well, as a matter of fact, it was almost exactly the same job that I'd had before, with the same title and the same designation - PLX, meaning Planning Division

Specialists program. Except that it had expanded a certain amount, in addition to the jobs that I had done as a special program director in the previous tour, it had expanded out to cover the BuOrd part of Atomic Energy programs - nuclear weapons, and also because no one in the planning division had really ever monitored it before; another one of my duties the budget, and more or less, administration of the ordnance plants, both the naval reserve NYROX, as they called them. In other words, the production facility.

One of the tragic things in that move was, I was also to be in that capacity of being a sort of a leg-man and a liaison for the deputy chief of the bureau, who was Admiral Deke Parsons. He was the deputy chief under Admiral Schoeffel, I think it was. And, Parsons, as you know, was one of the weaponaires in the Japanese Atomic Bomb drop. While I was on leave down here, for a matter of only about a week, because I'd had this long siege in Newport, Admiral Parson's went out to Bethesda, either for an annual physical or just a check-up, and he died there under examination; so that I never had the occasion to serve with him in this capacity.

Q: He was one of the Navy's great scientists?

Adm. M.: He was indeed, yes. Then, Admiral P. D. Stroup either fleeted up or was ordered in, and during this tour the chief was Admiral Red Schoeffel, and the deputy was Admiral Stroop. Also, by this time the planning division director who had, in all the previous years been a captain, really was changed to rear admiral, and we had Admiral Jim Ward, among others, as the head of the planning division. Research division had often had a rear admiral, as the head of research, and at this time that happened to be Rear Admiral Charlie Bergen. I don't know whether you've met him or not. So, in effect you had four rear admirals in the bureau rather than just two or three. Other than that the tour was very similar to the previous one -

Q: Well, in that you had taken on some added duties, you might talk about them. For instance, that area of the atomic weapon.

Adm. M.: In my previous tour they had arranged for me to get the seven or ten day course at Sandia Base in the atomic program, and in order to go to this course I had to obtain a Q clearance, which was the designation then for nuclear clearance - AEC matters, and that sort of thing. And so, in taking this job, that facet of the job, I had that background and it was largely in the idea of production again, because we were working on things like BETTY, the underwater atomic depth bomb, and that was one of the biggest Navy projects in the nuclear field, I would say. So, I had occasion to go to places like American Machine and Foundry where they were actually building the cases. In other words, the non-nuclear parts. And to Yorktown Mine Depot who was in on the program because of the nature of the beast. But that was really a small part of the job.

Q: Was BETTY related in any way to ASROC?

Adm. M.: Only to the extent that it was under water, and a submarine. BETTY was an aircraft-dropped depth bomb, period. No capacity for surface launching. That was the only strictly nuclear weapon that I can recall the Navy itself was working for because it had no relation to the other services, as some of these other things did.

ASROC, as I recall, hadn't come along yet. I think I ran into ASROC in later years.

Q: What about missiles?

Adm. M.: I've forgotten the years it happened but, TERRIER and TALOS had both come along from the BUMBLEBEE program, and I've forgotten exactly when the TARTAR missile came in, which was the smallest of that family. But, again, they had a program director for the missiles program so I didn't have any direct contact with that.

Q: Was WESSEG in being then?

Adm. M.: Oh yes; as far as I remember.

Q: What kind of cooperation did BuOrd have with WESSEG?

Adm. M.: I don't know that personally. I mean, I can't answer that.

Q: Your own particular office had none?

Adm. M.: Had none, yes. I think WESSEG dates back to the late-Forties, as a matter of fact. Now, we had a little more to do with WESSEG in the research in the Pentagon later on. I imagine most of those projects, if instigated by the Bureau, or if used by the Bureau, was done in the research division primarily or in naval operations. I certainly had no direct contact with it.

Q: Did you have anything to do with OpTevFor?

Adm. M.: No, not directly, although all of the reports by OpTevFor of BuWeps projects were pretty well circulated to the planning and research divisions and, as they went along, also to the production division - material division, I should say, which was a combination of the old production and maintenance, now called material division. Again, that was primarily monitored by the research and also, as I'll come to later, in Admiral Chick Hayward's outfit, which was the R and D for OpNav - he had one of four sections. One of his sections was, primary duty was liaison with OpTevFor, but that was OpNav R and D.

Q: Now, you said that you had an additional duty as a sort of an assistant to the deputy, and this was P. D. Stroup at this point?

Adm. M.: Yes. I worked a great deal with the deputy, more so than with the chief but, since this plan that Admiral Parson's had was of course never implemented. I think it was his personal plan rather than any bureau reorganization and I would say that I worked quite a bit, and closely and pleasantly with P. D. Stroup. He never adopted Admiral Parson's plan for this particular building.

Q: He didn't have Admiral Parson's know-how in the atomic area?

Adm. M.: It may have been that but, on the other hand, maybe this was something that Admiral Parson's felt was desirable and dreamed up, and then for one reason or another, P. D. Stroup never adopted it. And, since I had never been there with Admiral Parsons, and no one had filled the billet before me, I think it was a case of just his personal requirement and desire, rather than something that was written into the Bureau of Organization Manual.

The planning division got into, I think I told you last time, a great deal of budgetary matters; formation of the budget, defending the budget; and this is where I knew Gordon Pierson so well. He had become, by then, the director of the - we called it FI, whether it was fiscal or financial, I've forgotten, but anyway he was our top budget man.

Q: What were some of the problems in the area of budget in the middle Fifties? Economy?

Adm. M.: That's the word I was looking for, yes, and that's probably no different than it's ever been or ever will be - was the minute justification for every dollar you wanted, and the different program directors would get their budget together with their opposite numbers in research and shore establishment, and material and then you would face the grilling by Gordon Pierson and his people, which was a sort of murder board, as they called it. You're going to have to satisfy Gordon Pierson's people or you won't satisfy anybody. With final discussion with the chief and deputy your BuWeps budget would be put together. Then, long before going to Congress you faced the examination of the budget by the Navy Controller, and then a combined, as I remember, a combined screening unit from the Department of Defense and then Bureau of the Budget, now called Office of Management and Budget. So, we went through them before it was finally submitted to Congress. What the Bureau of the Budget cut out was - really you had no recourse. That was it. When I say Bureau of Budget, I mean DOD and Bureau of the Budget.

The Bureau of the Budget, and I suppose still does under the Office of Management and Budget, was a White House outfit, and they did a lot more than this Bureau of the Budget business, as the present name implies. Every service directive, I won't say every, but every important one had had to be approved by the Bureau of the Budget and they, again as I say, as the name implies, they were very much in the management game then, in spite of the title. Because of the size of the Defense Department budget, they had experts - I'd rather say specialists - who were most cognizant of, for instance Army programs and the Navy programs, and the ordnance programs, so that you saw the same people every year, and they were quite familiar with the programs and operations, or supposedly were.

Q: As I recall it, it was a very small staff but a staff

of highly trained experts. Was Stans there then, as director of the Bureau of the Budget?

Adm. M.: I'm trying to think who it was. I don't think it was Mr. Stans.

Q: Well, what connection did your planning section, in the Bureau of Ordnance, have with Op-06, was it? The long range planning, the ten-year forecasts?

Adm. M.: We had a section that used the OpNav plans of various - what did they call it? Short, mid-range, and long.

Q: The long was ten years.

Adm. M.: We had a section that generated the ordnance requirements to fit these plans depending on, mobilization of the Reserve Fleet, and the duration, and that sort of thing, and in the planning division we had a section whose name I've forgotten now, who generated what we call ordnance status reports and material status reports, to satisfy whatever plan was applicable.

Q: Would that mean say, with the long-range planning group in operations, that ordnance would have something cooking that would not materialize for ten years?

Adm. M.: The long-range planning group was an extremely valuable and saavy group, but they were thinking well ahead of the actual strategic plans groups. In other words, when I say the ordnance people had to fit the mobilization plan, I'm talking strictly of the two and five-year, and not so much the projection of what's going to happen.

Incidentally, you mentioned the value of driving squads when we were talking about the Industrial College. Later in OpNav with Admiral Hayward, and I won't go into that at this point because it's out of chronological order, one of the members of the long-range planning group was one of my driving partners, and so I know much about the long-range planning group, through talking to him every day. We had quite a mixture then. This will come along when I have moved to the Pentagon. We had someone in Op-05 - aviator. We had someone in personnel, and then we had this Marine officer who was in the long-range planning group, and we had a man in the logistics section, and myself in R and D, so that we almost covered the OpNav Directory.

Q: Almost looked as though it had been planned. This was a car pool that you selected your members. Incidentally, what was the status in this period when you were in BuOrd?

Morton #5 - 354

What was the overall status of research in terms of what the Congress was willing to appropriate, in terms of what the Department of Defense expected? That sort of thing.

Adm. M.: We never were satisfied with the budget we got. No one ever is but, I don't think there were any drastic cuts in any - In other words, I can't remember any particular program that was simply thrown out. They were either cut back or deferred, or something like that. The trouble we had a lot of times was mostly the people in the office of naval research. There was a very strong feeling against what we call basic research.

Q: Pure research?

Adm. M.: Pure research. Basic, or pure. But, we weren't too much involved with that except by you might say, liaison between our research people and ONR. Now, the office of naval material, as opposed to the office of naval research - I'm getting off the subject of your question. They were another group that used to ride herd on the bureaus, in connection with these plans to meet CNO's mobilization plan. They would very carefully screen what we prepared and go over it with a fine tooth comb, not necessarily in connection with the budget, but continually. These plans, as I say, were prepared by one of the divisions in

the planning division, not a program director; and they
went into you know, D-plus 60 plus 12, or N-plus six, then
12, even down to the factory that was going to make these.
We will say a five-inch projectile, or a TERRIER missile,
and they'd carefully go over that, continually. As a matter
of fact, we had an up-dating report every month, as I
remember, and it was a rather involved thing and they
must have had fifteen or twenty people working on this
thing, this division. What we need in peacetime; monthly
expenditure; what we had on hand now, then; what to
mobilize; and you'd have to list these commercial factories
or naval ordnance plants, whichever, to show when they
would get in production, how much we were counting on them
to make, and how it totaled to meet the overall plan. A
lot of the non-BuWeps factories; in other words, non-
government factories, non-Navy, were what they called
NIROP which I think I mentioned - Naval Industrial Reserve
Ordnance Plant - and they were commercial firms outside
of the government but were definitely picked to be the
producer of, we'll say the five-inch projectile or the
such-an-such fuse. We went to a few of them. I remember
there was one up in Hayes, Pittsburgh. I don't remember
the name of that plant, but they had developed, in recent
years, under BuOrds auspices, a means of turning out the
three-inch projectile, and possibly the five. But, from
one piece of raw material. In other words, it's like the

old saying "untouched by human hands." And, they would just stamp this in like a big assembly line, and finally come out - entirely automatic. It would come out with the body of an antiaircraft projectile. It was a fascinating place. I wish I could remember the name of it. Of course, in those days it was just idle. We went up there to see the procedure but they were not at that time making them. This was one of those NIROPs that was set up in case of mobilization.

Q: You said, just a little bit earlier, you intimated a certain amount of lack of enthusiasm, shall I put it, for pure research. Why was that? Is not pure research necessary before you can have specific research under way?

Adm. M.: Oh, yes. I think possibly members of Congress and possibly even members of the Defense Department, or even CNO, as far as that goes, never understood - maybe I'm prejudiced because of my time in the bureau - never understood why you'd spend money on basic research which, in some cases, never turned out to be worthwhile. In other words, if someone has an idea; what makes grass green? is a famous phrase they use, until you try something that somebody's brainstormed and find out, either it's worthwhile and has an application, or else it doesn't work. Until you conduct that research nobody knows. ONR had its fight to keep the basic research budget going.

Q: But, it doesn't seem to me a very difficult concept to appreciate.

Adm. M.: Well, I don't know. You still see in the papers some fellow in Congress for instance, screaming away. Proxmire screaming about what makes husbands and wives get along and not get along. I can't remember what university was doing that by Government funds but one of them was. You remember about a month ago when Proxmire? Well, that's the sort of thing. The idea of what possible use can this ever be, is just hard to get over to someone. The whole answer is nobody knows what it's going to be used for.

Q: Well, I suppose you can confuse the picture by illustrations such as you've given me. I mean, research in terms of human relations, but, when you're dealing with creation, so to speak, that seems to me a little different.

Adm. M.: Well, it is too, but, on the other hand - I can't particularly remember many items of basic research but my impression is that the average person in pure research, or basic research, he doesn't know what he's going to be able to do with this. If he did, it then becomes applied research, and is a totally different kettle of fish.

To go back to your question about the difficulties. In addition to never getting what you felt you needed in the budget, as I said some days ago, I think the ship building program largely in the terms that, whether something goes ahead or not and in what volume. Because that's big numbers, you see, and if they decide instead of, for instance, building a carrier each year for the next eight years, they're only going to build two, that's the sort of thing that's real big money - shipbuilding program.

Q: I thinkyou did tell me something about the relationship of this outfit with the Ships Characteristics Board. Is there anything more to add at this point?

Adm. M.: That's right. No, as far as I remember it was the same relationship, and the same program director who happened to be the one for - I'm talking about the office now, not the individual. The program director for gun and fire control systems was sort of _ex officio_ BuOrd's man. Of course, the chief of deputy went over it if it was a real important ships characteristic. But, he was a working member; got the agendas, suggested it, represented the bureau.

Q: Well, Tom, during this tour of duty with BuOrd, in this

planning division, we know that the Special Project was set up under Raborn, and POLARIS was getting under way. Now, is there anything that you can say about that relationship?

Adm. M.: Yes. Admiral Raborn started that thing. Do you remember what year?

Q: Yes, he took the job in December 1955.

Adm. M.: December '55. Right. Well, I remember his ardent recruiting in getting key people out of the bureau, because that's where some of them were that he wanted. My biggest dealings with them was really later on, again under Chick Hayward.

Q: Yes, because it was then well under way.

Adm. M.: Right, and by that time our friend, Gordon Pierson, had gone down there, and so forth. PERT had come along, and I think most of my dealings with the special projects office was largely because having, again been in the driving pool with Admiral Red Raborn and he was then a captain. And, at that time of course, he was in the BuOrd research division for aircraft weapons.

Morton #5 - 360

Q: I believe that at this particular period - '55-'56, some of the powers in BuOrd were a little bit upset at the setting up of a special project -

Adm. M.: This was very true.

Q: Was that reflected in your outfit?

Adm. M.: Yes, it was. Not in our relations with Red Raborn's gang but, it was a fact that basically, our senior people, and some of us minions, I guess, felt this was an ordnance program and why shouldn't ordnance do it? Whereas, the thinking, as you know, was that it was more than ordnance; it was the whole ship.

Q: And of overriding importance?

Adm. M.: Yes, and to give it a honcho who would have considerable authority and responsibility, and could keep the thing together rather than have it split. But, the resentment against the formation of SP - that's what we call it anyway, the POLARIS group, special projects - there was resentment, very much so. I imagine there was in BuShips, maybe even Rickover's outfit, I don't know.

To go back to the senior people in BuOrd. I think I mentioned that Schoeffel was chief then, and P. D. Stroup was the deputy chief. I think I'm wrong on that. I believe when I arrived there the second time that Schoeffel was the chief and Withington was the deputy. And then, somewhere during my tour Admiral Schoeffel was detached, I believe to go to sea as a carrier division commander. Withington moved up as chief, and that's when P. D. Stroup came in, just for the record. And this is going strictly by memory. But, I'd forgotten that Admiral Withington came in sometime before I left, until you mentioned him just now.

Q: It was September of '56 when you left the bureau.

Adm. M.: That's right. In the summer of '56 - I'm now leading up to my next assignment - the detail officer let me know that I'd been selected for what was then called "The deep draft command" which was almost a requisite to promotion. And, he let me think it over a bit and said there were available an APA - the Cambria, which was then in Sixth Fleet, and would be when I reported and my other choice was an AKA - the Capricornus, who was then in Norfolk, in Little Creek with her squadron, but was due to go to the Sixth Fleet. Well, I had friends that had been skippers of both APA's and AKA's and it was rather interesting that when I'd say, "Which would you take?" they were almost unanimous in - regardless of the ship they had - in recommending the Capricornus - the AKA, for two reasons. One was, as I had thought all along, the full Sixth Fleet tour is a highlight in a guys career, rather than going over and taking one and coming back in a month. But, the funniest thing was they all, or nearly all, said, "Tanks and vehicles can't talk back; people can. Take the AKA by all means." So, based on those two bits of advice I asked the detail officer to send me to the Capricornus.

Q: Well, that's a very profound reason.

Interview #6 with Rear Admiral Thomas H. Morton
Place: His residence in Annapolis, Maryland.
Date: Thursday morning, 8 January 1976
Interviewer: John T. Mason, Jr.

Q: Well, Thomas, it's good to see you in this New Year.

Adm. M.: I'm congratulating you on remembering that. It was '76.

Q: And good to resume this series. In the year 1956 - in September of that year, you took over command of a ship known as the Capricornus. Tell me about the Capricornus.

Adm. M.: AKA-57 was her designation. She was designed to work with the amphibious forces, of course. She was a converted merchantman, 469 feet long, as I recall, and something on the order of 13,000 tons.

Q: She was a sizeable ship, then?

Adm. M.: Yes, she's a good sized freighter. The AKA designation, as opposed to the APA which are the troop transports - or really combat transport, the AKAs, as you know, were designed to carry a minimum of Marines and a lot of heavy equipment, not only for the Marines on board but the Marines in the rest of the squadron.

Q: When you say a minimum, in terms of this particular ship -

Adm. M.: I think we carried between one and two hundred, mainly for maintenance, and their officers. Of course, the APAs carried - the opposite, you might say, a minimum of gear and a maximum of combat personnel.

In this particular squadron, in the year I was with it all of our troops were Marines. They were assigned for specific operations, and were not normally aboard. In other words, except in the Mediterranean, they were aboard for a particular exercise and then left us.

She was a member of ComPhiTron 6, which consisted of one AGC - the Taconic, two APAs - the Monrovia and the Rock Bridge, the Capricornus of course, and an LSD, which in this case was the Spiegel Grove. Of course, the Taconic, as the flagship was heavily equipped with communication equipment for the squadron commander and his staff, but also carried a considerable number of troops. The APAs - their sole reason for existence was the combat troops.

Q: Now this was a unit of the Atlantic Fleet?

Adm. M.: Yes, PhibLant. The commodore was Captain Freddie Laing. When I took her over she was as an individual unit, not with the whole squadron. She was overhauling at Todd Shipyards in Brooklyn, New York. I took over in September or October and we had about another month left - and we completed that overhaul, which was a routine one - no particular damage or difficulty, just a routine overhaul, and then we went to the NAD - Earle in New Jersey for our ammunition, and then back to Norfolk where we joined the squadron.

Shortly after that, as is routine in the fleet - or was at that time, we went as an individual ship to Guantanamo for the usual post-overhaul refresher training. The ship did very well in Guantanamo. We got several "Excellences" in the various drills, one of which was accuracy in anchoring. I don't remember the others. We got about five grades of Excellent which, if I say it myself, is pretty good - especially for that type of ship, where you have single screw, and very little power and -

Q: Fairly clumsy?

Adm. M.: Clumsy, yes - no maneuverability to speak of. But anyway, in the five or six weeks we were at Guantanamo we did very well on the whole.

About the only thing of real interest down there was

that they used the visiting ships - particularly of the amphibious types, the bigger ones - for what they called Dependent's Cruise - not our dependents but the wives and children of people on the base who had very little interests outside the base. I mean, Cuba was not much help to them.

Q: Pretty much confined?

Adm. M.: Yes, they were, and the purpose of these two or three-day cruises - they fitted you in with your exercise schedule and simply assigned you to make this trip. We happened to go to Port-au-Prince, Haiti. I don't remember exactly how many wives. There were not many children, and I think the children had to be at least 12 or 14. But anyway, it was a break that they all looked forward to.

Q: You just gave them a good time?

Adm. M.: We just gave them transportation, and then they were on their own when they got there. As I remember the schedule, we left around four or five o'clock in the afternoon - probably a Friday, but I don't really remember - and got into Port-au-Prince the next morning after daylight, and then we stayed at anchor so that they could completely - you might say abandon ship - and enjoy the full day in Haiti, plus that night. And then - if my dates are right -

then we'd sail Sunday morning and got them back to Guantanamo Sunday afternoon or Monday morning, I've forgotten.

Q: It was definitely a morale builder wasn't it?

Adm. M.: It was very much a morale builder at that time. I don't know whether they're still doing that sort of thing, but the APAs and AKAs were very well suited for this because we had the vacant Marine quarters. We gave them Marine officer's quarters, and we blocked off part of sick-bay. In other words, we gave them the best accommodations that we could. They teamed up two or three or four in a room, of course. But, it was very successful and, as I say, they looked forward to their rotation of this recreational cruise, as you might guess.

Q: Yes. I suppose they couldn't go over to Caimanera?

Adm. M.: Well, that had sort of died out. The old days in Caimanera and Boqueron, and so forth - they'd disappeared. They'd gone and, I suppose, even if they did, or could have that sort of -

Q: Well, they disappeared with the advent of Castro?

Adm. M.: Well now, Castro didn't come in until later. We

hadn't had the sawing of the water pipe, and all that because that came in '59. This was '56.

The other thing of interest on a trip down there which I forgot to mention is that - again, as a means of transport for people - we took two groups - or really we took one group of UDT personnel, who did their winter training, in those days - in this case it was St. Thomas. Whether they went other places or not. So, we had a day or so in St. Thomas, which is a fine liberty port, when we dropped these officers and men there for their winter training. And our other assignment was a considerable cargo of cement - concrete and so forth - for the Marines at Vieques. I believe we dropped the UDT boys at St. Thomas and then went to Vieques to unload this material for the Marines.

This was the only time I had a chance to really see Vieques. The commanding officer of the Marine detachment asked two or three of us over there, just to tour around and see it - and they had a small, typical, West Indies town, and that was about all, but it was interesting to be ashore in Vieques for the first time.

Other than that, the refresher training was pretty much routine and we went back to Norfolk to join the squadron and get ready for the departure for the Sixth Fleet in May. Somewhere in between - we'll say - January and May, we had several actual amphibious exercises for the squadron as a whole. I remember one of them - we went down and picked up the Marines and material at Morehead City, and then took them out and the landing was conducted on one of the beaches in either Virginia or Carolina - and I've forgotten which one it was - but anyway, that was my first amphibious exercise, as a complete exercise.

Q: The landing of your equipment, from your ship, came how much after the landing of the men themselves?

Adm. M.: It was all scheduled and the squadron commanders, or the Phib group commander, who would be an admiral - it was all in his -

Q: Discretion?

Adm. M.: Well, in his Op plan. It was all phased in and the boats did the usual circle with the troops and we unloaded the heavy gear - and it was timed so that the landing was more-or-less synchronized. I don't remember the details now.

Then, before going to Europe, we were given a very minimum number - three or four maybe - of nuclear projectiles, and the idea was that these fitted the heavy guns of the Marines - and the red tape and security of that was enormous. I think I had the only key to the magazine, or maybe two different keys - and you had to have a 24-hour guard. The magazine was either converted or erected on the deck - on the main deck, as I remember - up near the superstructure. And, so we were given that solely for the Mediterranean trip and unloaded it when we got back. I don't know how much of this is unclassified now - but, anyway, that's of interest. I mean, we know there are atomic projectiles in Europe anyway -

Q: Oh yes - and the security and secrecy is governed by the Atomic Energy Act itself, isn't it?

Adm. M.: Yes, right. There was a very carefully selected group of gunner's mates who checked the magazine temperatures and physical security, and all that - but, as I recall, the only keys were in my cabin safe at the time, and we had to sign up for receipt of the one or more projectiles, and so forth - and very few of the crew knew they were there - only the people who needed to know knew what they were.

Well, time came - sometime in May - to deploy to the Sixth Fleet and, again I had the pleasure and privilege of taking the squadron to Europe. I was the senior skipper, as it happened - and the commodore, Captain Laing, was long scheduled to attend a meeting in New York where he was getting some sort of award from the Navy League or a similar organization. And it happened to coincide with the transit to Europe so that, in his absence, I took the squadron over - and he joined us there, at Gibralter, or somewhere.

Our turnover with our previous amphibious squadron was held in, as I recall, Taranto, Italy, which was the first time I'd been in that port, and it was the scene of a rather prominent naval battle - you remember - between the British and the Italians.

Q: Devastating to the Italian Fleet.

Adm. M.: Yes, it was. Aircraft torpedoes, a lot of it, I believe.

Q: It could have been seen as a warning for what might happen at Pearl Harbor.

Adm. M.: Yes, true. The impression of Taranto, in the one, or two, or three days we were there being turned over from our predecessors - the impressive thing was the - such places as the Navy buildings there, and the - as usual - the Officer's Club, and so forth. They were stupendous Mussolini marble palaces, there's no question about that. They were rather impressive. We saw some of the Italian Navy there - in the course of our stay.

Q: This tour of duty in the Med was how long?

Adm. M.: It was the usual four or five months - just like my two previous cruises in a destroyer and a destroyer division. They were all gauged to be less than six months - and when you take in transit time. Depending on the schedule, it would run four and a half - five months, five and a half - away from home port and in a regularly assigned fleet.

The main amphibious exercise there, which came some time later, was the full-fledged NATO deal - I'll try to think of the name of it, but anyway, it was in Sardinia - in the south end of Sardinia. It was fully NATO and they had ships of most of the NATO Allies' Fleet, such as minesweepers, destroyer escorts, and that sort of thing.

Q: Did any French units participate?

Adm. M.: I'm sure they did. We also, each had NATO observers aboard. We had a very fine Italian Army officer who was there with us for that exercise. He was an Army adjutant, but extremely knowledgeable in amphibious work, and he was pleasant company. The adjutant, as I understand it is similar to - you might say - a personnel warrant officer in the Navy; in the Army too, I guess.

Q: Who was CinCSouth at that time?

Adm. M.: Let's see. I get my trips mixed up. You know, I just don't remember. We had a succession of them in my Atlantic cruising and I've forgotten exactly who was there then.

Q: Who was Sixth Fleet?

Adm. M.: Let's see. Sherman was my Sixth Fleet Commander in '48 and '49. I remember now. The Sixth Fleet Commander was Cat Brown who had been, fortunately, a very good friend of my family's, and his wife was too - and so when we saw him here and there, he was extremely nice to us. He gave a very fine luncheon party, by the way, for the skippers and senior officers. I guess we were in Cannes.

Q: Did Sue go to the Mediterranean?

Adm. M.: Yes. She went, and so did John. I think I mentioned in previous sessions with you that it was very convenient for Sue to be able to visit England and then come down to the nearer ports - accessible from England.

The first time we went - in my days in the Compton in '48, John was only one and a half so she left him with family and friends. Then, we were able to go to Naples and Cannes - and then the second time, in the division, in '52 and '53 she did the same trip with John - who by then was old enough to make it. He was then six or seven - and then this time, of course, he was now ten so we were able to get to Naples again, and Cannes. Then, in addition to that, we met in Valencia, and on the way around Sue and John were able to stop and see the Leaning Tower of Pisa, and so forth - and then, some very nice days in Barcelona, and then met me in Valencia.

Going back to the first port after Taranto. The Spiegel Grove and the Capricornus went into Cartagena, in Spain, and the squadron commander and the other ships went into Alicante. It was just a case of splitting the visiting ships.

Q: But not during the NATO operations?

Adm. M.: No. This was just a leave port.

Q: As U.S. units they were then?

Adm. M.: Yes, right. The darndest thing happened in Cartagena and the red tape became terrific. The Capricornus moored out at the mole, and the Spiegel Grove, the junior ship, was small enough to go in right along the beachfront of the town, where there was a sea wall and moorings - and I remembered when we were mooring about the same time that the quartermaster, or someone, said, "The Spiegel Grove had broken the Spanish colors." And I was busy - and then they said, "Now, they've hauled it down." I thought nothing of it, except I got to wondering, what did they - especially as the junior ship - what did they break the Spanish national ensign for? I thought no more about it and the thing came down right away. It was purely a quartermaster's mistake, I suppose. But anyway, the Spanish official I had to make my senior officer's calls on, as the senior officer of the two ships, was a Spanish admiral. I suppose he was a regional commander, or something - governor - more than just a naval district, in any case, and he sent a young Spanish Marine major out to be my sort of guide - escort, interpreter and whatnot. This boy's name was Leon - his last name, and he was born and raised in Brooklyn. But his family had moved to Spain, or moved back to Spain - whichever, when he was a little boy, and he was now a career Marine officer in the Spanish Marines. On the way in he said, "What are you going to tell the admiral about that Spiegel Grove incident?" And I said, "I just heard that the colors were broken and then immediately hauled down. I have no idea why the Spiegel Grove would do it. There was nothing that called for either ship showing the Spanish colors in any case." And, he said, "Yes, but they broke the Republican flag", which of course, I hadn't known - and apparently had created considerable stew in the whole town - and not only in the military - in the Navy, but in the town itself - even just the five seconds they saw this thing. So, I went in practically cold to see the admiral. He was truly furious, and so I had not much of an explanation for him, but I told him that I'd go to the Spiegel Grove and - well, possibly the skipper would accompany me on a call.

But, as it turned out - the Republican colors are the red and purple as opposed to the Spanish actual flag of red and yellow, with more or less the same insignia in the middle of the flag. Well,

Well, one thing led to another. There was much apology and all that business, and he asked me, or the Spiegel Grove skipper said, this flag had come from the Naval Supply Depot, with all of the others, in Scotia, New York. And the admiral said, "Well, why do you get your flags in Canada?" and it turned out he was thinking Nova Scotia - and he was trying to find out whether some maneuvering in the U.S. Navy personnel had deliberately handed this Republican flag - which, he explained is just like a hammer and sickle to the Spanish people. Well, God, confidential messages flew back and forth between me, speaking for the Spiegel Grove, and the Sixth Fleet Commander, and the squadron commander up at Alicante - and it must have taken three or four classified messages to finally end this furor.

Q: Did the State Department people get involved?

Adm. M.: I don't know. I imagine so - through, probably, ComSixthFlt. But, we had a time with that. Otherwise, the stay was very pleasant.

Q: Did you ever get to the root of the thing?

Adm. M.: The only explanation was what we'd told the Spanish admiral - was that the ship had ordered flags for the Mediterranean countries, and they'd been sent with a 1936 Republican flag. There was no other explanation. It was just one of those cases that if any other ship had carried that flag, or any other Spanish flags like it, they just never had occasion to use them.

Q: The other suspicious element about it was the Spiegel Grove didn't have any occasion to use it either.

Adm. M.: Well, of course not. That's right. They had no reason to have it and they had no reason to fly it, as far as that went.

 The relations with the Spanish admiral improved in the course of our stay and the town forgot the incident, I guess, and everything went pretty well.

 Then another stop - this time with Sue and John -

was in Naples, and the ship, led by the petty officers, not me - the petty officers had decided to adopt a little Italian girl, under the Foster Parents, or whatever it was. Well, that was quite a pleasant thing. Of course, I didn't take part in it - as the skipper. It was entirely at the instigation of the crew, and this little gal came with her family, and she was photographed, and photographed, and photographed with me and with the leading petty officers, and so on - and they had made her a great big cake down in the messhall, and loads of gifts that they'd gotten for her - and the contract was that the ship, or rather the crew, sent so much a month for her upkeep.

Q: For how long a period of time?

Adm. M.: I think each one was a year with the idea that you could renew it. And of course, she, herself was picked by the organization. I say Foster Parents but I don't remember - there are others like that.

Q: Was this typical? I mean did this always happen?

Adm. M.: No, it didn't. It had happened, and they'd heard of other ships doing it - but, as far as I know, we were the only one at that time in Naples, and the whole squadron was there, and other ships too.

Q: So it was just inspired by somebody on board?

Adm. M.: Either one PO had been in another ship that had done it, or heard about it, or something.

Q: And, it's permitted by Navy regs?

Adm. M.: Oh, yes. We didn't even have to get authorization because it was actually done by the crew on their own.

Q: Did you have experience with other instances of them raising money for a particular project, or anything on board ship?

Adm. M.: No. As a matter of fact this wasn't done by the ship officially. In other words, we had nothing in the plan of the day or the morning orders on this. No member of the crew was directed by me or anyone else to contribute - and I won't say it was the ship as a whole. The men who wanted to do this - they were the ones that contributed.

Not only did it build up a lot of interest in the crew itself but it created a lot of interest in the Naples area, among the Italian people. I got ahold of this by going out with Sue and John to get them myself. I got ahold of six Naples area newspapers - and they were very,

very free with the number of pictures they showed, and the write-up which you could understand. I don't speak Italian, but you could see that the thing was enthusiastically received. Of the six papers, the only one that had nothing was the one that was pointed out to me as the Communist daily and of course, they didn't mention the ship, or the incident, or the little girl, or anything else. I think it was a very successful maneuver which I can't take any credit for because it was dreamed up by some of my crew.

As I said, after Naples we went out on some operation or another, and my family had time to stop at Pisa and Barcelona, and then join us in Valencia. Well, Valencia was a tragic visit - at least for the Capricornus. We'd no sooner got there than we found out we had an epidemic of Asian Flu aboard - and it wasn't in any of the other ships. The ship was restricted entirely from any liberty - and there we were, with the squadron, but we were just confined to the ship - and it didn't pass off until we'd gotten back to sea a week or ten days later. So our time in Valencia was completely wasted by being restricted. We were on a rather large mole and it had enough place for people to play softball and throw a football around and that sort of thing, so they had some exercise - but, that's all they had. That was liberty. And the other ships went gaily on their way ashore, and so forth.

An interesting point was that when this first case

was discovered - just about the time we moored, I think - or shortly after. Well, Sue and John had met the ship and they were aboard, and then there was a problem of getting them ashore - which really was a problem. So the ship's doctor simply okayed their release on his own, and of course, I did too, because I didn't want to scare them. Well, as luck would have it, in the hotel at Valencia - Sue and John at least saw the town, even if I didn't - John came down with Asian Flu. So, the skipper of the Taconic and his doctor went out to see - well, he was sort of looking after Sue anyway, a great friend of ours - and so his doctor treated John in this hotel for his Asian Flu, and kept him under quarantine until he got over it. And the number of cases was a very high percentage of the crew. I can't say whether it was a half or a third - I've forgotten now. It went on for a long time, and it wasn't until, as I say, we got out to sea, say ten days later that the thing died off. But, that was quite an experience, and not a very pleasant one.

Q: What kind of preparation on board the Capricornus did you make for shore leave and visits to these various foreign ports? What did you do with the crew?

Adm. M.: Well, we operated very much the same way we did in the destroyers that I mentioned before. We had the

Sixth Fleet Directory, and this directory would give you a very good idea of what you recommend the boys see and do, and any out-of-bound area that they couldn't go in, and that sort of thing.

We almost invariably - in all three of my tours over there - we arranged ahead for tours for people who wanted them. I mean through either our local tour agency or American Express, or some such organization as that - and they'd come aboard with their plans, so these boys - particularly in Cartagena - were able to go say 50 or 60 miles for a bullfight somewhere else. Or, if they had time - I don't remember whether we sent any to Madrid, or not, but in any case, a lot of them in the Naples stay would go to Rome, and in Cannes - I don't think they had time to go to Paris - but they went to other French cities. It was pretty well laid on, as it was everywhere else. Greece, for instance, had a variety of tours there, and Athens was easily accessible - about 12 miles, I think. But, they could go to the more famous ruins if they wanted to. There was no particular strain on them. A lot of these - especially the senior petty officers - had been to Europe many times, and even to some of the more familiar ports before, so you had no real problem with giving them the information on what they might want to do.

Of course, as a matter of routine we furnished a certain percentage of the shore patrol so, except for getting out the information to them - and the information to the Sixth Fleet, as I say, was very, very good - that was really all you had to do - tell them what was available and so forth.

Q: What other fleet operations did you engage in, in addition to the one off Sardinia?

Adm. M.: When we left Cartagena - I believe it was at that period, which was one of our first ports - the usual stew broke out in either Lebanon or Syria, or somewhere - Jordan maybe. I don't remember which because these things happen all the time. And there had been some amphibious visits off Jordan, I believe it was, in the event that troops had to go ashore, so we were suddenly alerted to go and stand by for an operation in one of those mid-East countries, but I've forgotten which. But the thing cleared up by the time we got almost there and nothing came of it. The major operation was the one in Sardinia.

Q: The British had amphibious units in the Mediterranean at that time?

Adm. M.: Yes, they did. I don't think there were any in the Sardinia operation - there may have been. I'm not sure. It was a NATO Fleet all right, but whether we were the only troops landing, I just don't remember. When you try to reconstruct these things of twenty years ago you don't remember all the details. That was about it, I think.

The fact that the amphibious ships never went to the Trieste-Venice area because they were noncombatant, is a disappointment because those are among the two popular ports. But, as I told you, with these bombardment plans, and that sort of thing, they only sent combat ships up there. I can't think of any other highlights of that cruise, Jack.

For the big operations - like the Sardinia ones - a Phib group commander - rear admiral - was invariably flown with his staff over to the Med to join whatever amphibious squadron was there - to conduct it, because of the command relationships of the general officers of Marines, and that sort of thing - of the other services - other nations. So, although a Phib group commander did not stay the whole Mediterranean tour, he was always there for a major landing.

Q: Was there any expectation - This was before the Suez Crisis. Was there any indication that there might be something happening there?

Adm. M.: I don't recall it. No, the only operation I can think of which was carried out to completion was the one that we felt that we might have to do in the Middle East. In Jordan, either the year before or the year after - and this I don't remember - when we were not there, in any case - the Marine's actually did land there and - it was probably Lebanon. In any case, it just happened that the commanding general of the troops that landed there was Sid Wade, a classmate of mine at the Naval Academy - senior Marine officer and senior officer ashore. But whether that was '56 or '58, I can't recall. I know it was before or after we were over there.

Then there was - unless you have any other questions - then, being relieved and back to Norfolk - Little Creek I should say. The amphibious ships sometimes were anchored at Little Creek and sometimes were moored at the regular Navy piers in Norfolk - depending on activity or what was coming up and that sort of thing. So, when I say Norfolk was home port it could be Little Creek, which is a terrible place to get in and out of, if you know it. There's very little bus service and very difficult and distant for a taxi, and all that. Being based at Little Creek is not much fun for the seagoing people.

Then - I guess it was September or October -

Q: You only stayed a year with her then?

Adm. M.: Yes. A year was the so-called deep draft duty. This deep draft duty in those days was a sort of stepping stone to your major combat command, if you were lucky enough to get one - and it was one type of qualification along the line - whether it was an AGC or APA, AK, or even something like a tanker.

Q: Yes, a tanker. Very often it was a tanker.

Adm. M.: It was more frequently than any others because of the numbers of them.

Q: Well, then you came back to the Department in Washington?

Adm. M.: Yes, then I went to the Pentagon for the first time - my other tours in Washington having been in Main Navy with the Bureau of Ordnance or the Bureau of Weapons - and I reported to Admiral Chick Hayward's research and development.

Q: Had you known him before?

Adm. M.: Only by reputation. I'd met him a couple of times in the Bureau of Ordnance, but only in passing. I never knew him, but of course his reputation was Navy-wide. He was a phenomenal gent. I've been in his office and seen him wrestling with two telephones, his secretary, and someone in the room, all at the same time. He was able to juggle things that way, and that's the way he loved to operate.

Q: That's a good word to underscore - love to do. He loves to do it.

Adm. M.: He did. He was a fast mover - and he was an operator in the favorable sense of the word.

Q: Well, tell me the scope of the planning branch.

Adm. M.: Hayward's outfit then was called 03 C - 03 Charley - and it was a small group that was, as you see, under the deputy chief - deputy CNO Operations, by the designation 03.

Either while I was there, or later on, they set him up as 09 - Op-09 - as a separate deputy chief - just in the organizations there. He had a group of about - I'd say - not more than 30 of us. He had a - I don't remember the exact title - a programming division, which was primarily responsible for the inevitable budget, computation and administration. Then our planning group was, I'd say, six or eight officers and civilians, who were sort of his - I'd say - personal staff, and then we had a third group who was the liaison with OpDev 4 and foreign navies regarding research and development. I said 30 all together. I doubt if it was that many - probably 20 to 25 total.

But that was an extremely interesting year. It was only a year because of the feeling that - thanks to him - that it was time for me to get my major combatant command - which I did.

The highlights of the year with Chick Hayward - there were several. He knew a tremendous number of people - in especially the scientific world - and he was on first name terms with most of them, and just in going in and out of his office, I remember having a long talk with Dr. Teller - the nuclear wizard.

There were three major things that I got involved in there in that capacity. The first one was - Admiral Wright and Admiral Burke had proposed - or Wright had proposed to Burke, and he'd given it the okay - that we set up a NATO undersea research and development station in Europe. And the site was picked in Italy - La Spezia - and I was Hayward's representative in the committee that set this up. We had Admiral Hogle from Admiral Jerauld Wright's staff. We had people who had been engaged in foreign assistance matters, and so forth. But Hayward was given the job of bringing them all together - and one of the interesting things we had to do then was to select an operating company. The theory had been decided that a university or corporation would man this thing, under joint NATO-Naval command.

Q: What was the objective of this underwater plan?

Adm. M.: The idea was to get weapons research - detector research - all the facets of ASW.

Q: Sonars, and things?

Adm. M.: Yes, sonar - including things like sonobuoys - anything that pertained to ASW to have it in a joint multination station in Europe.

Q: Well, why a multination station? Why not U.S.?

Adm. M.: Well, the idea was to pull NATO together, and facilitate the exchange and that sort of thing - where you'd have officers of several navies working together on a particular project - or ships of several navies. That was set up. We finally - having had bids from ITT and Stanford Research Institute and Temco, I believe it was called - we finally selected Raytheon Corporation to set up the station and to be responsible for the manning of it, particularly from the civilian scientist point of view, from all nations. So Raytheon got the contract and I would say it was commissioned, probably a year later, maybe. We had one of our antisubmarine officers who was in the Pentagon, who was sent over as the first commanding officer. The idea was that the commanding officer would usually be an American - at least to start with.

Q: How was the matter of classification handled?

Adm. M.: That had to be handled through us, or through the antisubmarine warfare division. You had to have a specific okay that this particular thing could be released. Then, the other nations had the same type of classification. In other words, it was like our working with the British during the war, in that we respected each other's classification. Something thrown into the ASW center was sanctioned by the originating nation with the understanding that that particular classification would be observed by the others - and, as far as I know, it was.

Q: Well now, Tom, would this not, in a way, limit the amount of experimentation with certain pieces of ordnance because, say the U.S. had greater knowledge in a particular area than the British and the French and the others, and therefore did not want to reveal everything to them?

Adm. M.: That's true.

Q: So the effectiveness of the experiment was limited, was it not?

Adm. M.: It was. It was indeed because, as I say, each country okayed a portion, or a certain part of a project, to go to the center, and, like anything else, it was restricted - very much so - but it was one of these things that Jerauld Wright insisted on setting up as his - in his capacity as SACLANT. So it was called, I think, the SACLANT ASW Center.

Q: It would turn out to be an exercise but, because of the limitations upon it, not a complete exercise?

Adm. M.: It was no more restricted than the information that we could exchange with other nations - except it was a sort of a melting pot where that information could go. It had restrictions on it, just like discussing with the Italians or the British a particular weapons system or technique.

Q: Yes, but to pursue this just a bit further. In case of a conflict, the use of what was permitted on this NATO level was somewhat less say than what was possible -

and therefore, in case of a conflict what would happen? It's like fighting with one hand behind your back.

Adm. M.: True. It is - although, I'm given to believe that the SACLANT staff was fairly harmonious with all the nations, from the operational point of view. I can't tell you exactly how well this panned out or worked because it wasn't commissioned 'til after my time was up there.

Q: Was Hayward enthusiastic about this Wright proposal?

Adm. M.: I think we all realized some of the difficulties we'd have - particularly in staffing - and some of the things you and I have been talking about, but when Mr. Burke and Mr. Wright say they want something - whether you're Hayward or Morton, or who you are, that's what Mr. Wright and Mr. Burke get.

Incidentally, I understood later on that Raytheon had wanted out, and I believe the second contract to operate it - administer it - was Penn States' Ordnance Research Laboratory - so called ORL, which had done a lot of fine work with the Bureau of Weapons - and I don't know who's running it now. I understand it's still going - but how effectively, I can't say.

Incidentally, because of the international involvement here, one of the people who was extremely helpful and interesting to work with was from the Department of Defense - Tracy Vorhees. Does that name ring a bell with you? Tracy Vorhees had had quite a fantastic career. He wasn't Assistant Secretary of Defense, but he was something pretty well up in it. And he'd been a Director of the Long Island Railroad. His fame, a year before this - in 1957 or '58 he was the complete number one operator in the Hungarian Refugee situation - if you remember when we set up the camps - I think New Jersey and other places. Tracy Vorhees was the honcho of that whole operation. He was an interesting character and a very effective man - and very helpful to have someone influential in the Department of Defense, on this little committee.

Q: You say that was one of the three projects that you got involved with.

Adm. M.: Well, the others were not really as - didn't carry along the length of time this one did.

Another one was that we had in the ASW field, a thing called CANUKUS agreement. The abbreviation is Canada U.K. U.S. - called CANUKUS - and they met periodically - twice a year, I guess - and they rotated where the meetings would be. And, again I became Hayward's representative in this - but of course, we had numerous people and technical help from the antisubmarine warfare division of OpNav. But, anyway, the one I happened to attend was an extremely interesting one - it was held in Halifax - Canada being the host country, in rotation. And, I guess we were up there with the British and the Canadians for about - maybe a week. It was really more a clearing house than anything else. It's the sort of thing that you always felt would be more effective if we weren't glued to a formal agenda, and that sort of thing - but at least it was one way of exchanging information. Now you ran into the same classification that you mentioned in the case of the SACLANT Center, you see - what we could discuss and what we couldn't - and they had the same ground rules.

Q: This was limited to antisubmarine warfare too?

Adm. M.: Yes. At least that was the conference I attended.

Q: Does it continue as a working agreement?

Adm. M.: I don't know - and I'm not even sure it was restricted to ASW but our particular phase of it happened to be ASW, and I believe that was its only field. I could be wrong.

Q: Was this perhaps an outgrowth of that Canadian Defense

Board that we participated in?

Adm. M.: It might have been. I don't know the history of it. I don't know how or when it was set up, Jack, but it had been going some years, I think. The Navy in Halifax had a fantastic number of excellent scientific people on the staff - and also some excellent, what were then coming along as computers - that sort of thing. They really seemed to know what they were doing, as did the British, of course. Most of the people we observed in that week, and most of the material we saw, was entirely Canadian, because we happened to be in Halifax.

Again, I don't know whether that still continues or not, and how effective it's turned out to be. It wasn't new at this time.

Q: Now, the third project?

Adm. M.: Well, the third project was really a sort of weekly progress meeting held by Admiral Red Raborn's special projects - POLARIS group.

Q: Oh, you sat in on those?

Adm. M.: These were the CNO Supervisory Meetings - over Admiral Raborn. Again, I was Admiral Hayward's representative.

They had people from Admiral Raborn's SP, and then they had everyone in OpNav you could possibly imagine would have any connection with the POLARIS programs - the submarine division, the ASW division, the communications, BuWeps, BuShips. It was an informational committee - so CNOs people would know what was going on.

Q: Was WESSIG involved?

Adm. M.: No, I think not. I'm sure they weren't. I was going to say because they were tri-service group. I don't remember any WESSIG participation in this meeting. It was all Navy - it had some of Admiral Rickover's people from his section - and of course there were a lot of people involved here because, as you know, it was not the missile itself. I mean not the missile alone - it was the launching and the ship.

Q: BuShips people were involved?

Adm. M.: Oh, very much so, yes - although, of course, Raborn had his own people for that - but BuShips was involved in this. It was an exchange meeting.

Q: Did you reach outside the Navy? Was Electric Boat involved?

Adm. M.: No. A contractor, when he was called in, usually went right to Raborn's group. In other words, this was an informal, in-house progress report -

Q: That's interesting.

Adm. M.: Not in the detail that PERT went into in SP - but general information.

Q: And Raborn was there, was he?

Adm. M.: I don't think he was always there. The one who I remember who was there was - later a rear admiral - Frank Pinney, a very good friend of mine. He was usually the SP representative, as I recall.

That was, as I recall, a weekly meeting. It might have been bi-weekly - but in any case it kept everybody who could possibly have any interest, or even inputs as far as that goes - was represented. It must have been about 40 people, I would say.

Then, one interesting trip I made - again as Hayward's representative - with other people from the various bureaus in Ops, so-called. Admiral Rickover wanted to take a group up to see the Westinghouse plant in Pittsburgh which was doing considerable work for him - and he arranged the plan and everything, and a Navy plane took us up and we had an all-day tour of the plant - and seminars with his people, and with the Westinghouse people. It was a true Rickover day. In other words, you scarcely had time to eat lunch - but it was a very interesting day. And the reason I mention it is because - untypical of Admiral Rickover, when we got aboard to come home - it must have been dark by then - 7 to 8 o'clock, and we took off to fly back to Washington - after all this grueling leading us around, and so forth, and flight scheduling - what should the admiral do but tell the plane's stewards that, "The bar is now open." None of us had the faintest idea that this was going to happen. It sort of made our day in a way because everybody was fairly well pooped - but, on came the Scotch and soda, or the Martinis, or whatever you wanted - and as many as you wanted, courtesy of old Hyman Rickover. I mention that only because it was - it might be typical again. Maybe he does do that often - but we certainly were surprised.

Q: But, it isn't typical of his reputation.

Adm. M.: No, it certainly isn't that.

Well, aside from the sort of routine in-house thing - Another thing. I mentioned three. Admiral Burke wanted to arrange a seminar on Unconventional Warfare - you know guerilla's, deception, all that sort of thing - and Hayward's group was the one to honcho this one. We worked fairly hard on this. Captain Gentry - then number two to Hayward, and myself were the ones most involved.

Q: Well, what did you draw on as sources?

Adm. M.: Well, it was rather interesting. All this took weeks - months, to arrange. We decided to hold it at the Auditorium at White Oak - in the Naval Ordnance Lab, White Oak, which is now, I think, called Naval Weapons Center. But, anyway, they had a very nice laboratory and facilities - parking, and so on. And we collected some people we thought could help on this - from the services, from commercial research groups such as Stanford Research Institute and various universities - and asked them, by name, to give us some ideas - and they did, and that led to other names and so forth. One of the ones that came down for several days, and had a lot of good ideas, was none other than Henry Kissinger.

Q: From Harvard?

Adm. M.: Yes.

Q: What was his particular knowledge?

Adm. M.: He didn't take part in the seminar - but mainly, "You ought to talk to so-and-so, and so-and-so."

Q: He had made a study of this subject?

Adm. M.: Yes, he had - apparently. So, we finally got the thing organized and got the subjects in hand and picked the speakers - and I think we had three or four days of meetings and probably two or three speakers a day with question period.

Q: Did you have access to Mr. Thompson and the Malayan experience - the British in Malaya?

Adm. M.: No. We finally ended up with this thing being - maybe not as restrictive as Admiral Burke wanted it to be - but we had political people. We had so-called experts on Communism. Each speaker had some facet of this whole problem - intelligence.

Q: Now, how prevalent was guerilla warfare in various parts of the world at that time?

Adm. M.: Well, it wasn't too much I guess - 58 - but it was more than guerilla warfare. It was - you might say sabotage, actual jungle guerilla warfare - almost any part, as opposed to what you might call conventional war.

Q: Did your UDT people participate?

Adm. M.: I think we did have some of them. I've forgotten the subjects now, and even the speakers. We ended up with one fellow who was a reporter from Time magazine, another was a political professor at the University of Virginia, I believe. Then we had an editor of a couple of the newspapers. I believe the Christian Science Monitor might have been one - I'm not sure.

Q: Why did they come into this picture?

Adm. M.: They came in because these people we started with - before it sort of snowballed - had said, well now look, if you want to talk on such-and-such, you want to get ahold of him, if you can. I mean, it was a case of getting ideas from our initial nucleus - some of who became speakers themselves - and others, it was a sort of word-of-mouth thing.

Q: It strikes me as being - encroaching on the CIA provinces. Were they involved in it?

Adm. M.: No. Not to my knowledge. But, again it's like

your NATO-SACLANT Center - this is what Arleigh Burke wanted, and he apparently had it all cleared with somebody.

Q: But did he reveal his motivation for it?

Adm. M.: Just the idea that it was something the Navy should know about - and, in his opinion, didn't know enough about.

Q: So the net result of this series of lectures and bull sessions was what?

Adm. M.: Well, the auditorium at White Oak held several hundred, and we had to, not only pick the speakers and arrange the agenda, and so forth - and write the letters inviting these people. Of course some of them had conflicts and we had to get someone else. But finally it all worked out, and I suppose there must have been about 300 there, from all parts of the Navy. I think we did invite a token from the Army and Air Force, but it was predominantly Navy - both civilian and military.

Q: Was there a report, in distillation form, of what transpired? None whatsoever?

Adm. M.: None. No. I can't remember what the classification

of this thing was. I don't know whether it was classified or not Jack - I've forgotten. It may have been. I know that we had tight security on the doors - possibly not to prevent unclassified. Whether it was just to hold it down to the invited list or whether it was true security, I don't know - but the same group attended all three or four-day sessions.

Q: Well, that was a fascinating endeavor. Certainly down Chick Haywards' alley.

Adm. M.: Yes, exactly. These were the sort of things that the higher ups just said, "Well, who can we get to run that? Let's get Chick Hayward to run it." And this is the way they did it. He kept his hand in, and as I say, his chief of staff, Captain Gentry, very much did - but, I felt I was a little bit fortunate for being one of the working members of all these various things. So, it was a very profitable year.

To show how good he was to his people, for instance. Chick Hayward. He was the one that said that he didn't want to lose me - I mean, I'm saying this sort of thing immodestly. But, he said, "33 is beginning to get the combat commands now. Wouldn't you want me to go to work on this?" And, of course he did - and, as I said before - this was the reason I was only there a year. Now, how much Hayward really had to do with my assignment - and my assignment upon that particular month, I don't know. I didn't see him a great deal after that - but we were away on leave when I was selected to flag rank - and I got three calls - one from my sister Emily Mustin, and one from Admiral Tommy Robbins - more about him later. He was then was they called the Potomac River Naval Command - and one from Chick Hayward, to tell me about the list. And, they'd all gone to the trouble of tracking me down in North Carolina, of all places - and more about that later. That was quite a story in itself. But, that's the way he would. He was loyalty down as well as had loyalty up. He was just that way.

Q: I think you were going to talk about your next command - major command.

Adm. M.: Yes. So, he arranged for me to go to BuPers and see what they had for me in the way of major combat commands so-called. It looked like the most appropriate - as far as time went - was the USS Columbus, then CA-74.

Q: She was a heavy cruiser?

Adm. M.: Yes. But BuPers did tell me - he said, "Now, if you take the Columbus - she's in the Far East now, and you can go out there. She is on the list for conversion to a guided-missile cruiser, and you may find that you won't have her too long." And, I mulled it over. They said, "We hope to be able to give you your full year, or 14 months - in combat command by transferring you somewhere else if the Columbus should go out of commission for three years." So, I thought about it - and at this time this wasn't entirely definite. It was possible - but the fact that she was going to be converted was indefinite, and the time of the start of the conversion was indefinite.

Q: She was then what? Attached to the Seventh Fleet?

Adm. M.: Yes. So, rather than wait - and with a sincere promise from BuPers that I would get well over a year - or something over a year in that type of command, I decided to go rather than wait for another unit to be available.

Well, she was in the Far East, in the Seventh Fleet so I reported in to Admiral Smedberg, who was then Com-CruDesPac, and then went on my way.

I landed in Hong Kong after what seemed an awfully long air trip - and it was - and was met there by Admiral Miles Hubbard. The Columbus, by the way was the flagship of ComCruDiv 3. Admiral Miles Hubbard was in the process of being relieved by Admiral "Rebel" Lowrance, as the division commander, and I was then to relieve

Captain Ralph Johnson, in the Class of '32, who had been selected for admiral. That's why the ship had become available.

Q: Lowrance was a submariner, was he not?

Adm. M.: Yes - and a very fine man. He got to be one of my very best friends - and Sue and his wife. We visited each other's homes and that sort of thing - in years later.

So I joined the ship in Hong Kong, and Ralph Johnson, my predecessor, stayed aboard for the turnover until we got to the first stop that was scheduled for the ship in Taiwan. We visited two ports there in succession - Chi-lung and Kao-hsiung. I relieved Ralph Johnson during the first port - and of course we had the assistance of the Chinese naval pilots who, as all pilots, were excellent. I remember when Ralph left the ship. It was a very tricky entrance and harbor. He said, "Okay, I got her in here - now you've got to get her out," which was his parting remark, which I've never forgotten.

Incidentally, when I mentioned - way back in '36 or '37, that I went to Admiral Kalbfus' staff as the senior communication watch officer, Ralph was my predecessor there. The reason I mention this is that - twice, twenty years apart, I relieved Ralph Johnson who, incidentally, lives here now.

Anyway, we were in these two ports in Taiwan, and Admiral Lowrance and myself were invited to various dinners there. One was up at the Taiwan Defense Command, which of course was tri-service - and I saw a couple of my old friends from the Air Force staff in the United Nations - which was some fifteen years before. And also one - I guess it was Christmas, the ship in its various stops at these ports had gotten to know the Communication Intercept Station - it was Navy-administered but it was civilian. It was one of these sort of underground episodes that you probably have heard of. They called them - just Communication Station I think they called it, but it was a lot more than that. And that crowd was very nice to the ship's officers.

Q: They were largely CIA people, were they not?

Adm. M.: I guess so, yes. But, they didn't hesitate to put out a little lighter like this which you see so much in the Far East because the Japs and the Chinese make them - with their insignia on it. It may not have been Communications station - but anyway, that's what they were known as.

By New Years Eve we'd gotten into Yokosuka and of course had a chance to get up to Tokyo - just for a day. I'd seen Tokyo on the way down to Hong Kong. Tokyo was one of the stops - and incidentally, it was nearly an all-day stop, so I'd seen quite a bit of the city at that time.

Now the Columbus' time was now winding down. It was definite that she was going to be out of commission some years so - we sailed from Yokosuka, I believe, and came home without the rest of the Seventh Fleet. We just came home as a unit.

Q: You were only with her then a very short time?

Adm. M.: Up to then, yes - but of course that was early January. We got back into Long Beach and almost immediately started making preparations to have this conversion done at Bremerton Yard.

Q: I take it your family did not go out to the Far East with you?

Adm. M.: No, they didn't because I knew this stay was going to be short. They met me in Long Beach when I came back from the Far East, and stayed there for several weeks - but we had the problem of John and his schooling and so what we decided to do was have them come back here and let John finish - he was then at Severn - and let him finish the year at Severn.

Then we decided - later on - that the Columbus was due in Bremerton about the 10th March, as I recall - and most of the intervening time between January and March was taken up in numerous - red tape, forms, and so forth, for this conversion - including Board of Inspection Survey inspection. But, anyway, in early March we reported at Bremerton Navy Yard - and that picture there is deliberately taken by the yard as a preparation for a before and after shot.

Q: That was before?

Adm. M.: That was as we went into Bremerton. The ship was scheduled for a three-year conversion. She was to become CG-12 as her new designation. The Albany and Chicago may have been a sister ship to the Columbus - I'm not really sure. But, we had a lot of work to do - and the yard went right to work right away - and then we had the phasing-out of the crew. We'd gone up to Bremerton with almost the full crew. I think we'd unloaded some of them at Long Beach.

Q: Well, what was the complement?

Adm. M.: 1600 - possibly. I'm a little hazy - again, getting ships mixed-up - but 14-1600-18 - somewhere along there. So there was considerable work by the officers - particularly the exec - in preparing the phase-out schedule.

We could let so many of a certain rating go first and this went on a sort of almost weekly schedule of release of men. It involved naming them and giving their rates - and then also getting them orders - to tell them where to go next. So, the time in the yard went fast.

Meanwhile, the family had come out. I had found out at Bremerton - I'd gotten a little place to live and I'd found out that he could enter the local school there - with his part year credits. So they came out to spend the rest of the time. We left Bremerton as a family - Bremerton for Long Beach - my new duty about the 15th of May, I would say - somewhere along there.

Q: By that time you'd turned the ship over to the shipyard?

Adm. M.: To the shipyard. Incidentally, the yard commander was a great friend of mine and a peach of a guy - Bobby Snyder so called. He was "Chips" Snyder's son - engineer admiral, and was a real peach. We saw a lot of the Snyders - and a lot of the other yard officers - having been there these two months.

One of the things that we attended officially was the keel laying of the Iwo Jima which was then one of the then new troop carrying helicopter carriers. I don't think the Iwo Jima was the first one but it was one of the first - and she was not a conversion - she was built from the keel up.

Bobby Snyder, as the admiral of the yard officiated at the laying of the keel in this drydock.

Being in the yard, and being with the ship gradually winding down, we personally had had a very interesting two months. The olympic peninsula in the northwest has countless places of interest and beauty to go. We went to the Oregon coast - we went to the Washington coast - we went to Port Angeles - we went to Mount Ranier - all that sort of thing - and, as you know the skipper of a ship in the Navy yard is not too busy, and so the Friday night to Sunday night, or Monday morning weekend was a thing you just took for granted.

Q: Your activities were largely confined to personnel matters then?

Adm. M.: That's right - for the first time. So, we took advantage of the fact that we could see the country, and John would know the area. We particularly were interested because this was where we had married and honeymooned, as I mentioned some interview ago. The family affection for the Northwest is great.

So that ended the Columbus - and the last personnel on the ship was my steward and myself. We had already gone through with what crew we had left and hauled down the flag and turned the ship over to Admiral Snyder.

Q: Just a footnote now - did they adhere to the schedule for her conversion, and was she converted in time?

Adm. M.: To the best of my knowledge - yes. When I said three years, I'm not sure whether it was a little less - but she came out, essentially on time as the CG-12 - and went out of commission about a year ago as such - and so she had - well from '59 - she had eleven years as a going missile ship. The only time I ever saw her was when she had made - either a reserve cruise or a Navy League cruise.

Q: After leaving the Columbus. Tell me - you say BuPers was true to their promise -

Adm. M.: - and had me ordered to command of Destroyer Squadron 23, then home-ported in Long Beach.

Q: And this was still calling itself the Little Beavers?

Adm. M.: Yes. They were known - still known - as the Little Beavers. Of course the ships were totally different than they had been, but as you remember, the squadron - DesRon 23 - the Little Beavers - were the ones that Arleigh Burke made famous in World War II.

I have to digress a little bit. John, Sue, and I drove down from Bremerton, and stopped in various places along the coast - giving them their first view of San Francisco, for instance. We stayed there overnight. And then we had a very pleasant stop with Admiral and Mrs. Kelly Turner - the famous amphibious commander.

Q: Where were they? In Pebble Beach?

Adm. M.: Monterey - or Carmel - Monterey, I believe - but one or the other. In any case, Admiral Turner had been my Navy boss at the U.N. - as I mentioned, back in '46 or '47, and he and his wife had become great friends in those days and insisted that we stop by and see them. He was one of John's godfathers. So, we had a very pleasant day with them. We didn't stay overnight but we had lunch, as I remember - and of course, the admiral's collection of albums and photographs was fabulous. One of the things I remember he told me - he said since the war he had many senior officer friends in the Japanese Navy who had made a point of coming by to see him at his home there - some years after the war and, I remember he said that the almost unanimous opinion of the ex-Japanese officers was that the U.S. submarine is the one that won the war - that they would say it was not the atomic weapon, and it was not the aircraft - it was the submarines that really starved the mainland into submission. He found that very interesting of course. I think he subscribed to this. It's certainly one of the major factors - but the Japanese actually named that as one.

So, we then came down to Long Beach, and had rented a very nice house over in Palos Verdes, if you know that area. Then, in the various sorties on operations, my turn would eventually come around - to design the screen and operate the screen for sortie. I'd mentioned this being done before - but this was the first time where I myself had actually taken my turn to do this.

The operations there were fairly routine. I can't think of anything particularly - there were no major cruises that we went on. I stayed with the ship until the First of March, I guess, the next year it would be.

Q: Now, was this with the First Fleet? Who was First Fleet?

Adm. M.: Yes. First Fleet, I think, was Admiral Libby. I'm pretty sure he was. The Edson made two cruises - not operational ones but - you might say ceremonial. One was - we went up to Monterey. The Edson alone, I say now - not the whole squadron. The Edson to represent the fleet at Monterey for Commodore Sloat Day. I think this was the anniversary of the landing by a Commodore Sloat - his landing sailors in the Monterey area. My history isn't very good on that. Admiral Yeomans had the PG School. He was the senior officer present by reason of rank -

and we were the visiting ship, and it was one of these rounds of parades, dedications, and so forth.

During our stay there - and the family went along - Admiral and Mrs. Turner asked if we could find a blank spot in the schedule - which, staying there for a week or so we did and - you mentioned Pebble Beach. We went down to Pebble Beach to the Country Club with them for a very fine luncheon, and had the pleasure of meeting for the first time, Admiral Spruance, who lived in that neighborhood and was a great friend of Admiral Turner's. So, after all of my service under Admiral Spruance's Fifth Fleet, I finally met the gentleman. I found him fascinating.

Q: What was he like in retirement?

Adm. M.: I would say rather quiet. I don't know whether that's his reputation or not. He certainly wasn't the swashbuckler his opposite number in the Third Fleet was. I have the book by Tom Buell which I must get around to reading.

The other - you might call it non-operational trip - was to Seattle to visit the Sea Fair, which is an annual civic celebration and occasion in Seattle - and I went up there, again with the Edson by herself - and Admiral Rebel Lowrance, who had been my old boss in the Columbus, was still the cruiser division admiral in another ship -

another cruiser. But anyway, we had this very gay week of Sea Fair, and quite a nice reunion with Admiral Lowrance - Rebel, as we call him.

Q: This was sort of the flower circuit, wasn't it?

Adm. M.: Actually, the Rose Festival is Portland, but it's the same sort of idea. One of the features there is this hydroplane race - unlimited hydroplane race, which is an annual part of Sea Fair - in addition to the International Balls, and that sort of thing.

Q: Was that because of Lockheed?

Adm. M.: No. You mean Boeing?

Q: Boeing - I mean.

Adm. M.: No, I don't believe there's any connection. These unlimited hydroplanes are the same ones that race for the President's Cup in Washington - you know, the tremendous rooster tail.

The Canadian skipper of the Frazer invited four or five of us, I think, from the cruiser and the Edson to come aboard for the day and observe the hydroplane race, as his guest - and that was quite an occasion. We went aboard the Frazer at Sands Point - the Naval Air Station - and then went out into Lake Washington or Union, whichever it is, and had just a perfect finish line view of this terrific race - with the television or radio telling us what was going on. It was a very interesting day and a very nice luncheon.

Another part of Sea Fair was SecNavs visit. He gave a reception. I'm trying to think now whether it was Franke or Gates. Yes, I believe it was Secretary Franke. It was nice to see him, and meet him - and also, incidentally, the former superintendent down here - Bill Mack - was Secretary Franke's naval aide at the time.

That was about what Sea Fair amounted to - and then the various routine operations continued out of Long Beach. They also had each squadron commander, at one time or another, go down to San Diego to ASW School. They always feel that you never get enough of that - so I had a two week course down there for squadron commanders. And they'd take us a couple at a time, when the ship was in port.

Q: Were there any war games at this point, and if so, what was their nature.

Adm. M.: None that I recall. That's why I say our major long-distance trips in the Edson were really ceremonial visits more than operations.

Q: Well, I was wondering, with the Japanese out of the picture what kind of war games the fleet would engage in.

Adm. M.: I don't remember any major fleet problems out there. Most of it was antisubmarine operations - for our part - and gunnery, of course. But, there were no major long-range, long time problems.

Q: Did you get involved in any way with Alaska or the Arctic?

Adm. M.: No, not at all. When my relief was on the way, we had sailed for deployment in the Seventh Fleet - and after a stop at Pearl Harbor, and calls on CinCPac - CinCPacFlt, we went on to Guam where we were to stay a few days - and my relief arrived in Guam, and relieved me there.

Incidentally, I had been to Guam before and I don't think I mentioned in connection with the Columbus but - on the way back home from the Far East with the Columbus, we stayed in Guam for about a week. The idea was - just as they'd done at Pearl Harbor before the war - they were trying to keep the know-how and personnel in the ship repair facility at Guam - so the policy then was to have any ship visiting Guam - the fleet would schedule them for a week or ten days to keep this investment going. It was all minor stuff - we gave them as much work as we could. In the Columbus there was quite a bit - because of the long time in the Seventh Fleet. So, the Edson and the rest of my squadron at Guam didn't have too much for the ship repair facility to do - but this was the idea. They were mostly Filipinos, and they were afraid that if we didn't keep them busy, and paid, they would go home. They were limited - just as that title implies - a limited ship repair facility.

Q: Was this absolutely essential to the fleet - to have repair facilities on Guam?

Adm. M.: It was then considered so, yes. It was part of the game - and this policy I mentioned was to make sure that it continued to function, with as much business as they could send. The people at Guam - Commander Marianas. Well, they arranged for me to get a helicopter trip around the island - and that was extremely interesting because having been out there in the war - offshore - you could see the - they'd point out these wrecked tanks and that sort of thing, here and there - and submarine hulls up on the beach - either having been shot to pieces or run aground - and there were marks of the war still there to be seen - they just must have left them there - and seeing it by helicopter was a quick and handy way of seeing this thing.

Q: This evidence of World War II - does this remain apparent elsewhere in the Pacific?

Adm. M.: This is about the only one of the battle islands that I've seen since the war. Of course some of the atolls that I'd moored in with the North Carolina - I've never been back to any of them - and Guam is the only one that I've personally seen. Now, how much there would be, for instance, on Saipan, or Attu, or Okinawa - I don't know. It isn't a voluminous amount of wreckage but they have left something - not so much as monuments but, just left them there. Some U.S. - some Jap tanks. I imagine the submarines were probably all Jap.

One of the things that they recommended that I do was to promulgate to the squadron - A very interesting sight was the dumping of the garbage off a cliff out there. It was then used as a standard garbage disposal place and they had it built so that the trucks could come up and dump - and then they had railings for safety all around - and the sharks would immediately hit - by the score. It was fantastic.

Q: Feeding ground for them?

Adm. M.: Yes - and it was something that they thought the visiting ships would like to see - and we did - and I think each ship sent 50 or 60 men up there. They arranged the buses.

Q: To visit the garbage dump.

Adm. M.: To visit the garbage dump - and I suppose that tides were such - tides and current were such that what the sharks didn't eat never came back and bothered any beaches - it went on to sea, I suppose. But it really was impressive - the numbers and the violence of these creatures.

Q: I would think also it would be a deterrent for using any of the beaches on the island.

Adm. M.: Well, I think so - I think all the swimming was done inside. Now, I don't say near the naval base. I don't think there was any outside swimming. Other parts of the islands down at the south coast may or may not have been used for swimming - but it was a little scary. You know, you felt, if I stub a toe look what's going to happen to me down there. But it was a spectacular sight.

Then at Guam I was relieved by a good and old friend who, incidentally lives in Annapolis - Captain Tom

Cunningham, if you know him. He was our relief as ComDesRon 23. And then I flew home from Guam via Midway and several others - and we booked to Travis - and then from there commercial home to Annapolis, with orders to report to - as the commander - then called the Naval Weapons Laboratory Dahlgren.

Interview #7 with Rear Admiral Thomas H. Morton
Place: His residence in Annapolis, Maryland
Date: Tuesday, February 10, 1976
Interviewer: Dr. John T. Mason, Jr.

Q: It's good to see you on this beautiful day which gives promise of an early spring - whether we get it or not.

Last time you were talking about your command of the so-called "Little Beavers" destroyer squadron. I think you have a few other remarks to make about that command.

Adm. M.: Yes. There are just some interesting sidelights that happened in DesRon 23, in which the Edson was my flagship. I didn't mention that during the period in Long Beach there with the destroyers we were part of ASW Group 3 which was a command that was activated for specific exercises and the tactical command of the group commander was used over us for specific operations. Admiral Colestock, who I believe lives here now, was the ASW Group Commander. This, as I say, was for special operations - and really made no change in our organization in the Destroyer Force Pacific.

The ASW carrier was invariably the flagship, and the squadrons assigned to that group - to some extent - rotated but, we were always in Group 3 with him. He was always an aviator because of the ASW planes and the dunking sonars and things like that - but invariably the ASW group commander had a chief of staff - a captain experienced in destroyers - so that we had the normal link-up of air and surface ASW work; and they were always in tactical command.

One of the things that was interesting that I wanted to mention was that one operation at sea, the group commander wanted to see me as the squadron commander, and so we went alongside to transfer me by high line, to have this hour or two conference with the admiral and staff. And I got an MSG shortly after I got settled down which, in so many words said, "Dear Commodore: I'm glad you made it. We thought you'd want to know this is the first time we did this" - meaning the high line transfer of personnel.

Q: Aren't you glad that came afterwards?

Adm. M.: I still have that. Then, after I returned to the Edson, after the conference, I went by helicopter and and was lowered down with a winch and sling on the fantail of the Edson - very successfully, thank goodness. And again, the Edson skipper said, "Commodore, we thought you'd want to know this is the first time we've done this, too." So I had two means of ship-to-ship transportation, neither of which my flagship had ever done before.

Q: Let me ask, perhaps this is the logical place, to ask about the state of AS warfare at that time. Were there new techniques being employed?

Adm. M.: Yes. Well, the dunking sonar -

Q: Dunking sonar?

Adm. M.: One that's carried by a helicopter and lowered down into the water at a particular spot. And they could use it as either a group of them, with a sort of moving screen, or in the case of an actual contact, they would be able to detect the range and bearing of the contact.

Q: What depth capability did this sonar have?

Adm. M.: I don't remember how low down they could take that thing - but that wasn't too important really, because when you stop to think of it, a dunking sonar could easily go down below the level of the destroyers sonars. In other words, they had - perhaps more depth, but not a great deal more than the destroyers did. They didn't really have to go down too deep.

Then, other things were coming along. A few of the ships were experimenting with a thing called the DASH, which was a destroyer ASW. I can't remember what the H was for - but the acronym was DASH - and that was ship-launched - and then it would carry to the spot and then go into the water and become a torpedo. It combined the speed to go through the air a certain distance - and then the torpedo, when it got there, could home on the submarine.

Q: Sort of a magnetic nature, was it?

Adm. M.: Sonar - and had it's own sonar and its own directional capability.

The thing that I mentioned last time we met was the great responsibility put on the squadron commander who was designated as screen commander. Now, I understand, in connection with this Belknap collision with the carrier in the Mediterranean - I understand now that in a good many cases, particularly the carrier in a screen, the screen is maneuvered, ordered, shifted, and so forth, by the OTC, and not by the squadron commander. As a matter of fact, Lloyd Mustin told me this - and I think he's probably correct. And he feels very bitter about taking away the responsibilities and duties of the squadron or screen commander in such maneuvers. He wonders perhaps whether the Belknap collision was due to the fact that the destroyer commander - the unit commander present - had no real say in what the Belknap was doing.

Q: Was there not a court of inquiry on this matter?

Adm. M.: There is one - has been, yes - but I don't know the results, and I don't think he does either. But it was just a - as he called it - downgrading of the destroyer unit commander, and the fact that someone - more or less inexperienced with destroyer screens - was ordering these maneuvers. How much that had to do with the actual collision, I can't say.

The only other thing was - both in the Columbus and in the Edson there was considerable entertaining for me to do - and of course the Columbus was beautifully fitted-out with a large captain's cabin and mess and so forth, so during those days I was able to have any number of foreigners, civilians, military and their ladies to dinners in various places. And, also in the long journey home - the Columbus by herself, coming back from the Far East, I was able to have every officer up to dinner, which I did - either to dinner or lunch - in groups of six or eight.

Of course the Edson was much more cramped but still had adequate - what you might call - flag quarters. I was glad to have the chance of my own mess in both those ships because when I - going all the way back to the division command and the Hyman - I knew that most division commanders ate in the wardroom. I immediately put in my own system on this and insisted that I have my own mess in my own cabin. I felt that the skipper of the flagship should not have the division commander leaning over his shoulder at every meal - and I've always felt that way. Of course the squadron commanders have their own mess anyway.

These are just some thoughts I had since we last met - and now, we can go on from there.

Q: Well now, we got to February of 1960 when you became the Commander of the Weapons Laboratory at Dahlgren, Virginia. All right, sir.

Adm. M.: The experience at Dahlgren was a wonderful one. It was, perhaps, my very favorite shore duty - with possibly the experience at the United Nations in New York, years before, as the close runner-up.

Q: Now, tell me why it was such a happy experience.

Adm. M.: Well, you were in - to some extent free of the Washington bureaucracy, not entirely so - but it was not the sort of spinning of the wheels that you find in the

Pentagon and in the old Main Navy. It was also the only time that, in my shore duty tours, that I was truly in command - and command to me is something that - really, you might say I joined the Navy to move up to - So the fact that it was a pleasant and interesting station, more or less free of Washington and, as I say, a true command made it a very fine tour for me.

In connection with Washington, as all the shore establishments were in those days - and I suppose they are now - we were under the Military Command of what was then called the Potomac River Naval Command, and under the technical command of the chief of Bureau of Weapons. Admiral Stroup was the chief of bureau the whole time I was there, and when I took over, Admiral Mendenhall was the PRNC at the time - but was later succeeded by Admiral Tommy Robbins who, during that tour, and in later years in Washington, Admiral and Mrs. Robbins became among our very best friends. That was the command relationship.

The fact that I was commander of a shore station meant a lot of things that I'd never really thought of before - or realized would happen. You become - not only a commander, but also you become the chief of police and the almost senior chaplain for taking care of families - and all aspects of the community are referred to you in - you might say - in extremis. We had all sorts of things like that which - not necessarily to worry about but I mean, if a sailor boy or a civilian beat up his wife he would get called by the duty officer at 2 o'clock in the morning to have that duly reported to you. That sort of thing.

I said "senior chaplain" rather facetiously there because we had an excellent chaplain named Ben Hughes - Lieutenant Commander - who was able to take care of family crises, financial difficulties, and that sort of thing - through the Navy Relief and whatnot.

And while I mention the chaplain - the little church on the station at Dahlgren is rather interesting. We had - again something I'd never seen, but I'm sure you'd be familiar with - we had a four-sided altar, on a sort of turntable, so that we could have the Protestant altar, or the altar for the Jewish faith, or the altar for the Catholics - and then the fourth side of this turntable was a non-sectarian plain blank wall so that you could use it for things like Boy Scouts, or other meetings not to do with the Chapel - why we had it that way. It made it very fine. The chaplain was actually Protestant, but we had a trio of Catholic priests - to some extent - young ones, in a mission in Colonial Beach, which was only ten or fifteen miles away, and they took turns conducting the Catholic service with the chaplain, and other services that the Catholic faith required. We also had available a Jewish rabbi, but there were not too many of the Jewish faith there so that we didn't see him as much. We got to be very good friends with the three priests and Sue and I, and John were often invited down to their quarters for dinner and that sort of thing - and we saw them a lot at Dahlgren.

The laboratory was then organized - the technical part. This may, or may not be of interest - the technical side had three main laboratories. The K Lab, so called, was the computer part of the work. The T Lab was the terminal ballistics laboratory.

Q: Terminal?

Adm. M.: Terminal ballistics - such as armor plate and bomb analysis after impact and that sort of thing. And then the third one was the W Lab for weapons. I'll go into them a little bit later.

In addition to that of course, we had the administrative department. We had the public works, and we had our own police force and our own fire department, and of course we had the fiscal division - budget and finance. Under the administrative officer were the main part - the bulk of the enlisted personnel. There were only about 100, 120. Incidentally, the population of Dahlgren - as far as workers of all types - was about 2,000. I'd say 50 or 60 officers and 120 enlisted men, and the rest civilian - of both scientific and service personnel. By service I mean budget and public works.

Incidentally, in 1960, when I took over, I was rather fortunate, because for some years before - the budget cuts in Washington and the reorganization of the bureaus and that sort of thing, had almost condemned Dahlgren to closing. But, with the advent of the vast computer program, and that sort of thing, Dahlgren had taken on a new life and was safe for the reasonable future, as far as staying in commission.

The bulk of the enlisted men I mentioned were in what we called the Waterfront Division, and they had the important job of patrolling the river when we were actually firing. They had regular patrol boats with experienced crews and -

Q: To keep fisherman away, and that sort of thing?

Adm. M.: Yes. Fishermen and private yachts and that sort of thing. The charts of the river were extremely well laid out in that anybody would know where the danger areas were, but you always have the fellow who is either ignorant or careless. So they kept the private boats on the river out of trouble.

Now, the W Lab had several functions. Of course, they did most of the firing, and that sort of thing - and they had two rather interesting departments which I might mention. They had the HERO Division, which was "hazards of electronic radiation on ordnance" - and they had all sorts of turntables, and instruments and things - that they could take a radar for instance, or a transmitter, and play it on a - particularly on an airplane - on the turntable - and they could chart exactly where, at what angles and distances and so forth, the aircraft ordnance would be hazarded by this radar transmission. They'd had accidents aboard ship from this sort of thing - radars training on armed aircraft on deck. And this division had the purpose of minimizing this danger, by various methods, such as shielding and safe distances and that sort of thing - and they did a very fine job, and a very important one for the Navy - in my opinion.

The other interesting division of the W Lab was the CAD Division, which was "cartridge activated devices." Now, the bulk of these were such things as ejection seats, and that sort of thing - and they were continually developing these cartridge activated devices for various and many uses other than ejection seats. Those were two rather important - small, but important divisions of the W Lab.

Q: Was there anything that pertained to submarines and escape mechanism under that division?

Adm. M.: I don't recall any at the time. Most of it was aircraft.

Now the T Lab - terminal ballistics was the one that investigated the dispersal of bomb fragments and the efficacy of armor plate and that sort of thing. And, over at a place across the creek, but still on laboratory property, we had the Pumpkin Neck Facility - named because this particular peninsula was called Pumpkin Neck. Over there they had these large circular stockades - circular screens - and they could detonate bombs of fairly high capacity, and then would study the fragments pattern after - in various angles, and so forth - and that was the main source of our noise, and broken china and broken lamps, which occasionally happened down there. It was just one of those things that you put up with.

Q: I might ask about the attitude of civilians who lived in the surrounding area. Did they object sometimes to the excessive noises?

Adm. M.: Because of the size of the place, they were reasonably far away. In other words, the quarters on the laboratory were the ones that were much the closest. Now there were some outside, but most of them were Dahlgren employees anyway - and it's just like these people who choose to live near an airport. These people owned these houses - large and small - and lived there by choice with their eyes open.

Q: Well, that doesn't necessarily apply around airports because I've seen threats of suits, and so forth - most recently in connection with the Concorde.

Adm. M.: I know. Well, that's why I mentioned it. I think it's absolutely ridiculous, when you put an airport in an isolated position such as Dulles once was, and then immediately the industrial and residential developments start around the airport, just because it's there and has the roads. And how anybody that can build a house, or buy one, near an operating airport and then complain about the noise - I've never understood this.

Q: Charge it up to human nature, I guess.

Adm. M.: I know. I think they have absolutely no right to complain about the Concorde.

Q: Did you have any problems with so-called environmentalists down there?

Adm. M.: No, we didn't, though we had one man - I think he was in T Lab - a man named Payne - and he was our game warden, as additional duty, and he was very active in, particularly the wild life point of view, and he was officially the Virginia Game Warden working on government property.

Q: I was thinking in terms of protecting the wild life, and being agitated because of some of your experiments, and the threat that this might have to the life of -

Adm. M.: Of course the ecology hadn't come along as strong as it is these days, but on the other hand, Dahlgren had been functioning since 1917 and it was sort of taken for granted that these things might happen - but there were never any official complaints because of the fact that, after all it had been forty years or more that it had been going on.

Q: There must have been some interesting things in this particular lab - the T Lab - at that time - projects that were to the fore. Can you recall any of them?

Adm. M.: There was a good bit of work going on SHAPE charges, which of course had come in during World War II.

Q: SHAPE charges?

Adm. M.: They were originally a German development but the British and American - both I remember used them, in my experience in London. They were actually shaped charges. They were sort of like - you might say like a funnel, and the design of the bomb, or charge, was such that it focused like you focus a flashlight beam - and they were very much used in World War II for demolition - blowing up bridges and that sort of thing.

Q: I see. Pinpointing things.

Adm. M.: Pinpointing, yes. Much more oomph on a very small area than you'd get from just a plain charge.

They were still, but to a greatly reduced degree, testing armor plate - at various thicknesses, angles, and so forth.

You mentioned the complaints from outside. The only cases that I remember were - in some of the firings down river the people with houses on the shoreline occasionally had such things as broken windows and cracked ceilings - and, we just had an automatic sort of procedure to handle this and were able to pay them indemnity right on the spot - after due investigation. But this didn't come up a great deal because of the fact that the distances were allowed for safety, and it was only the rare, big bang, or something like that that would do any real damage.

But that was not a cause for any animosity because we took care of it so quickly and promptly there was never any back-firing.

One of the things down the river, by the way, was Blackstone Island - or St. Clemente's

Q: Blackstone Island?

Adm. M.: Blackstone Island - and also called St. Clemente - and this had been used during the war as a target area for large caliber projectiles, but was no longer in the firing range now, but it was an interesting place to go. It had a big, 40 or 50-foot concrete cross on it - and the reason for this cross was the fact that the <u>Ark and the Dove</u>, when they'd come to settle what turned out to be Maryland - before they went ashore near St. Mary's they had their first Mass on this island. In other words, the ships dropped the people there and had a Mass, and then they went onto the Maryland mainland.

It was interesting during the last few months that I was there, the <u>Baltimore Sun</u> predominantly, started a campaign to try to get that released to the State of Maryland.

Q: It was Federal property?

Adm. M.: Yes, it was still part of the station - and after

collecting all the data, and so forth - while I was there, the machinery went forward to release the island to the state of Maryland, which was done either before I left or just after. I played a small but important part in this transfer. I don't know exactly what they're using it for now - of course it's no longer Federal property - it was released.

Q: It has been uninhabited though?

Adm. M.: Yes, it was completely uninhabited. You could take the gig down there - with a party - and it was an interesting place to go - completely barren and waste but the cross itself made it quite a landmark.

Q: Would it be, in any sense, a substitute for Vieques?

Adm. M.: It had been, but not since World War II.

Q: Perhaps the Navy's sorry it released it, then?

Adm. M.: The firing down the river in the 1960s was such that we didn't need a land target really. I mean, it didn't require it - it was air bursts or rockets, or something like that, and we didn't actually need a long-range land area for impact.

Now, going to K Lab - the computer. Of course, they were the most important of the three laboratories there. The K for computer merely was an arbitrary symbol because of the fact that the Command organization - commander, deputy commander, and so forth - were designated by the symbol C.

The computer organization was the largest of all - and really I guess the most important, since it had gone from the old type of proving ground to the Naval Weapons Laboratory - and also the Dahlgren computers had been the Navy's best known, and best, for many years as the computer game evolved. Nearly all of ours were IBM - or the bigger ones were IBM, but with others always being considered when a new installation was going in.

One of the most important things that grew up in these two years that I was there was the Space Surveillance Laboratory, which was located there because of our great computer capacity - and became really an independent command - an operational command - for satellite tracking.

Q: Was it related to NASA then?

Adm. M.: No, it was not related to NASA, but we did report our tracking results to NORAD - in Colorado - as part of not only the air defense angle but the fact that these were up there. This Space Surveillance Command came into being in early '61 and was there solely - as I say - because of our capacity in these computations.

To staff this command, they had to take some of our people - transfer them - and there was a certain amount of bitterness about this new outfit, and I sort of fought it bitterly up in the Bureau of Weapons - but, looking back now - and even at the time when the thing was settled - I realized that a research shore station should not also be an operational command, which this was. So, it was evolved and the Commander of Space Surveillance was a subordinate to the Commander of the Naval Laboratory.

Q: He was under you?

Adm. M.: He was under me, but largely because he was there. In other words, his command and mine worked very closely together, but he had his own operational commanders, and so forth, separate from the laboratory.

The computers also got quite a lot of interesting side work. They worked very closely with the War Games Division of CNO, and they also had a most important thing in the fire control printouts for the POLARIS submarines. This was entirely done at Dahlgren.

They also had considerable liaison work with the Marine Corps on amphibious operations - that is this sort of war game concept of amphibious operation. We had a few Marine Corps officers there just for that purpose.

The POLARIS fire control plan was probably one of the most - not famous - but best known of Dahlgren's programs. We continually had submarine officers and staff officers from the various squadrons come down there and just see how we evolved these things for them. Now, this meant the actual fire control data for - you might say - any target that POLARIS would conceivably fire on and from any part of the world. So we were really the fire control computer for the submarine - or at least developed the guts to go into their computer.

I remember Admiral Grenfell, who was then ComSubLant. Incidentally, I'll go into that. We had an awful lot of visitors down there - official and otherwise - foreign and U.S. Admiral Grenfell came to get the presentation on POLARIS - and with several members of his staff - and we had the standard presentation we could give him. And, it fell - I won't say it fell to Sue and me - but it was our pleasure to be able to entertain these visitors. The thing was scheduled so they got all their work done in the morning, and then we would adjourn to lunch at the club - if it was a very large party - but usually at our quarters. Admiral Grenfell had been president of my class, and the senior officer at the Industrial College, so I knew him fairly well - peach of a man.

I think he was due about 9:30, but at 9 o'clock we

got this call from his aide back in Norfolk who said, "You might not know it but the admiral always had Metracal for lunch." And, here we'd planned this huge sit-down dinner or fancy buffet and all that food - we always had some of the Dahlgren people, too.

Q: What a blow to a hostess.

Adm. M.: Yes. Well, our hostess sent the steward we had up to the commissary and they didn't have any so finally she - without trusting our good Filipino steward to go out in the village - she forced herself out, and finally got some Metracal and brought it back - at 10 o'clock or so, and, of course the admiral was in our hands by then and the luncheon wasn't til maybe 1 or 2 o'clock so there was plenty of time. But anyway, when the admiral arrived after the tours of Dahlgren and the presentation, and so forth, we jokingly said, "Admiral, we've got your Metracal." And he was furious. He said, "That damn aide. I'm going to fire him. He ought to know that I have Metracal every day for lunch, but when I'm on an official visit, I certainly don't want it." He said, "You keep the Metracal and give me anything you have, but give me the same thing as the others." That's what he got. I never knew what happened to that aide. I know he must have caught hell though.

Q: At least he got straightened out. What about your relationship in terms of this lab with CinCLant?

Adm. M.: None directly I would think. In connection with what? The POLARIS job, you mean?

Q: In connection with the computers and so forth.

Adm. M.: No, because the results of satellite tracking and that sort of thing were really of interest to, as you say, NASA and NORAD, and that - but none directly with the U.S. Fleet that I can think of. Those were the remarkable results - to see these things. As these satellites broke up - such as our Vanguard when we finally got it up in the air, up in space - then they'd begin to disintegrate and we could identify the original satellite, including all the Russian's. They were all plotted. And then we could even identify things like wires and springs where they were disintegrating in space - and you could see an expanding group of garbage - as they call it - debris, as these satellites finally wore themselves out.

As I remember, when a satellite, of any type, got down to - my recollection was 89 seconds - then it hit the atmosphere. In other words, regardless of its size or anything else, its speed determined the altitude that it would orbit in - and with a gradual diminishing of staying away from the earth. In other words, gradually descending - and as I recall, it was either 86 or 89 seconds. No satellite could avoid just coming into the atmosphere and burning up -

Q: And it burned up completely when it came into the atmosphere? There was no danger of particles falling?

Adm. M.: I never recall, during that time, of any particle falling anywhere. As a matter of fact, I think that's still true today.

Q: Well, that's a comforting thought.

Adm. M.: Yes, it is. It's sort of the idea of the meteorite. There are relatively very few that hit the earth. There are some. There were occasional scares in the last few years where somebody reported something falling, which may well have been. But, on the other hand it usually turned out to be something off an aircraft, or something.

We had lots of that type of visitors there, including the foreigners. We had French and Norwegian, and of course a lot of British - plus the people like the Assistant Secretaries of the Navy and Assistant Secretary of Defense, and various flag officers - and it was quite a chore, but a happy and interesting one to entertain these people because invariably the lunch was on the schedule - and we had one steward in training, and he did the best he could for a four-stripe commander - but it was hard work but tremendously interesting -

Q: And all these visitors were largely people who spoke the same language? Ordnance? In addition to these momentary visitors - day visitors, or what have you - were there any foreigners who came and had access to the studies that were being made?

Adm. M.: Yes, there were several. They'd come and stay maybe a week or so. In addition to that - in the HERO Division, at hazards of electronic radiation - one of our key officers was a Wing Commander Gray, Royal Air Force - and he was there as a permanent officer. In other words, he had a full tour at Dahlgren assigned by the RAF, through the British Embassy. He was one of the station's regular officers.

Q: Now, we had counterparts abroad?

Adm. M.: Yes, we did. I don't know who they were. But, Gray was an acknowledged expert on this and it was mutually beneficial, both to us and the RAF and the British to have this fellow there. He was really good at it.

Q: Were there any experiments which were withheld from foreigners?

Adm. M.: Not in his purview. The HERO thing - the British and Americans were working on it pretty closely together.

Q: It was a mutual problem?

Adm. M.: Right - a mutual problem.
　　Incidentally, on that entertainment thing. It was really an expensive proposition for me, personally, because they had this rule long in effect, that I was reimbursed for any foreign group that came there, including any Americans who accompanied them, but if it was strictly an American group - Navy, Air Force, whatever - it came out of my pocket.

Q: What was the justification for a policy like that?

Adm. M.: Well, I don't know that. Although you were expected to do it, I suppose you might say that - someone could say, "Well, you didn't have to give a luncheon." But, why not, it made it much more interesting. The foreign thing was cut and dried because of the fact that it was financed under the MDAP - by the CNO people - and, you'd very promptly get a personal check.

Q: Were you permitted to serve liquor?

Adm. M.: Oh, yes, very much so.

Q: And that was compensated, too.

Adm. M.: The cost of a foreign party was accepted by my voucher. It was never questioned. Incidentally, speaking of liquor, we had a very fine Officer's Club - Officer's and civilian scientists, of course - and a very fine NCO Club - and they both had wine messes. In other words, we were considered an isolated station - which was very true because there were practically no liquor stores in the little hamlets outside.

Q: What relationship did you have with the testing facilities?

Adm. M.: Nothing direct - except that they would ask us for help if they needed it - in some of the development of new ordnance.

Q: What was it known as - ComDevFor?

Adm. M.: It used to be called ComOpDevFor and then they changed it to ComOpTevFor. We would send our teams out, as requested by them - and very often did. Now, the picture you saw of the Little Rock firing the missile there. That was taken by our crew, and that particular picture was developed and framed to give me as their commanding officer. There was a continual flow like that - but usually, either Dahlgren offered to send experts, or they asked Bureau of Weapons to have us send some. And, of course, I suppose the same thing applied at the Mine Depot and others.

Q: Did they still have the Mississippi in your time there?

Adm. M.: No, the Mississippi had gone out by then - or was about to. I just don't remember where I was when the Mississippi decommissioned - because she was an old ship of mine. I can't answer exactly when she did go.

Q: Did you visit their testing facilities over there?

Adm. M.: Where's this?

Q: They were stationed in Norfolk, were they not?

Adm. M.: Oh, yes - no, I never personally went down there - whether it was the Mississippi or not, I didn't go down. We had plenty of experts that we could send - teams, large or small, for whatever the project was - and did. But, I never personally went down.

Q: Now, Patuxent was developing quite thoroughly. Did you have any relationship with them?

Adm. M.: Practically none, really. I think we had relationship - like cooperation you might say - exchange of ideas. Patuxent test flights, and all that sort of thing were really not in our sphere of interest.

Q: Except for the ejection - you were talking about that.

Adm. M.: Oh, now that - yes. Undoubtedly our people did work with Patuxent on that - and probably with the Bureau of Aeronautics - but, not in a formal way, with Patuxent.

We had some - not to the point of research, but we had some informal and close relationships with the Army at Fort A.P. Hill, because they happened to be a station near us. A.P. Hill was the one who got in some trouble two years ago. Too many people visiting the hunting lodges and shooting deer and whatnot - sort of like the Rockwell-Lockheed business of today.

On the social line - when we got there, I was horrified to find out that since 1917, I guess, the Commander had always been "at home" every Tuesday - or every Thursday, and people would come with their white gloves and calling cards. And, I stopped that as soon as I entered the station because I figured, from other places I'd been stationed, that was sort of getting archaic - and also, I didn't feel like spending one day a week with my family, waiting for someone else to come - with possibly none coming. So, we went down the list and gave two big receptions for civilian and military - mixed, of course. And, in those two parties - of say eighty or so each - that was considered all the calls made and returned.

Q: Did Susan go along with this modernization?

Adm. M.: Oh, yes - very much so. She didn't like this white gloves attitude either.

Some of the things we tried to do down there - When I say we, that includes Sue. She wasn't involved in all of them but for instance, she found - in spite of the altar guild and the various organizations which she participated in on the station - that there'd never been an enlisted wives club, so she got some of the senior petty officers and their wives, to sound them out as to interest, and by the time we'd left there the enlisted wives club was a very successful and going concern, which I give her credit for because I had nothing to do with that really - except to okay it.

Q: What sort of objectives would a club like that have?

Adm. M.: Why, it was just the idea that here you had 100 enlisted men - 120 and maybe, say 50 of them had wives on the station - I'm guessing at the number - and that no one had ever given them a chance to get together and plan for - say Christmas, or whatever they wanted to do, unless they did it on their own - so the idea was to have a formal club with elected officers just as you'd have at a woman's club anywhere, of any kind. No particular objective except to give them something of interest.

Q: Adding to the social structure of the command?

Adm. M.: Yes. The other thing that happened - in my last year there I guess, was the beginning of construction for a housing development - the town houses and detached houses - outside of the station. A lot of people did not want to live in Dahlgren quarters. I'm talking now about the civilians - technicians, scientists, whatnot - but there was not enough housing really, except in the Fredericksburg area, for them. So Bittersweet - or whatever the name of the project was - was started and it was very welcome and much needed. The quarters at Dahlgren - or the senior scientists and senior officer's quarters - are very fine indeed, but then as you went down through the grades - both military and civilian, and of course enlisted - they got progressively inferior, so that a lot of our junior people lived in a place which had the World War II nickname of Boomtown, and Boomtown was more or less deteriorating, and then when they built the addition and the new computer lab down there a lot of Boomtown had to go so the quarters situation was getting a little tight and this outside housing was a welcome thing - and I hope was successful.

Q: Was there any difficulty in getting the necessary funds for that project?

Adm. M.: No. It was getting the commercial interests interested. In other words, they were not government housing loans -

Q: Oh, they were not?

Adm. M.: No, but it was a case of the Bureau of Ordnance and the Bureau of Yards and Docks getting somebody interested in showing them what the possibilities were, and why it was needed, and how it would be - frankly, a profitable thing for them. I hope it worked out because it certainly was badly needed.

Q: You were talking about how much housing? How many units were you talking about?

Adm. M.: I think it started out at around - I'm guessing when I say 40 - something like that. We had a lot of our senior people in the civilian side - the scientific side - who lived in Fredericksburg by choice. They preferred it to government quarters which, by reason of their rank, they would rate at Dahlgren but, just by their own choice they wanted to live outside.

Another thing that was interesting was the fact that the scientists at K Lab - and Field Lab - got the inspiration, in the summer of '60, to work with the school authorities in King George County to have any students who wanted to get work for remedying deficiencies or outside studies - and we had about six or eight of the K Lab people who actually taught these classes every Saturday morning. It was very well received in the community of course, and I'm sure was a great help to the students concerned. Now, these were men - most of them young men - who evolved this idea all by themselves - just wanted to see if it would go, and it did go very well - and I don't know how long it continued, or whether it's still going on. But it was strictly a volunteer thing, and something to offer to the outside community.

Dahlgren had its own school for dependents of all personnel, right on the station - and that carried up through the eighth grade - and as far as I know, when the children went out to the ninth grade - in high school in King George, I think they did very well there. The school was very well administered by Mr. Settle, who was the principal - and had been for years - and he had full-time teachers.

Q: I've heard various men say that when stationed at Dahlgren one of the things they enjoyed so very much was hunting. What about your proclivities in that area?

Adm. M.: Well, I'm not a hunter or a fisherman - but particularly the hunting - now this Lloyd Payne that I mentioned was a technical employee and also the game warden - we would have guests down there during the season for hunting and he would always organize the thing and pick the area, and so forth. The Mustins were down and Dick Landford, down the road here, then a congressman from this area.

Q: Probably the Moorer's too. Were they not there?

Adm. M.: No. But that was very successful.

Now, another thing. Again, I'm not a golfer either, but there was a very nice course right in the middle of the station. It winds around among the roads and quarters and things and, it's golfers heaven down there really, they always said. It's a flag course and only nine holes, but well kept - and if you were a golfer or a hunter you were certainly in the pink down there.

We also had a concrete skating rink which would be flooded every winter, and of course ths swimming pool at the club was a fine one. We had bowling - lots of facilities for anybody who wanted to use them - tennis courts.

Q: It was a self-contained community?

Adm. M.: It was entirely self-contained - and it really had to be because you had to go miles to go anywhere really, so you had to have the facilities for the relaxation of both the men and their families - of all ages and grades.

There was a lot of boating too. A lot of them had their own private boats, and we had a little marina which was not government land but was right outside the station - and we also had inside the station, for small craft, what we called the Dahlgren Boat Club, and they were authorized to keep their various small sail boats and that sort of thing there. It was a membership thing. So, you had a fairly large marina outside for the bigger private boats, and then a facility inside the station for the smaller - sail boats and outboards and that sort of thing.

So there was plenty in the way of recreation but, as you say, it was in the confines of a relatively small town.

The 4th of July was a real big day down there. The commander's gig and his family and guests traditionally led the boat parade - and we had the Mustin's, among others, down there for that. And, we had one fellow who was one of the pioneers in this water ski soaring. He'd attach his skis to his towing boat and then he'd - in these big sort of bat wings - go flying up. Sort of like this - what do they call it - on the mountainsides. They're doing it a lot now?

Q: Gliders.

Adm. M.: Yes. Hand gliding is it? Some name like that.

Incidentally, part of the 4th of July ceremonies - events - was an afternoon swimming meet, and Lloyd Mustin and I being ardent, old swimmers - and Lloyd particularly his reputation as a young man - we entered the 50-yard or 100-yard dash against two young men at Dahlgren. There was this big fanfare over the public address system, "Rear Admiral Lloyd Mustin and in Wing three our commanding officer, Captain Morton," and so forth. Surprisingly enough, with Lloyd's collegiate reputation of years and years ago, one of these young fellows at Dahlgren was the son of somebody down there who'd beat Lloyd. The order of the ones that I knew - remember - Mustin was second and Morton was fourth - in a race of four people - but it was fun.

Other things you had to do there in that community - I had to give the graduating address at the school every year - and all that sort of thing. As I say, you were mayor and chief of police and everything else.

The term commander, in those days, came from the fact that during the war and post-war period the commanding officer down there was a flag officer - Admiral Bill Kitts, and others - and when, in later years - '50s - the command reverted down to a four-stripe billet, they never changed the name to commanding officer. They left it as the Commander, U.S. Naval Weapons Laboratory, for some reason I don't know - so that the title was Commander rather than CO.

Those quarters down there - particularly the Commander's quarters - were absolutely beautiful. I would say they are probably the finest captain's quarters that I know of in the Navy - they really were.

The sort of quarters for the senior civilians and the commanders and up - lieutenant commanders maybe - were really equally good. They were built in the days when people built houses and somehow Dahlgren got the money to do all this back in the post-war period.

Incidentally Dahlgren - I think dates to 1917 - but it started in World War I as an adjunct or annex - an early detached annex of Indian Head, Maryland - and somewhere along there, either during World War I or in the post-war years became a separate command.

During the time there we tried to carry on a Dahlgren tradition which had gone on for some years of knowing the sort of prominent people in the area - well outside the station - and we entertained - we for them and them for us while we were there, and among them was Admiral Ballentine who I served with in the United Nations, and also had gotten to know him very well when he had the Sixth Fleet carriers. He and Mrs. Ballentine, by then were old friends. He had retired and they lived at Dogue in a beautiful old rambling farm house there. And there were others there who lived in the area between Dahlgren and Colonial Beach with very fine homes. Camden was one of them, where I believe the Pratt family lived. Stony Point was another. Stony Point was - he was very prominent with one of the steel companies in Pittsburgh. They were an interesting group - they really were, and very much worthwhile in keeping touch with and having them over and we being with them in their homes.

Q: That was a nice respite, was it not, and one in your own area - in your own field?

Adm. M.: Yes.

Q: And a much more relaxed command?

Adm. M.: Yes, it was an ideal command from that point of view and, as I say, it was my only shore command which was one of the reasons I liked it. I would have stayed there by choice rather than go anywhere else - at least for the next year or so.

Q: But that was not your fate?

Adm. M.: That was not my fate when the selection board put their rear admiral stars on me. I was no longer welcome at Dahlgren. I wouldn't say that, but it was not a flag billet so that was it.

Q: So, it all came to an end in September of '61?

Adm. M.: Yes. I usually took my large portion of my leave in that sort of season - August, and we went down to the Great Smokies Cataloochie Ranch, which was a wonderful spot. We'd been there in '60 and '61 - and some years later it became an all-year-round event rather than just summer and fall. We still hear from the owners and they're thriving and year round. They had a nice lodge, wonderful country food, and nice little cabins - or cottages and Sue and our son and I went down there those two summers.

We went into Ashville to visit friends - which was only about ten miles from Cataloochie - and from there we went to see the Vanderbilt estate - Belmont - and from there we went with our friends to a small cocktail party in Ashville, and we got back to our friends house where we started off in Ashville and John had stayed there with them and he came running out and said, "Dad, you made it." "Made what?" He said, "You're an admiral." Apparently, what had happened was that, as I think I mentioned some interviews ago, my sister Emily had called up and traced me down there through the duty officer at Dahlgren. And Admiral Chick Hayward was another who called up. I missed talking with my sister and Admiral Hayward - Chick. And then the third person who called - just after we got back to the house - was Admiral Tom Robbins, who was, as I said, was my military boss at the time - and Tommy couldn't do less than just read me the whole list - all 35 of them - to see how many I knew - and of course, I knew them all. There were a great number of my classmates on that particular year.

So when we got back to the ranch - Cataloochie - they

had a great big 50-foot banner with "Welcome, Admiral" on it, and had a picture of Sue riding a horse, I guess, with Old Dog on it, and Johnny also riding a horse, and me drinking a martini, on this poster. And then I got several calls there from various people, and the owners said that the operator had called up and said, "What's with all the calls for this guy Morton? Did he get married or something?" The local operator was completely baffled by this barrage - so that was quite a thrill, I must say.

When we got back to Dahlgren I found that all the officers and senior civilians were gathered in the big back patio of the quarters and there were stars and things all over the windows and eaves. They'd really decorated the place - and every one of them was there by the time we arrived. We found out later that they were very ingenious on the timing. Somebody had remembered that we'd taken our beloved cat, who we had had several years, and put him in the kennel about five or ten miles away - during our stay down at the ranch. So they made arrangements with the kennel people that as soon as we picked up the cat to call the duty officer at Dahlgren - or my secretary - whichever it was - so that's how they organized the thing and had it all ready.

Q: Well, that meant you had to leave Dahlgren. Did it mean also that you had to go to some newly selected flag officer's indoctrination group?

Adm. M.: Well, I guess I went to one of the junior ones. The one that I went to from there - and I went fairly quickly because they sort of immediately had the relief on the way. I went up to relieve Brick Blackburn who was then going to sea in a carrier division - as the war games assistant to CNO. This is the job he had and it's the one that I'd worked with quite a bit down at Dahlgren because of our computers.

Q: But did you not have, in those days, also a group meeting of newly selected flag officers?

Adm. M.: Yes, they still had that, and I guess still do. Some years they'd had about a four or five day meeting in Washington where you had certain briefings, and all that, of various kinds; and then receptions and cocktail parties. The only one that I was able to make, because of the fact that my relief had arrived, and I had to leave before the end of August, they excused me from joining this whole working week - so they asked me if I would like to come up to the Decatur House for a reception with the selectees.

You're right. They had that four or five day gathering.

Q: Well, what is the content of that indoctrination then - that week long indoctrination?

Adm. M.: Of course I wasn't there, but I had seen the agenda of others - previous ones. I think it was a sort of a seminar like the presentation by the Bureau of Personnel and by -

Q: By each of the bureaus - I see.

Adm. M.: Yes, that sort of thing.

Q: I wondered if it didn't heavily accent ordnance.

Adm. M.: No, not at all. I imagine ordnance had a presentation - and probably CinCLant Fleet. They had various - and of course a lot of fiscal and budget work - but, as I say, the only thing they felt that I should come to was the reception at the Decatur House, which was quite pleasant.

Q: Well, now we're entering a new and interesting assignment in September of '61 when you became assistant for war gaming in the office of the CNO. Tell me about the scope of that particular job.

Adm. M.: It was just as it sounds - presenting to CNO and the OpNavs any study that we felt would be of interest or that some OpNav office had requested us to do. One of the biggest studies during my tenure there was the submarine and aircraft barrier - more or less across the North Sea - to prevent the Russian submarines from getting out into the Atlantic.

Q: It was from Spitzbergen?

Adm. M.: Yes, up in that area - Baltic, and so forth. We used all sorts of empirical assumptions and types of craft, types of weapons - the homing torpedoes and so forth - dropped by air, and others - antisubmarine torpedoes fired by - so we evolved the barrier scene and the number of various types required, and made a study that showed - at least in our opinion, and the submarines opinion - that given this particular force that there'd be very few Russian submarines get through undetected.

Q: Your determination was that it would be relatively successful, then?

Adm. M.: Yes, it would. Not necessarily killing of Russian submarines, but the fact that they would not get out in the Atlantic in great numbers. Now that dragged on for some time. These things take months, you know - there's detailed work in them. Meanwhile, we were passing stuff to Dahlgren to do.

As I say, my predecessor there was Brick Blackburn. Tom Moorer had been war game assistant when I was with Chick Hayward.

Q: Yes, he had been - and had a great deal to do with the Joint Chiefs.

Adm. M.: Yes. That was our big project. I don't remember exactly how long I stayed in, what was then called Op-06.

Q: You were there until 1962 - July of '62, so it was less than a year.

Adm. M.: Less than a year - that's right.

Q: Now, let me ask about that. When you were developing a project like this one in the North Sea, did this occupy your entire attention, as a group of war gamers?

Adm. M.: Pretty much so. In other words, there might have been minor projects here and there, but the general work of my staff - my office - was entirely with the current project which was, for a large part of my stay there was this.

Q: How many were there on the staff?

Adm. M.: Let's see - we had - I'd say six or eight officers at the most - with a few young personnel - that sort of thing. It was a small group - very small.

Q: Of specialists?

Adm. M.: Yes.

Q: Were these ideas always generated somewhere else or were they generated sometimes within your own organization?

Adm. M.: It could be either. Some particular OpNav office could ask us to do a certain study, whereas in this case I think it was our own idea - with the interest in that sort of Russian submarine affair. I think we offered to do it and they gave us the go ahead.

Q: Well, I would gather then that these studies had, very often, more relevance to the present situation than do some of the contingency plans and that sort of thing that we develop.

Adm. M.: Yes, I think that's right. It could be highly hypothetical or imaginative - or it could be something that applies to this month, this week. But, it's a detailed grind to do one of those things.

Q: What do you mean by that?

Adm. M.: Well, I mean it takes so much meticulous work - and any number of assumptions. This, I think is one of the weaknesses of wargaming. There's too much dependent on too many assumptions. I mean, what percentage of time will a torpedo operate correctly? And that sort of thing. The assumptions you make are so enormous in number that when you feed it in to the problem as a whole you really wonder what accuracy you have. It's an interesting study but it's one that could be way off base if the thing actually took place.

Q: Is it also based in part upon say, the lessons learned in the last war - and the assumption there being that the next war is going to be a continuation of the last war?

Adm. M.: Well, we took the more modern weapons that were avilable. The torpedo I think was the Mk. 48 - I could be wrong on the Mach number - which of course was just coming into development then. I'd say it was based on the experience of the last war plus advances in such things as sonar and torpedoes and radar - aircraft. You had to start somewhere, you see. It would be too much of a big problem to hook this in with - say an atomic attack or something like that. In other words, it was an isolated problem.

Q: What role did existing information avilable from intelligence sources play in the drama?

Adm. M.: We had lots of material from ONI. We could get almost anything we wanted in the way of Russian submarine capabilities, numbers, where based, and so forth. We had unlimited sources such as that - with no trouble of getting them.

But, as I say, I am a little skeptical about wargaming, when you really come down and say 10% this and 20% that. I can't conceive of the fact of being accurate - necessarily accurate.

Q: Wherein does this kind of wargaming differ from the classical type we used to hear about at the Naval War College?

Adm. M.: Where they actually played it on a board?

Q: Yes.

Adm. M.: Well, it presumably would solve the same problem, but much more accurately. In other words, the war games, as we used to call them at the War College - In the old time war college games, that the judgment of the commanders involved in the game entered more than it would in these intricate computerized games. In other words, the wargaming in OpNav when I was there really left nothing to anyones judgment. It was cut and dried, with no command judgment whatsoever - except maybe strategically. But tactically operating an aircraft, or a destroyer, or submarine, or whatever, there was no capability of taking any human judgment into effect.

Q: Because of the computer?

Adm. M.: Because of that, yes.

Q: Now, explain to me how all the data was fed into the computer. How was it organized, or collected, or what?

Adm. M.: Well, you start off by saying that a particular classification of ASW aircraft - barrier flown - that the radar will detect a snorkling submarine at such-and-such a range, and with so much accuracy. And then you have to take into effect what is the submarine going to do when he knows he's been tracked. Is he going to submerge or, if it's night, is he going to zig zag?

Q: How far can he escape?

Adm. M.: Yes, right - but all down sort of in theory, mathematically correct, but, again subject - very seriously I think - to the assumptions going into it. But, there was no way, at least in those days, of determining well, what is the aircraft pilot going to do, or what can he do under the terms of his barrier?

Q: Does he have any options?

Adm. M.: That's right. I really think they're an interesting exercise, but I was never too enthusiastic about them.

Q: Have any of these exercises been actually tested?

Adm. M.: Not that I know of.

Q: That would be the answer, would it not?

Adm. M.: That would be the answer, yes - true - and probably it would come out totally different.

Q: The one you worked on was exclusive of the involvement

of any atomic weaponry?

Adm. M.: That's right.

Q: Are there other war games that involve atomic -

Adm. M.: There were some going on in the Joint Chiefs of Staff - in their special study group which, incidentally I went to from the war gaming - Navy wargaming office - and when we come to that I can give you a little bit on that period.

In addition to the wargaming itself, we had occasional questions from the fleet - particularly, staff officers would come in and ask us to do this and that on a sort of small scale job - just really for curiosity more than anything else, I think.

As one of the flag officers in what was then called 0-6 - and it was Admiral Sharp by the way - we attended his briefings and de-briefings, in each case, of a JCS meeting. It was automatic. We'll say the JCS met Tuesdays and Thursdays - I've forgotten the way it was actually - and he was the sort of working deputy for CNO. If CNO didn't actually attend, why Sharp was his representative.

Q: And CNO at that time was Arleigh Burke?

Adm. M.: Arleigh Burke, right. Now, wait a minute, was Burke still there? No, I think Admiral George Anderson had come in by then - and then by the time that I left the Navy, I think Admiral McDonald was the CNO. I believe Burke still was up.

Q: Burke was there until - well, a short time after Senator Kennedy became President.

Adm. M.: Yes, '61 - because I remember Admiral Burke very well in the Chick Hayward days - but I think he'd retired by then. It was George Anderson most of the time I was there.

Q: You said, a little earlier, that the barrier scheme - implied the barrier scheme was evolved from this particular study. Was the barrier across the North Atlantic - the early warning system - was that somewhat different?

Adm. M.: That was different to the extent that the early warning - if I understand your question - was primarily for enemy bombers or missiles - that sort of thing - whereas this was strictly against the submarine. So the Dew Line and that sort of thing didn't enter into this picture.

Q: It seems to me there's some kind of similarity though,

isn't there — some affinity, at least?

Adm. M.: Yes, there is — but, on the other hand, all the early warning systems that we speak of as such are for airborne aircraft and missiles and whatnot, whereas we were strictly working against surface, surface-snorkling, or submerged submarines.

Q: Now, how would your findings in a war game of this sort — how would those findings have any impact on long-range planners in the Navy?

Adm. M.: Well, every time that you'd finish one of these studies you gave a presentation.

Q: I'd asked about the presentation to the interested parties, and whether it was done with graphics — or how you did this?

Adm. M.: Well, it was done with the geographical charts — in the case of some statistics, the bar chart, or mathematical curve — whatever was appropriate to the point you were trying to make. Largely, you might say tactical charts, which actually showed the position of the aircraft on the barrier and supporting surface ships and that sort of thing — with actual geographical presentation, you might say — primarily.

Then you'd have sort of subordinate tables which showed your probabilities of this and that. If A happens, what happens to B, and that sort of thing. So, you could be graphical or topographical, or it could be mathematical curves - whatever best suited the point you were trying to make.

Q: I take it that this technique for wargaming in this time is something that all the services have adopted.

Adm. M.: Yes. They very much have - and, as I say, my next tour was with the JCS - that was a tri-service outfit which very much did its own work but had very close liaison with CNOs wargamers, and the Army's and the Air Force. I don't remember now the names of the other two services - divisions or units that did this work, but it was the same idea.

Q: And, is this also common as a technique with our Allies and enemies?

Adm. M.: I'm sure it must be, yes. I can't think in this modern day and age that we like to call it, how they could avoid doing this - although again, I stress, I'm skeptical about the results.

Q: You're skeptical because it largely obliterates the human element in it?

Adm. M.: That - and the wide range of assumptions that you could make and which you finally select as the most likely one. How reliable is the torpedo? How reliable is this and that? So you pick a number - .6 for liability. Well, is it really? I mean, who knows?

Q: Well, I suppose this is a hypothetical thing but if some commanding officer was assigned a task similar to this particular one, how binding would this particular study be upon him, as the commanding officer of something that had to be put into effect?

Adm. M.: I don't think it would be binding at all. I think that the usefulness of these studies is advice as to how to set up an operating plan or operation order - rather than to be binding on any particular aircraft or surface unit. Is that what you mean?

Q: Yes. When you gave the presentation before the CNO group, what kind of reaction did you get?

Adm. M.: Quite a few questions. Why did you do this? And would it have been feasible to do this? That sort of thing -

open discussion - but more the fact that you'd hear later on from the various OpNavs who had been present - individual questions relating to their field of interests - DCNO air people, DCNO ops people, or the submarine people - so you had this, not so much a detailed discussion at the presentation as you got from interested parties individually later on.

Q: Once they'd had a chance to study the -

Adm. M.: Right, yes.

Q: Was this effort broken down further in the department, in that say submarines made their own little war games?

Adm. M.: I would say no. As I said, we had fleet people, and probably OpNav people who came in and asked us to develop something for them, and I think they sort of left it up to us to be the sort of clearing house - and knowing that we could call on Dahlgren or anyone else that could help us, rather than duplicating what we were doing in their own shops. I think they, unquestionably had their own theoretical studies but not to the extent of detail that we carried them on.

Q: Did you have any other projects lined up for implementation?

Adm. M.: No. I think that's the only really major project that occurred while I was there - and, as I say, these take weeks and months so it was understandable.

Then, from there I went to what was called the special study group of the Joint Chiefs of Staff. That was, obviously, a tri-service group in the Joint Chiefs of Staff, and it was headed up by Air Force General Emrick, who was also J-6 of the Air Force staff. I mean his second hat duties was the special study group - and there we had a much larger group than individual services, and they were given assignments by the (in theory) JCS.

The big item there was a study of the advisability and the efficacy of small nuclear projectiles. In other words, the limited atomic war in Europe.

Q: As an adjunct to conventional forces?

Adm. M.: Yes - with again, complete detail on the geographical concept. In other words, actual large-scale maps of Europe and that sort of thing.

Down there it was sort of like I mentioned the way the British research worked during World War II. You were down there not necessarily as a naval officer. In other words you were - In the war in Europe, for instance, there was very little input of Navy there so you were just - that particular assignment was given to the study group and it didn't make any difference what your uniform was. Actually, I of course, was the senior naval officer, but that didn't mean that all my naval officers were sitting on their butts because we were studying an Army problem.

Q: You were expected, as a wargamer to show experience and to have your own input -

Adm. M.: That's right.

Q: - rather than Navy input.

Adm. M.: Again - I said that Dahlgren was a very fine shore assignment - again, my skepticism about all this was still bothering me, and the other thing that I objected to down there was the fact that, although we had no scientific or - I'd say civilian personnel in the Navy op war game, down there you were heckled by these Deputy Assistant Secretaries of Defense, and that sort of thing, who could just come down and tell a general or an admiral where to get off - and I'm just not built that way.

Q: You mean, in other terminology, they were called whiz kids?

Adm. M.: Well, that's the sort of people they were, you

see - and it was in the McNamara regime. I remember just before I left the Navy wargaming I went out to - as CNOs representative - for what Fort Leavenworth called the Combat Arms Conference - and they just wanted one Navy flag officer out there, so I was the one that went, and General Johnny Johnson then was head of Leavenworth - Harold Johnson I think his name was - three stars and had been prisoner of war for practically the whole war, in Japan, and later was to become Chief of Staff of the Army with four stars. Well, General Johnson was completing his tour at Leavenworth just after this conference that I attended and was assigned sort of temporary duty with the JCS special study group - and he was a tremendously fine office roommate, you might say - and we'd work up a paper of X number of pages, and then these whiz kids would come down and pick it apart. The sort of thing of, "Well, Johnson, I don't like this paragraph. I think you're on the wrong track" - that sort of thing - and it just hit me the wrong way. I mean, I just couldn't get used to this sort of thing - which is why I think it was building up to the fact that the whole Pentagon and McNamara's setup was not sitting quietly in Morton. It just was not the way I thought things should be.

I remember one particularly - there's no question, he must have been considered capable, he wouldn't have been where - Dr. Alain Enthoven, who was one of the most obnoxious, in my opinion. He was typical. He was probably the worst.

Q: But he was the chief of the whole group?

Adm. M.: Yes, and less and less did I like the Pentagon setup.

Q: Well, your objections - based on what? The fact that these men ignored specialized education and training on the part of the military?

Adm. M.: No, not so much as the fact that with all the work and all the ability and brains we had down there that the one whiz kid could come in and argue with the whole concept, or at least part of the concept - and tell a three or four-star general that he was all wet - "you've got to change that." It was a difficulty.

Q: Their objections were based on what?

Adm. M.: Well, they just figured that their - It almost looked like they could read a paragraph and then their snap judgment overruled what had taken weeks to evolve.

Q: One of the points I have heard emphasized by military

men was the fact that these people had a tendency to downplay or disregard completely experience, and wisdom gained by experience.

Adm. M.: This was part of it. I agree with that, but I don't think it was a deliberate - you might say contempt for the military as much as it was the fact that, "Well, I know better than you do," you see.

Q: But, the source of this "I know better" was based on what?

Adm. M.: In my humble opinion, the type of, if you want to call them whiz kids, that the McNamara Defense Department surrounded itself with - and this, as far as I can remember, or could see at that time, this applied to almost anything you wanted. It applied to strategic matters, tactical matters, budget matters, research and development matters - just these pip-squeaks, if you'll permit me to use the term, that were all through the Pentagon.

Q: They found their truth in what they call systems analysis?

Adm. M.: That sort of thing, yes. He was head of - That was his job.

Q: Enthoven?

Adm. M.: Yes - and probably could have been a perfectly nice guy, as far as I know - but just a pain in the neck to work with, and you might say, under. Not that he was on our necks all the time, but I mean some big phase had been completed - he'd come down, look it over and give you his reaction in about ten minutes. And, he had staffies with him who were equally bad.

Q: The result of this specialized study by the three services concluded what, as far as the use of limited atomic -

Adm. M.: Well, as I remember it ended up with about four or five possibilities - maybe two or three. And, you more or less left it up to the person who was going to read it, as to which he thought because we couldn't flatly say anything this way or that way. In other words, would the use of these artillery projectiles be feasible? Would it do you any good? And, what would the other side do? And, would it escalate into all-out atomic war? All these things were listed as possibilities with, as I remember, no particular pinpoint of this is what's going to happen. It was just a way of giving the - you might say high command - a series of possibilities of what would happen, with no flat-out saying that this will happen.

Q: The fact that you were dealing with this particular subject, in the possible use of atomic weapons in warfare - did this in itself prove to be something of an anathema to the whiz kid types?

Adm. M.: No, I don't think that really. I think they, like everyone else, felt that this is something that may never happen but may have to happen, and what would be the results of it? No, I don't think that they were trying to, you know, stick to conventional warfare, or anything like that.

Index to

Series of Taped Interviews

with

Rear Admiral Thomas H. Morton
U. S. Navy (Retired)

AMPHIBIOUS FORCE: p. 90-1;

ANDERSON, Admiral George: p. 473;

ASW (Anti-submarine warfare): p. the dunking sonar, p. 425; the DASH, p. 426;

AUSTIN, Senator Warren R.: becomes permanent U. S. Representative to the United Nations, p. 245 ff;

BALLENTINE, Admiral John J.: becomes Chief of Staff to Adm. Turner at United Nations, p. 247; p. 254; p. 256; p. 270-1; in retirement at Dogue, Virginia, p. 459;

BARUCH, The Hon. Bernard: he presents the subject of Atomic Energy to the United Nations, p. 257-8;

BLACKSTONE ISLAND (on the grounds of Dahlgren), p. 438;

USS BORIE (DD-215): p. 99-103;

BRAINARD, VADM Roland; p. 90;

BU ORD (Bureau of Ordnance): Morton's first tour in the Bureau (Nov. 1949), p. 292 ff; organization of the Bureau, p. 292-3; p. 311; second tour of duty in Bureau (Dec. 1953), p. 343; as Special Program Director this tour included duties in connection with atomic energy programs, the budget and the administration of ordnance plants, p. 345 ff; Administrative set-up in the Bureau in 1953, p. 345-6; budgetary matters, p. 350 ff; R and D matters, p. 354-7;

BURKE, Admiral Arleigh: his idea for a seminar on unconventional warfare, p. 398 ff;

BYRNES, The Hon. James: Secretary of State, p. 246-7;

CANUKUS: the Canadian-United Kingdom-United States group - meets on AS warfare matters, p. 393-4; Morton represents Admiral Hayward, p. 393-4;

USS CAPRICORNUS: Morton takes command, p. 361 ff; dependents cruises out of Guantanamo, p. 366; other missions in the Caribbean, p. 368-9; preparations for the European cruise, p. 369-71; a NATO exercise, p. 372-3; also 383-4; an incident in the Spanish port of Cartagena, p. 374; ship's liberty cancelled in Valencia because of Asian flu aboard, p. 380-1;

USS COLUMBUS (CA 74): preparations for decommissioning and conversation, p. 404-5; p. 408-11; entertaining required while serving as skipper, p. 427;

USS COMPTON (DD 705): Morton becomes skipper (Oct. 1947) p. 262 ff; family
                       makes headquarters in Newport, p. 264; carries mail for
                       U. N. presence in Palestine, p. 267-8; back to Newport,
                       p. 283-4; reserve cruise in NEW ORLEANS, p. 284 ff;
                       ship inspected by reporter to note employment of minorities,
                       p. 289-91; p. 310;

COOPER, RADM Joshua W.: becomes Commodore of DD squadron 12, p. 265; p. 268;
                         p. 272; p. 281;

CURLEY, George: son of Mayor Curley - friend of the Mortons, p. 325; p. 327;

CURLEY, James M.: Mayor of Boston...the story of the Mortons stay at the
                   Somerset Club in Boston and the Curley election for Mayor,
                   p. 223 ff;

DAHLGREN, Va.: Naval Weapons Lab): p. 422; Morton happy in this assign-
                ment, p. 428-9; an account of activities on station,
                p. 429-31; the several divisions and labs, p. 432 ff;
                the K Lab (computors) p. 440; space surveillance lab,
                p. 440 ff; the HERO project, p. 446-7; entertainment on
                base, p. 447; p. 451; cooperation with OpTevFor, p. 448-
                9; enlisted wives' club established, p. 451-2; a housing
                development, p. 452-3; remedial courses established for
                children, p. 454-5; recreational facilities, p. 455-6;
                Morton's departure from Dahlgren, p. 462; 477;

MS DELHI: fitted out with new U. S. 5 inch AA batteries (1940), p. 126;

DESTROYER DIVISION 122: Morton takes command (1952), p. 322 ff; roster of
                         ships, p. 326; p. 328-31 ff; race relations in the fleet,
                         p. 336-7; the homeward voyage from the Mediterranean -
                         a discrepancy in communications coverage, p. 339; a
                         discussion of ocean fog and ship's speed, p. 340;

DES RON 23 (The Little Beavers): Morton given command after decommissioning
                                  the CA COLUMBUS, p. 421 ff; part of ASW group 3 out of
                                  Long Beach, p. 423 ff;

DRY TORTUGAS: p. 61; p. 68-9;

DULLES, The Hon. John Foster: p. 260;

DUNKING SONAR: p. 425;

DUTTON, Captain Benjamin: skipper of BB WYOMING during Morton's midshipman
                           cruise, p. 52-3;

USS EDSON: flagship of Morton with Des Ron 23, p. 414; p. 416-417; two
            experiences of transfer at sea, p. 424-5; entertaining,
            p. 427;

EISENHOWER, General Dwight D.: p. 174-5;

ENTHOVEN, Alain: Chief of the 'whiz kids' in the McNamara Defense Dept.
                  p. 480-1; p. 483;

HMS EXCELLENT: p. 147;

FAHRION, Admiral Frank George (Spike): skipper of the BB NORTH CAROLINA, p. 184;

FLEET COMMUNICATIONS: p. 91-4;

FLEET SPORTS: hey-day in the 1920s and 30s, p. 84-5;

USS FRANKLIN: Morton's account of the attack on her, p. 208-210; p. 211;

FRAZER, Captain Chas. Leonard (Len): p. 106; p. 111; p. 115; p. 136; p. 164-5;

GRANT, Gen. Ulysses S.: names the two Howard boys (grandfather to Adm. Morton and great uncle) to the service academies, p. 8.

GRENFELL, VADM Elton Watters: ComSubLant - visits Dahlgren, p. 442 ff;

GROMYKO, Andre: p. 235; p. 238-9; p. 243; his first walk-out from the Security Council meetings, p.246;

GUAM: repair facilities on Guam, p. 418-9; the garbage dumps, p. 420-21;

HART, Admiral Thomas C.: as Superintendent of the U. S. Naval Academy, p. 25-7;

HAYWARD, VADM John T.: (Chick) Chief of R and D - Morton reports for duty with him, p. 386-7; plans for an undersea research and development station in Europe, p. 388 ff; p. 392; seminar on unconventional warfare as planned by his staff, p. 398 ff; p. 403-4;

HOWARD, Admiral Thomas B.: CincPacFleet (1915) - later superintendent of Naval bservatory, p. 1-4; p. 8;

USS HYMAN (DD-732): flagship for DD Div. 122, p. 326; p. 328; U. S. Navy representative at celebration in Tunis, p. 333;

INDUSTRIAL COLLEGE OF THE ARMED FORCES: p. 305; p. 311 ff;

ISRAEL: p. 267-8;

IWO JIMA: BB NORTH CAROLINA participates in operation, p. 200-2; marine spotter on shore directs the gunfire, p. 202-3;

JOHNCKE, Ernest Lee Jr.: roommate of Morton at the Naval Academy, p. 16-17;

JCS (Joint Chiefs of Staff): Morton joins the special study group to examine efficacy of small nuclear projectiles, p. 478-9; Morton objects to the pre-emptory manner of the Whiz Kids, p. 479 ff; conclusions of the special study, p. 483-4;

JOHNSON, VADM Felix: p. 289;

JOHNSON, General Harold (Johnny): p. 480;

JOHNSON, RADM Ralph C.: turns over command of COLUMBUS to Morton, p. 406;

KALBFUS, Admiral Edward C.: ComBatShips (1936), p. 88-9;

KAMIKAZI: The NORTH CAROLINA'S first view of the kamikazi, p. 197, p. 211-12;

KASHMIR: p. 258-9;

KENNEDY, The Hon. John F.: p. 323-5;

KIRK, Admiral Alan: p. 141-2;

KISSINGER, The Hon. Henry: gives advice on subject of unconventional warfare for the planned seminar, p. 399-400;

LA SPEZIA: site of NATO-NAVY undersea research and development station for Europe, p. 388; a contract put it under control of Raytheon, p. 388-91; p. 93;

LEASE-LEND: the London office presided over by General Aurand, USA - the Oerlikon and Bofors guns, p. 165-6;

LEE, Admiral Willis: p. 180, p. 191.

LOWRANCE, VADM Vernon L. (Rebel): p. 405-6; p. 415-6;

MALTA: p. 269-70;

MARIANAS Operation: participation of BB NORTH CAROLINA, p. 185; use of relief maps, p. 186-8; p. 192-3;

USS MASSACHUSETTS: shells used in her attack on JEAN BART, p. 157-9;

MINE WARFARE: status at outbreak of WW II, p. 112-4; p. 130;

USS MISSISSIPPI - BB: Morton gets duty on her upon graduation from Academy, p. 55 ff; detailed to patrol off Havana during a Cuban crisis, p. 61-3; p. 67-9; p. 76-7; mission to San Francisco for the dedication of the Bay Bridges, p. 86-7; p. 94; p. 96-7;

MOORE, Admiral Sir Henry: Senior British Officer on U. N. Military Committee, p. 262;

MOORER, Admiral Thomas: p. 43-4;

MORTON, RADM Thomas H.: family references, p. 1 ff; recollections of his father, p. 5-7; early education, p. 9-11; marriage, p. 224 and p. 306 ff; Admiral Turner asks Sue Morton to become hostess for the American delegation in London, p. 234 ff; p. 264-6; p. 270; Morton's accident in Newport delays his duty assignment in Washington, p. 342; living arrangements in Annapolis and Arlington, p. 343-4; family reunion in the Mediterrancean, p. 373; John Morton comes down with flu after his father's ship had been

quarantined in Valencia harbor, p. 381; p. 410-411;
a call on Adm. Kelly Turner, p. 412-3; vacations in the
Great Smokies, p. 460-1; selection for Admiral, p. 461-3;
personal disillusionment with situation in the Pentagon
under Secretary MacNamara, p. 479-81;

MUSTIN, VADM Lloyd: p. 455; p. 457-8;

NATIONAL WAR COLLEGE: see entries under INDUSTRIAL WAR COLLEGE.

NATO - and the SIXTH FLEET: p. 331-2;

NATO TACTICAL INSTRUCTIONS - and SIGNAL BOOK: p. 330-3;

U. S. NAVAL ACADEMY: Morton's difficulties with an appointment, p. 12-13;
p. 14-15; p. 18 ff; summer cruises, p. 27 ff; lacrosse
becomes principal sport for Morton, p. 33-36; comments
on the chapel service, p. 42-4; aviation summer, p. 44;
second class duties in summer with plebes, p. 46;
class of 1933 and commissions upon graduation, p. 48-50;
FDR is speaker at graduation ceremonies, p. 58-60;

U. S. NAVAL RESERVE: the DD COMPTON and other DDs take a series of cruises
with Naval Reserve members - based on New Orleans, p.
284 ff;

USS NEW MEXICO: detailed with BB MISSISSIPPI for patrol off Havana in a
Cuban crisis, p. 61-3; p. 67;

USS NORTH CAROLINA: Morton ordered as gunnery officer after his return from
U.K., p. 180-184; p. 189; p. 193; p. 195; p. 196-7;
takes over billet of BB NEW YORK for close in bombardment
at Iwo Jima, p. 200; p. 208-210; damaged inflicted upon
her by shell from an escort ship, p. 212-3; remarks about
her effectiveness with damage control, p. 214; bombing
of Jap mainland targets, p. 216-7; her return to U.S.,
p. 222;

OERLIKON and BOFORS guns: p. 166-7;

OKINAWA: participation of the BB NORTH CAROLINA, p. 206-7;

PANAMA: a fleet exercise, p. 82;

PEARL HARBOR: in 1935, p. 71-81; policy of Navy to give more repair work to
yard at Pearl Harbor (1938), p. 101; p. 131-4;

PIERSON, Gordon: p. 350; p. 359;

POLARIS: p. 359-60; CNO's Supervisory meetings, p. 395 ff; Dahlgren provides
fire control printouts for POLARIS, p. 441-2;

POST GRADUATE SCHOOL: Morton enrolls in ordnance engineering, p. 102 ff;
European war makes a change in P.G. courses but Morton's

group continued for two years nevertheless, p. 104-5; Morton sent for third year with the Royal Navy - gunnery, etc., p. 106; p. 111 ff; the first two years in Annapolis, p. 106-10;

PULESTON, Captain Wm. D.: skipper of the BB MISSISSIPPI 1933), p. 57;

RABORN, VADM Wm. F. Jr.: p. 303-4; p. 359; p. 395-7;

RADAR: p. 116-7; p. 128-9;

RESEARCH AND DEVELOPMENT - NAVY: see entries under:
VADM J. T. Hayward; also LA SPEZIA; three major projects that Morton was involved in as the representative of Admiral Hayward and R and D, p. 388 ff;

RICKOVER, Admiral Hyman: p. 396; his conducted tour of Westinghouse plant in Pittsburgh, p. 397-8;

RIDGWAY, General Matthew: p. 237; p. 253-4;

ROBBINS, RADM Thomas H. Jr.: p. 404; p. 429;

ROOSEVELT, President Franklin D.: speaker at graduation of 1933 class - N.A., p. 58-60; the great naval review of 1934, p. 63-6; p. 72; impact at news of his death, p. 218-9;

ROYAL NAVY: Morton goes for year of Post graduate study, p. 120 ff; British set up on ordnance, research, etc., p. 125-8; Morton learns about radar, p.128-9; p. 135-6; requests for information from the U. S. Navy, p. 137-8; various U. S. delegations, p. 141 ff; the Thanksgiving reception at Buckingham Palace (1942), p. 147-9; R and D in preparation for bombing of German dams, p. 150-2; Saint Nazaire raid, p. 155; Morton's trips to various Ordnance stations, p. 161-2; conducted tour with group of Russian naval officers, p. 162-3; social notes, p. 172 ff;

RUSSIANS - IN THE UNITED NATIONS:
see entries under: GROMYKO: also, p. 246; p. 248 ff; p. 252-3; p. 255-6;

SAC LANT ASW CENTER: see entry under: LA SPEZIA.

SAINT NAZAIRE: raid on German submarine base, p. 155-6;

SCHOEFFEL, RADM Malcolm F.: p. 360-1;

SEVERN SCHOOL: p. 9-13;

SHERMAN, Admiral Forrest: in command of 6th fleet - his strictures on hats, beards, p. 270-1; p. 272; p. 282;

SHIP'S CHARACTERISTICS BOARD: p. 300, p. 358;

SIXTH FLEET: see entries under: ADMIRAL FORREST SHERMAN: J. J. BALLENTINE: USS COMPTON; data on the fleet, p. 275-6; p. 278-82;

SOLBERG, Captain T. A.: p. 147; p. 172;

USS SPIEGEL GROVE (LSD): p. 364; the flag raising incident in port of Cartagena, p. 374-7;

STARK, Admiral Harold R.: p. 142;

STEVENSON, The Hon. Adlai: p. 260;

STROOP, VADM Paul D.: p. 346; p. 349;

TARANTO, Italy: p. 371;

TORCH - Operation: p. 141-2; p. 157-8;

TRIESTE: p. 266-7; p. 281-2;

TUNIS: the celebration of the liberation of Tunis, p. 333 ff;

TURNER, Admiral Richmond Kelly: Morton ordered to staff of Turner who served as CNO's representative on United Nations Military Staff Committee, p. 233 ff; off to London with the delegation - Sue Morton becomes official hostess for delegation in London, p. 233-4; p. 241; p. 244; p. 252; p. 254; the Mortons call on the Turners in California, p. 412-3; p. 415;

UNCONVENTIONAL WARFARE: a seminar at the behest of Adm. Burke - Morton and one other develop plans, p. 398 ff; p. 400;

UNITED NATIONS: initial meetings in London - complexion of U. S. delegation, p. 234-5 ff; p. 240 ff; difficulties with the Russians, p. 246; p. 248 ff; atomic energy for peaceful purposes, p. 257;

UNITED NATIONS - MILITARY STAFF COMMITTEE:
see entries under: Admiral TURNER; also under UNITED NATIONS.
complexion of the committee, p. 236-8; p. 247-8; problems over composition of United Nations armed forces, p. 247-50; p. 249-52; p. 261-2;

HMS VICTORIA and ALBERT: p. 147;

HMS VICTORY: p. 147;

WAR GAMING (Op. 06): upon his selection as Rear Admiral (Sept. 1961) Morton becomes assistant for War Gaming in Office of CNO, p. 464 ff; a study for a submarine and aircraft barrier across the North Sea, p. 465-9; the presentation to interested parties, p. 474 ff;

WARD, Admiral A.G.: p. 184;

USS WEST VIRGINIA: in 1936 Morton becomes CWO on flagship of Admiral Kalbfus (ComBatShips) p. 88;

WRIGHT, Admiral Jerauld: p. 388; p. 391-2;

YORKTOWN MINE SCHOOL: p. 111-2;

www.ingramcontent.com/pod-product-compliance
Lightning Source LLC
Chambersburg PA
CBHW080627170426
43209CB00007B/1527